P. NOVA.

Communal Square

Episcopal Square

PARMA F.

P. S. BERNABA.

The Pennsylvania State University Press
University Park, Pennsylvania

Areli Marina

The Italian Piazza Transformed

Parma in the Communal Age

Publication of this book has been supported in part by a grant from the Graham Foundation for Advanced Studies in the Fine Arts.

Some material in this book was previously published in "Order and Ideal Geometry in Parma's Piazza del Duomo," *Journal of the Society of Architectural Historians* 65, no. 4 (2006): 520–49, and in "Magnificent Architecture in Late Medieval Italy," in *Magnificence and the Sublime in Medieval Aesthetics,* edited by C. Stephen Jaeger (New York: Palgrave Macmillan, 2010), reproduced with permission of Palgrave Macmillan.

Library of Congress Cataloging-in-Publication Data

Marina, Areli, 1964–
The Italian piazza transformed : Parma in the communal age / Areli Marina.
    p.   cm.
Includes bibliographical references and index.
Summary: "Explores the history and architecture of two city squares, constructed by rival political parties, in the Italian city of Parma from 1196 to 1300"—Provided by publisher.
ISBN 978-0-271-05070-6 (cloth : alk. paper)
1. Piazza del Duomo (Parma, Italy).
2. Piazza Garibaldi (Parma, Italy).
3. Architecture, Medieval—Italy—Parma.
4. Architecture and society—Italy—Parma.
5. Parma (Italy)—Buildings, structures, etc.
I. Title.
NA9072.P364M37 2012   711'.550945441—dc22
2011014230

Designed by Bessas & Ackerman, Guilford, CT
Printed in China by Everbest Printing Co., through
Four Colour Print Group, Louisville, KY
Published by The Pennsylvania State University Press,
University Park, PA 16802-1003

The Pennsylvania State University Press is a member of the Association of American University Presses.

It is the policy of The Pennsylvania State University Press to use acid-free paper. Publications on uncoated stock satisfy the minimum requirements of American National Standard for Information Sciences—Permanence of Paper for Printed Library Material, ANSI Z39.48–1992.

Additional credits: frontispiece, detail, fig. 2; title-page spread, details, fig. 12 (*left*) and fig. 53 (*right*); page v, detail, fig. 79; pages 22–23, detail, fig. 18; pages 104–105, detail, fig. 104.

For Bob

Contents

Part II: The Piazza and Public Life

Illustrations

1. Map of Italy. This material originated on the Interactive Ancient Mediterranean Web site (http://iam.classics.unc.edu). It has been copied, reused, or redistributed under the terms of IAM's fair-use policy. © 1998, Interactive Ancient Mediterranean.

2. Parma's episcopal square (now Piazza del Duomo) and communal square (now Piazza Garibaldi) created between 1196 and 1296. Detail from Paolo Ponzoni, *Pianta della città di Parma in prospettiva* (Piacenza: Francesco Conti, 1572), woodcut, after an earlier drawing. ASPr, Raccolta Mappe e Disegni, vol. 2, no. 13.

3. Aerial view of Parma's Piazza del Duomo, or cathedral square, from the northwest, 2004. Photo: Carlo Ferrari.

4. Aerial view of Parma's Piazza Garibaldi, the former communal government square, from the south, 2004. Photo: Carlo Ferrari.

5. Diagram of Roman Parma. Photo: Royal Air Force, United Kingdom, 1944, neg. 174278, used with permission from the Aerofototeca, Istituto Centrale per il Catalogo e la Documentazione, Ministero per i Beni e le Attività Culturali, Rome. © Foto Aerofototeca Nazionale—ICCD.

6. The city's two principal canals, the Canale Comune and the Canale Maggiore. Detail from Giuseppe Cocconcelli, "Compendio del Corso di tutti li Canali, Canadelle, Condotti, e Scoli sotterra-nei della Città di Parma," 1765. ASCP, MS, no. 1, cubo 7, cassetto 1.6, Canali e canaletti.

7. Diagram of Parma c. 1190. Photo: Royal Air Force, United Kingdom, 1944, neg. 174278, used with permission from the Aerofototeca, Istituto Centrale per il Catalogo e la Documentazione, Ministero per i Beni e le Attività Culturali, Rome. © Foto Aerofototeca Nazionale—ICCD.

8. Traces of the arcade of the imperial Palazzo dell'Arena, built into part of the city's Roman amphitheater, remain engulfed in the later masonry of the Collegio Maria Luigia on borgo Lalatta, Parma. Photo: author.

9. In this statue made at the time of Charles of Anjou's appointment as senator of Rome, he is seated on a classicizing curule chair. Arnolfo di Cambio, *Charles of Anjou,* c. 1277–81. Capitoline Museums, Rome. Photo: Erich Lessing/Art Resource, N.Y.

10. Parma's episcopal square, as represented in the late sixteenth century. Detail from Paolo Ponzoni, *Pianta della città di Parma in prospettiva* (Piacenza: Francesco Conti, 1572), woodcut, after an earlier drawing. ASPr, Raccolta Mappe e Disegni, vol. 2, no. 13.

11. Reconstruction diagram, the cathedral piazza of Parma c. 1195.

12. Detail of the facade of the Duomo, Parma. Photo: Seth C. Jayson.

13. Plan of the bishop's palace of Parma.

14. Aerial view of the bishop's palace from the northwest in 1961. Photo: Fotocielo, neg. 225359, used with permission from the Aerofototeca, Istituto Centrale per il Catalogo e la Documentazione, Ministero per i Beni e le Attività Culturali, Rome. © Foto Aerofotototeca Nazionale—ICCD.

15. Baptistery of Parma from the north. Photo: Seth C. Jayson.

16. Reconstruction diagram, the cathedral piazza of Parma, 1196–1216.

17. Baptistery of Cremona from the north. Photo: Seth C. Jayson.

18. Analytical diagram of the north elevation of the baptistery, Parma, illustrating how aspects of the baptistery's design derive from a 7-meter module. From an engraving by Piero Sottili after a drawing by G. Bertoluzzi, in Michele Lopez, *Il Battistero di Parma* (Parma: Giacomo Ferrari, 1864), fig. 4.

19. Rotation of the square by 45 degrees to derive successive measurements from the original base module.

20. Analytical diagram illustrating the dimensional correspondence between the baptistery and cathedral facades.

21. Platea Maior, Cremona. Detail of the map of Cremona in Antonio Campi, *Cremona fedelissima città et nobilissima colonia de Romani rappresentata in disegno col suo contado: Et illustrata d'una breue historia delle cose più notabili appartenenti ad essa et de i ritratti naturali de duchi et duchesse di Milano e compendio delle lor vite* (Cremona: Hippolito Tromba & Hercoliano Bartoli, 1585), after p. lxxviii. Courtesy of the University of Illinois Rare Book and Manuscripts Library.

22. Analytical drawing representing the process used in the siting of the baptistery of Parma.

23. Analytical drawing representing the Parma baptistery portals.

24. West portal, baptistery of Parma. Photo: Seth C. Jayson.

25. North (piazza) portal, baptistery of Parma. Photo: Seth C. Jayson.

26. Tympanum and lintel of the north portal, baptistery of Parma. Photo: Seth C. Jayson.

27. View of the baptistery from the strada al Duomo. Photo: Robert G. La France.

28. Reconstruction diagram, the cathedral piazza of Parma c. 1235.

29. Eastern facade, bishop's palace, Parma. Photo: Seth C. Jayson.

30. Detail of painted, ceramic, and masonry ornament on the eastern facade, bishop's palace, Parma. Photo: Robert G. La France.

31. Northwest corner of the Piazza del Duomo, Parma. Photo: Robert G. La France.

32. A building on the north side of the Piazza del Duomo, Parma. Photo: author.

33. Reconstruction diagram indicating the ideal square geometry of the cathedral piazza c. 1235.

34. Reconstruction diagram indicating the cross axes underlying the design of the cathedral piazza c. 1235.

35. Northeast corner of the bishop's palace, Parma. Photo: Robert G. La France.

36. Reconstruction diagram, the cathedral piazza of Parma in 1262.

37. South portal, baptistery of Parma. Photo: Seth C. Jayson.

38. Campanile, Parma, 1284–94. Photo: Seth C. Jayson.

39. Reconstruction diagram, the cathedral piazza of Parma c. 1285.

40. The campanile as seen from the strada al Duomo, Parma. Photo: Seth C. Jayson.

41. Reconstruction diagram of the cathedral piazza representing the sightlines from the strada al Duomo to the campanile c. 1292.

42. Analytical drawing representing the ideal 45-degree angle of view to the cornice of the campanile, Parma.

43. View of the entrance to Parma's episcopal square from the strada al Duomo. Photo: Robert G. La France.

44. The episcopal square seen from its center, looking south. Photo: Seth C. Jayson.

45. Reconstruction diagram of the cathedral piazza representing the axial relationships between its major buildings c. 1285.

46. Cathedral, campanile, and baptistery from the northwest corner of the Piazza del Duomo, Parma. Photo: Seth C. Jayson.

47. Parma's communal square, as represented in the late sixteenth century. Detail from Paolo Ponzoni, *Pianta della città di Parma in prospettiva* (Piacenza: Francesco Conti, 1572), woodcut, after an earlier drawing. ASPr, Raccolta Mappe e Disegni, vol. 2, no. 13.

48. Reconstruction diagram, the communal piazza of Parma c. 1220.

49. Medieval facades visible on Piazza Garibaldi, Parma. Photo: Seth C. Jayson.

50. Reconstruction diagram, the communal piazza of Parma in 1223.

51. Torello's communal palace. Highlighted detail from Paolo Ponzoni, *Pianta della città di Parma in prospettiva* (Piacenza: Francesco Conti, 1572), woodcut, after an earlier drawing. ASPr, Raccolta Mappe e Disegni, vol. 2, no. 13.

52. The Palazzo del Municipio, Parma, which occupies the site of Torello's communal palace. Photo: Robert G. La France.

53. Parma's communal square in the late sixteenth century. Detail from a copy of Smeraldo Smeraldi's 1589–91 map of Parma. ASPr, Raccolta Mappe e Disegni, vol. 2, no. 61.

54. The earliest surviving representation of Parma. Detail from *Pianta di Parma e del suo territorio con parte di Borghigiano e Reggiano disegnata dopo il 1460*. ASPr, Raccolta Mappe e Disegni, vol. 2, no. 85.

55. Piazza Grande (now Piazza Garibaldi). Detail from Pietro Sottili, *Reproduction of Bird's-Eye View of Parma c. 1570,* ink, 1873. Museo Archeologico, Parma.

56. Sandstone pier and fragmentary arch from Torello's communal palace, Parma, now engulfed in the Volta del Municipio. Photo: Robert G. La France.

57. Communal palace, Cremona, 1206–46. Photo: Seth C. Jayson.

58. Like the Palazzo del Municipio now on the site, Torello's communal palace would have been highly visible from the eastern branch of the former via Claudia/Emilia (now via della Repubblica). Photo: author.

59. Reconstruction diagram, the communal piazza of Parma in 1246.

60. Communal tower. Highlighted detail from Paolo Ponzoni, *Pianta della città di Parma in prospettiva* (Piacenza: Francesco Conti, 1572), woodcut, after an

earlier drawing. ASPr, Raccolta Mappe e Disegni, vol. 2, no. 13.

61. Stucco boss representing the city of Parma as if in a convex mirror, vault of the Sala della Giunta, Palazzo Municipale, Parma, c. 1675.

62. The communal tower dominates the cityscape in this fresco, *View of Parma, 1569,* by Jacopo Sanguidi, called il Bertoia. Sala d'Ercole, Palazzo Farnese, Caprarola. Photo: Gerardo de Simone.

63. Torrazzo, Cremona, begun c. 1235, completed up to the four-light window by 1267, and up to the spire by 1309. Photo: Seth C. Jayson.

64. Torre dell'Arengo, Bologna, by 1212. Photo: Scala/ Art Resource, N.Y.

65. House of the Podesta. Highlighted detail from Paolo Ponzoni, *Pianta della città di Parma in prospettiva* (Piacenza: Francesco Conti, 1572), woodcut, after an earlier drawing. ASPr, Raccolta Mappe e Disegni, vol. 2, no. 13.

66. Reconstruction diagram, the communal piazza of Parma c. 1266.

67. House of the Capitano. Highlighted detail from Paolo Ponzoni, *Pianta della città di Parma in prospettiva* (Piacenza: Francesco Conti, 1572), woodcut, after an earlier drawing. ASPr, Raccolta Mappe e Disegni, vol. 2, no. 13.

68. House of the Capitano, Parma. Photo: Seth C. Jayson.

69. Arched *ballatoio* that connected the House of the Capitano to Torello's communal palace. Photo: Seth C. Jayson.

70. The communal vault (*ballatoio*) over the former *cardo maximus* seen from via Cavour. Photo: Seth C. Jayson.

71. Reconstruction diagram, the communal piazza of Parma c. 1277.

72. Aerial photograph from the north showing the westward deviation of the Roman *cardo* just south of the communal piazza. Archivio Caproni, n.d., neg. 191571, used with permission from the Aerofototeca, Istituto Centrale per il Catalogo e la Documentazione, Ministero per i Beni e le Attività Culturali, Rome. © Foto Aerofototeca Nazionale—ICCD.

73. House with battlements and portico on the southwest border of the communal piazza (Torselli properties, later Palazzo Bondani). Highlighted detail from Paolo Ponzoni, *Pianta della città di Parma in prospettiva* (Piacenza: Francesco Conti, 1572), woodcut, after an earlier drawing. ASPr, Raccolta Mappe e Disegni, vol. 2, no. 13.

74. House and portico on the southwest border of the communal piazza (Torselli properties, later Palazzo Bondani). Giulio Carmignani, *Piazza Garibaldi,* watercolor, c. 1850. ASCP, Fototeca, Fondo A.P.T., Album Fotografici, 4330/A.

75. The market space now known as the Ghiaia extended north from the stone bridge, along the east bank of the Parma torrent, on the site of its pre-1177 river bed. Detail from Paolo Ponzoni, *Pianta della città di Parma in prospettiva* (Piacenza: Francesco Conti, 1572), woodcut, after an earlier drawing. ASPr, Raccolta Mappe e Disegni, vol. 2, no. 13.

76. Aerial photograph showing the Ghiaia from the north in 2004. Photo: Carlo Ferrari.

77. Reconstruction diagram, the communal piazza of Parma in 1281.

78. The New Communal Palace of San Vitale, now Palazzo Fainardi, from the southeast. Photo: Seth C. Jayson.

79. The communal piazza from the west. *Veduta di Piazza Maggiore di Parma,* in Attilio Zuccagni-Orlandini, ed., *Corografia fisica, storica e statistica dell'Italia e delle sue isole,* vol. 8.1 (Florence: All'insegna di Clio, 1839), Vedute pittoriche, tavola 2.

80. Reconstructed medieval south elevation of the Palazzo Fainardi. Courtesy of Juergen Schulz, "The Communal Buildings of Parma," *Mitteilungen des Kunsthistorischen Institutes in Florenz* 26 (1982): 301.

81. The Rocca di Torrechiara (PR). Photo: Seth C. Jayson.

82. Reconstruction diagram, the communal piazza of Parma in 1285.

83. Analytical diagram representing the ideal square underlying the communal piazza's design, 1285.

84. Analytical diagram comparing the surface area of the communal piazza to that of the episcopal piazza in 1285.

85. The New Communal Palace of the Piazza (*de Platea*), now the Palazzo del Governatore, Parma. Photo: Robert G. La France.

86. The communal piazza (now Piazza Garibaldi) from the south. Photo: author.

87. The eastern flank of the piazza, with the New Communal Palace of San Vitale, as seen from the opening of the deviated *cardo,* now via Farini. Photo: author.

88. *Rinceau* decoration of the north portal, baptistery of Parma. Photo: author.

89. Column fragment from the Palazzo dell'Arena, borgo Lalatta, Parma. Photo: author.

90. The ground story of the Parma baptistery displays an assortment of spoliated, colored-marble columns. Photo: Seth C. Jayson.

91. Faux spoil fluted plinth and column base carved from a single piece of *rosso di Verona,* baptistery of Parma. Photo: Robert G. La France.

92. Benedetto Antelami (attr.), *Archangel Michael.* Museo Diocesano, Parma (formerly on the baptistery's north facade). Photo: Scala/Art Resource, N.Y.

93. Benedetto Antelami (attr.), *Archangel Gabriel* copied after the *Archangel Michael.* Museo Diocesano, Parma (formerly on the baptistery's north facade). Photo: Scala/Art Resource, N.Y.

94. Schematic Corinthian capital from the loggia of the cathedral facade. Photo: Robert G. La France.

95. Corinthian capitals from the left jamb of the Parma baptistery's north portal. Photo: author.

96. Three-light windows from the House of the Capitano, Parma. Photo: Robert G. La France.

97. *Protiro,* or prothyrum porch, supported by classicizing *rosso di Verona* lions, central portal, west facade, cathedral of Parma. Photo: Robert G. La France.

98. Engaged Doric column shaft, northeast facade, baptistery of Parma. Photo: Robert G. La France.

99. Trabeated exterior galleries, baptistery of Parma. Photo: Seth C. Jayson.

100. Trabeated galleries of the ruins of the Septizodium. Giovanni Antonio Dosio (1533–1609), *View of the Septizodium, Palatine Hill, Rome.* Gabinetto Disegni e Stampe, Uffizi, Florence, Italy, n. 2524 A. Photo: Scala/Art Resource, N.Y.

101. Capital with knights at war, west face of the first major pier on the south side of the nave, cathedral of Parma. Photo: Seth C. Jayson.

102. Roland sounding his horn, Oliphant. Ghirlandina tower, Modena. Photo: Seth C. Jayson.

103. Arthurian reliefs in the archivolts of the Porta della Pescheria, cathedral of Modena. Photo: Seth C. Jayson.

104. Analytical diagram showing how in Bentham's panopticon penitentiary, a central observer commanded a view of the prisoners' cells, along the structure's perimeter. Jeremy Bentham, "Panopticon," from *The Works of Jeremy Bentham, Published Under the Superintendence of His Executor, John Bowring,* edited by William Tait (Edinburgh: Simpkin, Marshall & Co., 1843), vol. 4, after p. 172. Courtesy of the University of Illinois Library.

105. Analytical diagram representing the panoptic qualities of the episcopal piazza, Parma, c. 1292.

106. Analytical diagram representing the panoptic qualities of the communal piazza, Parma, 1285.

107. Episcopal complex, Pisa. Photo: Alinari/Art Resource, N.Y.

108. Piazza della Signoria, Florence. Photo: Scala/Art Resource, N.Y.

109. Campo, Siena. Photo: Alinari/Art Resource, N.Y.

Acknowledgments

The first kernel of this study sprouted in Marvin Trachtenberg's seminar on public space in Italy. For his enduring inspiration and support through the project's long maturation, my gratitude to him remains immeasurable. Juergen Schulz's groundbreaking work on Parma's communal buildings contributed to this project's launch. I remember with appreciation his kind words as I prepared to set off for my first research trip to Parma, in 1998, and the stimulating questions he has raised throughout the intervening years. Caroline Bruzelius, David Friedman, Dorothy Glass, Dale Kinney, and Debra Pincus have commented on (and gently guided) my work on Parmesan architecture and urbanism over the course of several years, formally at conferences and informally during several Roman, Venetian, and Kalamazonian conversations—I am grateful for their encouragement.

This project has benefited from the insights of many current and former members of the Institute of Fine Arts community, especially Jonathan Alexander, Leonard Barkan, Jean-Louis Cohen, Anne-Marie Sankovich (†), Gwen Ajello, Adrienne Atwell, Peter DeStaebler, Theresa Flanagan, John Garton, Mia Genoni, Max Grossman, Erik Gustafson, Michelle Hobart, Heather Horton, Seth Jayson, Anne Leader, Anna Beth Martin, Kathryn Moore, Lisa Rafanelli, Daniel Savoy, Michael Waters, and Amee Yunn. All have my thanks.

The American Academy in Rome and the Kress Foundation funded a two-year study trip to Italy during which I completed the first research campaigns for this study. I could not have finished this book without their generous support. Furthermore, the American Academy proved to be a most congenial environment for the development and maturation of ideas. I am grateful to dozens of members of the greater AAR community for correcting my mistakes, lifting my spirits, and leading me to productive new paths. They include Tom Andrews (†), Elizabeth Bartman, Kate Bentz, Lana Bortolot, Martin Bresnick, Sam Cohn, Anne Coulson, Brian Curran, Leslie Dawsey, Joanna Drell, Lella Gandini, Paul Garfinkel, Wendy Heller, Jack Hill, John Dixon Hunt, Johannes Knoops, Margaret Laird, Stephanie Leone, Lester Little, Michael Maas, Heather Hyde Minor, Vernon Hyde Minor, Pina Pasquantonio, John Pinto, Meg Pinto, Carol Rosenberg, Charles Rosenberg, David Routt, Ingrid Rowland, Stephen Sears, Nancy Sevcenko, William C. Stull, Richard Talbert, Peter Waldman, Genevieve Warwick, Ronald Witt, and Anne Marie Yasin.

I tested some of the research findings included here in several settings. I would like to thank

George Bent, Barbara Deimling, C. Stephen Jaeger, Mark Jarzombek, Carla Keyvanian, Andrew Ladis (†), Alick McLean, Lisa Reilly, Shelley Zuraw, the Italian Art Society, the International Center for Medieval Art, the College Art Association, the Society of Architectural Historians, the International Medieval Congress, and the University of Virginia for providing stimulating fora for the discussion of this material, both in and out of the conference hall.

Librarians and archivists throughout Italy and the United States have supported my investigations. My first thanks go to Christine Huemer (†) of the American Academy in Rome and her extraordinary staff. In addition, Jane Block and Chris Quinn at the University of Illinois in Urbana-Champaign, Lamia Doumato and Gregory P. J. Most at the National Gallery of Art in Washington, Germana Graziosi, who does double duty at the American Academy and the Norske Institutt i Roma fur Kunsthistorie og Klassic Arkeologi, Ivano Reviati of the Archivio Cartografico Urbanistico di Parma, Father William Sheehan and the staff of the Sala Stampati of the Biblioteca Apostolica Vaticana, the staffs of the Kunsthistorisches Institut and Biblioteca Nazionale in Florence, and in Parma the staffs of the Biblioteca Palatina, Archivio di Stato, and, especially, Roberto Spocci at the Archivio Storico Comunale have all been liberal in their assistance with this project. Special thanks go to Annarita Ziveri of the Soprintendenza ai Beni Artistici e Storici per le Provincie di Parma e Piacenza, who helped me obtain access and permission to photograph in several normally inaccessible places. I owe a particular debt of gratitude to the University of Parma's architecture program, and especially to Michela Rossi, Cecilia Tedeschi, and Paolo Mancini, for

their generosity with their time and professional expertise. Without Michela's unstinting support, the surveys of Parma's Piazza del Duomo and Piazza Garibaldi would not have been possible.

At the University of Illinois, Kathryn Anthony, Martin Camargo, Larry Hamlin, Dianne Harris, Anne D. Hedeman, C. Stephen Jaeger, Richard Layton, Heather Hyde Minor, Vernon Hyde Minor, Lisa Rosenthal, Manuel Rota, John Senseney, Nora Stoppino, and Jeryldene Wood have provided invaluable intellectual and/or physical nourishment in the later stages of this book. The Campus Research Board, School of Architecture, and Laing Endowment provided me with money and time to finish the manuscript, including a helpful publication subvention. Mario Chavez Marquez and Patrick Ainsworth, my student assistants, helped when help was most needed.

Robert G. La France and, especially, Seth Jayson brought their unerring art-historical eye and technical expertise to most of the photographs in this book. I thank them for their infinite patience during the multiple photographic campaigns we undertook together in Parma. Their pictures were always better than mine.

In a challenging publishing environment, The Pennsylvania State University Press remains a beacon for scholars of medieval Italy. I am grateful for Eleanor Goodman's advocacy for this project, and to the press's reviewers, editors, and editorial board, whose recommendations strengthened the book's arguments. I thank Ellie, Danny Bellet, Patty Mitchell, Keith Monley, Jennifer Norton, and Laura Reed-Morrisson for their parts in the special alchemy that transformed my imperfect words and pictures into a proper book. A grant from the Graham

Foundation for Advanced Studies in the Fine Arts generously supported the book's production. I am thankful, too, for the wise counsel of the 2010–11 community of fellows, visiting professors, staff, and fellow travelers at Villa I Tatti, the Harvard University Center for Italian Renasissance Studies, as the book went from manuscript into production.

There are a few people who have not had a direct hand in the formation of this text but without whom it would nonetheless not exist. Two deserve special thanks for being the first to treat me like a "real" art historian: Cynthia Hahn and Jack Freiberg of Florida State University launched me on the path of scholarship. I may have finished a bit sooner but been a worse scholar and a sadder person without the unwavering friendship of Mario Acuti, Monica Carbò, Meli Costopoulos, Drew Haluska, Ambra Maffei, Molly March, Mariceli Marina, Marimeli Marina, José Miguel Marina Torres, James Parchment, Giancarla Periti, Wadda Rios Font, Patricia Silva, and Stefano Ticci. I would never have become a scholar without my parents' abiding influence. My mother, Aracelis Font, taught me that learning is its own reward. My father, José Miguel Marina Cortés, instilled in me his love of buildings. They knew, even when I didn't, that I would end up writing books.

And as for Bob, who reread every word of this manuscript and trod every cobblestone in Parma: I thank him for sharing with me his boundless scholarly imagination, his Italy, and his life.

Areli Marina
June 2011

Abbreviations

ASCP	Archivio Storico Comunale, Parma
ASPr	Archivio di Stato, Parma
Chronicle of Salimbene	Salimbene de Adam, *The Chronicle of Salimbene de Adam*, edited and translated by Joseph L. Baird, Giuseppe Baglivi, and John Robert Kane (Binghamton, N.Y.: Medieval & Renaissance Texts & Studies, 1986)
Chronicon Parmense	Bonazzi, Giuliano, ed., *Chronicon Parmense: Ab anno MXXXVIII usque ad annum MCCCXXXVIII,* Rerum Italicarum Scriptores: Raccolta degli storici italiani dal cinquecento al millecinquecento, edited by Ludovico A. Muratori, Giosuè Carducci, and Vittorio Fiorini, 9.9 (Città di Castello: S. Lapi, 1902)
DBI	*Dizionario biografico degli italiani,* 73 vols. (Rome: Istituto della Enciclopedia Italiana, 1960–2009)
DBP	Lasagni, Roberto, ed., *Dizionario biografico dei parmigiani,* 4 vols. (Parma: PPS, 1999)
Statuta 1	Ronchini, Amadio, ed., *Statuta Communis Parmae digesta anno 1255,* Monumenta historica ad provincias parmensem et placentinam pertinentia (Parma: Fiaccadori, 1855–56)
Statuta 2	Ronchini, Amadio, ed., *Statuta Communis Parmae ab anno 1266 ad annum c. 1304,* Monumenta historica ad provincias parmensem et placentinam pertinentia (Parma: Fiaccadori, 1857)
Statuta 3	Ronchini, Amadio, ed., *Statuta Communis Parmae ab anno 1316 ad 1325,* Monumenta historica ad provincias parmensem et placentinam pertinentia (Parma: Fiaccadori, 1859)
Statuta 4	Ronchini, Amadio, ed., *Statuta Communis Parmae anni 1347: Accedunt leges vicecomitum Parmae imperantium usque ad annum 1374,* Monumenta historica ad provincias parmensem et placentinam pertinentia (Parma: Fiaccadori, 1860)

About the Reconstruction Diagrams

The reconstruction diagrams of Parma's Piazza del Duomo and Piazza Garibaldi are based on a 2005 laser-assisted survey of the sites conducted by architects Michela Rossi (formerly professor of architectural drawing and historical documentation at the Dipartimento di Ingegneria Civile, dell'Ambiente, del Territorio, e di Architettura of the Università degli Studi di Parma and currently professor in the Department of Industrial Design, Art, Communication, and Fashion of the Politecnico di Milano) and Cecilia Tedeschi (currently an instructor in architectural design at the Università degli Studi di Parma).

Gray lines represent the city's current state. Black lines represent hypothetical medieval building lines, based on my research findings. Yellow shading indicates the buildings under discussion. Red lines indicate new, widened, or improved streets. North is at the top of each diagram.

The schematic diagrams representing the ancient Roman and medieval city are superimposed upon aerial photographs of the city center made in 1944 by the British Royal Air Force, before Allied bombing and postwar reconstruction altered the urban fabric. North is at the top.

Introduction

In the twelfth and thirteenth centuries, cities dispersed across Italy's Lombard plain achieved political independence and transformed their urban centers in rapid succession (fig. 1).[1] In Parma, a midsized city sited in the plain's heartland, between superpowers Milan and Bologna, the ruling elites created two magnificent civic squares framed by nine imposing new structures, including a freestanding baptistery, two bell towers, and six palaces, between 1196 and 1296 (fig. 2). These spaces survive today as the Piazza del Duomo and Piazza Garibaldi (figs. 3 and 4).[2] Parma achieved this remarkable transformation in unlikely circumstances, as the thirteenth century was marked by continual civil disorder, sporadic famine, military and diplomatic confrontations with international powers, and frequent intercity warfare.[3]

In this study, I demonstrate that planners in Parma employed rational, geometric principles to transform the city's urban core. In part I, I analyze the thirteenth-century development of Parma's two most important public spaces from heterogeneous assemblages to harmonious ensembles. I conclude that both the episcopal and communal squares were carefully crafted environments pervaded by order and animated by the desire to produce panoptic vistas of the major monuments defining the sites' perimeters.

The form and fortunes of Parma's two principal medieval squares intertwined with the political and urbanistic agendas of the city's dominant political factions. The piazzas gave physical shape to their embattled patrons' political imaginations. This statement flies in the face of two commonplace (if gradually abating) misconceptions about Italian medieval urbanism. Parma's piazzas were neither the ad hoc agglomerations of buildings that medieval urban projects have historically been characterized as being—a point already eloquently made by Marvin Trachtenberg and therefore needing no further explication here—nor merely unproblematic, collective expressions of communal pride, although the exaltation of local, civic prestige was certainly part of the equation.[4]

In part II, I reintegrate the real, physical space of the two piazzas produced in the course of the thirteenth century with the ideological space of their patrons. I do not aim to explain the formal and iconographic choices of the sites' builders by recourse to some ephemeral spirit of the age, but to provide the modern viewer with sufficient cues of Italian Duecento culture to decode the visual and cultural language

Fig. 1 Map of Italy.

Fig. 2 Parma's episcopal square (now Piazza del Duomo) and communal square (now Piazza Garibaldi) created between 1196 and 1296. Detail from Paolo Ponzoni, *Pianta della città di Parma in prospettiva* (Piacenza: Francesco Conti, 1572), woodcut, after an earlier drawing. ASPr, Raccolta Mappe e Disegni, vol. 2, no. 13. North is at the bottom of the map.

P. NOVA.

Communal Square

Episcopal Square

PARMA F.

P. S. BERNABA

CASTEL

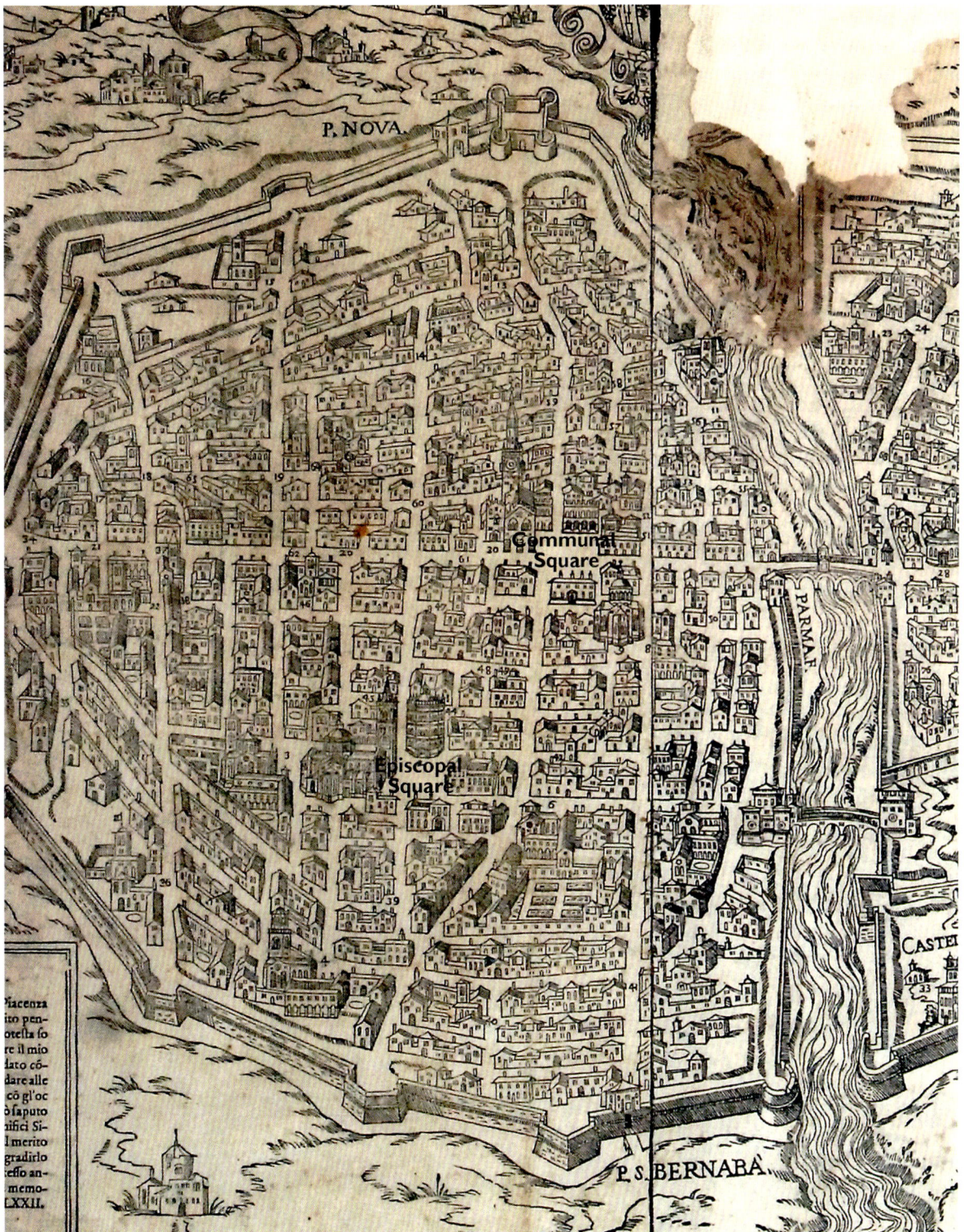

3

inscribed in the squares. I cannot achieve a seamless narrative, even if one were desirable; there are too many fissures in the historical fabric. My goal is to weave together sufficient strands to reveal the sites' semantics.

Fig. 3 Aerial view of Parma's Piazza del Duomo, or cathedral square, from the northwest, 2004.

Fig. 4 Aerial view of Parma's Piazza Garibaldi, the former communal government square, from the south, 2004.

This study differs from other works on medieval Italian architecture and urbanism in three ways. First, I center my inquiry on urban space, rather than focus on isolated buildings. Urban landscape and architecture, figure and ground, are examined together. Second, I consistently seek not only to reconstruct the two sites' period form but also to recapture their practical and symbolic function and their place in the production of civic consciousness. Third, I demonstrate that the political and artistic leaders of the pioneering commune of Parma engaged in deliberate, geometrically idealizing urban design a century before the patrons of the better-known Tuscan piazzas were born.

Although the cultural and urbanistic revival of Italy was pioneered by the communes of the Lombard plain, such as Parma, the intriguing relationship between their civic life and the carefully crafted physical setting from which it emerged has received little attention. The impulse that gave shape to the Italian piazza also shaped the emerging idea of the city-state.

A Tale of Two Cities: The *Civitas* and the *Urbs*

"A city (*civitas*) is a multitude of people united by a bond of community, named for its 'citizens' (*civis*), that is, from the residents of the city (*urbs*). . . . Now *urbs* (also 'city') is the name for the actual buildings, while *civitas* is not the stones, but the inhabitants."[5] So Isidore of Seville begins the chapter on public buildings in his encyclopedic collection of all human knowledge, the *Etymologies*. Isidore's seventh-century compendium remained, after the books of the Bible, the best-known and most influential text in western Europe throughout the Middle Ages.[6] The view Isidore presents of two coeval and interwoven systems, the city as social network (*civitas*) and the city as physical phenomenon (*urbs*), encapsulates medieval understanding of the city. Modern scholarship on the medieval city, however, has tended to divorce the *civitas* from the *urbs,* forming two discrete discourses, one on the social, economic, and institutional history of the city and another on its material manifestation.

This dichotomy presents special problems for students of twelfth- and thirteenth-century Italy and the urban transformations undertaken by communal governments, clerical authorities, and wealthy citizens. Historians, seeking to recapture the *civitas,* continually refer to this building boom as the material expression of its patrons' power and authority. However, they seldom elucidate with any specificity how these ideas were given visual form. Indeed, many accounts give the impression that it does not matter whether the structures that housed the new communal governments were brick, wood, or stone, had arcaded or trabeated loggias, or were crowned by battlements or plain roofs. Authors state that new town squares functioned as stages for civic ritual, but seldom pause to analyze those spatial arrangements. Thus, although architecture and urban renewal are frequently invoked as essential ingredients in the formation of the political culture of Italy's medieval communes, few historians have attempted to explain how these new building ensembles and spaces incarnated its notions of authority or how the new shape of the city encoded its political aspirations.[7]

By contrast, when analyzing Italy's medieval architectural and urbanistic culture, art historians have concentrated their attention on formal questions, architectural authorship, the characterization and development of period styles, or monographic studies of individual buildings, architects, or patrons. There are few book-length studies on medieval Italian cities as architectural environments, and those do not necessarily address how their architectural culture shapes and expresses their distinct civic culture.[8] In other words, the relationship between the *urbs* (the physical city) and the *civitas* (the social entity) remains inadequately explored by modern scholars. Because of their formative role in medieval urban culture, north Italy's new piazzas are fruitful terrain in which to examine this question. Parma's middling size and disproportionately large political importance in the Middle Ages, as well as its relatively well-preserved and documented piazzas, make it an ideal case study. I set out to ask—and answer—what seem to me the fundamental art-historical questions about Parma's medieval squares: Why do these buildings and sites exist? Why were they made this way? Why do they look the way they do? How do they work, or, in other words, how were they understood by their principal audiences? In doing so, I uncover an approach to understanding the form of the *urbs* that benefits from its symbiosis with the *civitas.*[9]

I mined four bodies of material to develop answers to these questions. The first was the physical evidence of the sites themselves. Even in their fragmented form, Parma's great piazzas still have much to tell about their original and evolving material history to the patient and attentive viewer. The second was the body of contemporary primary literature composed in Parma or relating to Parma. My reconstruction of Parma's political, social, and artistic circumstances at the time of its urbanistic transformation emerges from this heterogeneous mass of chronicles, legislative statutes, notarial documents, poems, papal bulls, imperial decrees, and inscriptions. (Though by its very nature this evidence captures the experience of a small, elite fraction of the Parmesan population and relegates the ordinary inhabitants to the sidelines, it is precisely this elite segment that master-minded the piazzas and constituted their most significant audience.) The third was the small but revealing group of historical representations of the city. These include maps, surveys, prints, mural paintings, sculpture, and historical photographs from the sixteenth to the twentieth centuries. Although visual representations of buildings and places are never unproblematic documents, they can, when used in combination and checked against other evidence, provide information unobtainable elsewhere about the sites' past appearance. Finally, aspects of the secondary literature on late medieval western European civilization, including Parma and northern Italy, informed my analysis of Parma's political and visual culture. Together, these materials enabled me to understand the conditions that resulted in the piazzas' formation, to develop a clear view of their building history, to analyze the conceptual approaches that underlie their design and ornamentation, and to see them with "period eyes."[10]

Analyzing Urban Space

Although the overall composition of Parma's medieval communal and episcopal squares survives, the sites have undergone several modifications in the intervening centuries. I used two key procedures to recapture their period appearance and to develop a credible theory of their place in civic consciousness. The first was to treat the space of the piazzas with as much rigor and attention as the buildings shaping their perimeter and therefore to place urban space at the center of inquiry. I addressed the urban landscape and architecture together,

seeing them as parts of a larger whole. The traditional art-historical approach of singling out the individual monument skews the results, negates the close interrelationships between buildings and their sites, and obscures the importance of shaped open space within the city. I paid particular attention to points of connection between buildings and between buildings and site—that is, materials, propor-tional systems, formal vocabulary—and to the physical, spatial relationships between them. At the core of my study was firsthand examination of the sites. I considered the forms of the spaces, the scale and shapes of the buildings framing them, the materials in evidence now, their relationship to the city fabric around them, and current traffic patterns. To capture the sites' forms, I gathered the best available surveys—those used by the city of Parma in the conduct of its public works. Eventually, I commissioned even more detailed surveys of the two piazzas; these were carried out in collaboration with architects Michela Rossi and Cecilia Tedeschi of the School of Architecture of the University of Parma.[11] In addition to documenting the plans of the two squares, the survey measured the elevations of the main building facades along their perimeters.

I supplemented these graphic representa-tions of the sites with extensive photographic documentation and examination of surviving historic views, including early modern maps and prints from Parma's Archivio di Stato, the Archivio Storico Comunale, the Biblioteca Palatina, and private collections.[12] A survey of textual sources complemented my study of the sites and their visual representations. Primary sources that were invaluable in reconstructing the piazzas' building chronology, form, and function include the *Chronicon Parmense* (fourteenth century), the chronicle of Salimbene de Adam (thirteenth century), the four sets of medieval statutes of Parma (thirteenth to fourteenth centuries), and the *Liber iurium communis Parme* (twelfth to fourteenth centuries).[13] Most apparent contradictions in the primary sources were resolved by going back and forth between the written sources, the visual sources, and the evidence provided by the current form of the piazzas, with one aspect informing and inflecting the conclusions reached by another approach. This integrated strategy constitutes the second key to elucidating Parma's medieval piazzas.

I was guided by three useful historical studies on medieval Parma and its urban form: Ireneo Affò's eighteenth-century history of medieval Parma, Marco Pellegri's essay "Parma medievale: Dai Carolingi agli Sforza," in *Parma: La città storica* (1978), and Juergen Schulz's 1982 article "The Communal Buildings of Parma."[14] Although it was written in the eighteenth century, Affò's history remains the most detailed treatment of Parma during the thirteenth century. Pellegri's essay, based on the state of research at the time of publication and intended for an audience of nonspecialists, provides an accessible chronological overview of Parma's urbanistic history between the eighth and the fifteenth centuries. Schulz's groundbreaking study of the history of the communal buildings of Parma, which rectifies several misunderstandings in the buildings' chronology, greatly facilitated my work by introducing me to Parma's basic historiography and providing a point of departure for my own interpretations. I supplemented these principal secondary sources with a myriad of specialized treatments of different aspects of the history of Parma and the Lombard plain.[15]

My method was informed by the work of other scholars engaged in the study of medieval Italian urbanism. Models in the use of primary sources to elucidate and interpret the medieval city include Francesca Bocchi and Elisabeth Crouzet-Pavan.[16] David Friedman's analysis of the towns founded by Florence in the fourteenth century alerted me to the importance and subtleties of overall composition and geometrically derived design.[17] Trachtenberg's examinations of urban space in Florence reminded me to think of the two piazzas of Parma as three-dimensional artifacts with a distinct materiality, not as two-dimensional plans.[18] Alick McLean's attentiveness to the uses of Prato's Piazza della Pieve heightened my sensitivity to the ways in which ritual animates public space.[19] Like theirs, my project derived from the conviction that buildings and public spaces are shaped by human enterprise to advance human agendas. Societies produce social spaces for their own self-presentation and representation, as Henri Lefebvre has argued.[20] As material embodiments of these social spaces, Parma's piazzas are ripe for art-historical investigation. To date, scholars have pursued the identification, dating, construction history, and, occasionally, iconography of the individual structures bordering Parma's medieval piazzas without considering the implications of these findings within the larger, spatio-visual system of the piazza and the town, or as an expression of the patrons' and planners' spatial practice at a specific moment in time. What I undertake in this study is the reconciliation of these two approaches.

I faced two major challenges in carrying out this analysis of Parma's urban space. The first was the fragmented state of research on Parma's medieval buildings. While some buildings and sites attract repeated attention, such as the baptistery and cathedral, others are virtually unknown.[21] Furthermore, the existing scholarship is often limited to discussions of dating, style, and authorship. The dearth of archaeological evidence compounds these limitations.[22] Since Parma's two great medieval piazzas remain at the center of a vibrant, modern city, their continuous habitation has altered their historical form and renders archaeological investigation difficult. The second challenge was the lack of a modern historical study of thirteenth-century Parma. Reinhold Schumann's analysis of the formation of the Parmesan commune extends only to the early twelfth century; Roberto Greci's studies of the city's economic history begin in the late fourteenth.[23] Most specialized historical treatments of Parma concentrate either on its perceived heyday, when the city was the capital of the Farnese duchy of Parma and Piacenza (1545–1735), or on the modern period (especially 1814–47). The gap is partially filled by heterogeneous studies of narrow subjects, a tradition begun by the antiquarian scholars of the nineteenth century and continuing today.[24]

The approaches outlined above helped me to overcome these barriers. Excessive or exclusive reliance on one or another type of data could have distorted my view, but using them together resulted in a system of checks and balances that enhanced the accuracy of the project. Used in constant dialogue with one another, these methods continually reminded me of the sites' temporality and their dialectical nature and enabled me gradually to shape a plausible narrative of their development. Careful study of

visual and textual historical sources and painstaking analysis of the sites—including photographic and graphic representation and measurement—can, in combination, enable the diligent scholar to reconstruct a hypothetical building history of the medieval city and recapture its urban image of itself.

Parma in the Middle Ages

Parma's patrons and builders did not begin construction of Parma's medieval piazzas on a tabula rasa. At the end of the twelfth century, Parma retained the underlying urban system that had organized the city at least since the first century B.C.E. Despite Paul the Deacon's well-known eighth-century statements to the contrary, the urban infrastructure of the Roman world had not entirely vanished from the peninsula.[25] Parma had been one of several Roman colonies along the via Emilia, the consular road that traversed the Po River plain, linking its fertile fields to the Adriatic ports. It was founded on the east bank of the Parma torrent (a tributary of the Po) in 183 B.C.E. and resettled in Augustan times. Like many other Roman colonies, Parma had an orthogonal street plan oriented to the cardinal points, and a rectangular forum at the intersection of the colony's *cardo maximus* (running north–south, corresponding to the modern via Farini and via Cavour) and *decumanus maximus* (which ran east–west and coincided with the intramural course of the via Emilia, fig. 5). A stone bridge spanned the Parma, linking the colony's *decumanus* to the extramural, western path of the consular road. A rectangular fortification marked the boundaries of the city, though it comprised earthworks and palisades rather

Fig. 5 Diagram of Roman Parma. The large yellow quadrangle corresponds to the hypothetical placement of the city's Roman walls. The small yellow squares represent the principal city gates.

Fig. 6 The city's two principal canals, the Canale Comune (A) and the Canale Maggiore (B), enter the city together at its northern boundary. The Canale Comune follows the path of the Roman *cardo maximus,* while the Canale Maggiore wraps around the *curtis regia* and then proceeds south to the east of the city's Roman perimeter. Detail from Giuseppe Cocconcelli, "Compendio del Corso di tutti li Canali, Canadelle, Condotti, e Scoli sotterranei della Città di Parma," 1765. ASCP, MS, no. 1, cubo 7, cassetto 1.6, Canali e canaletti.

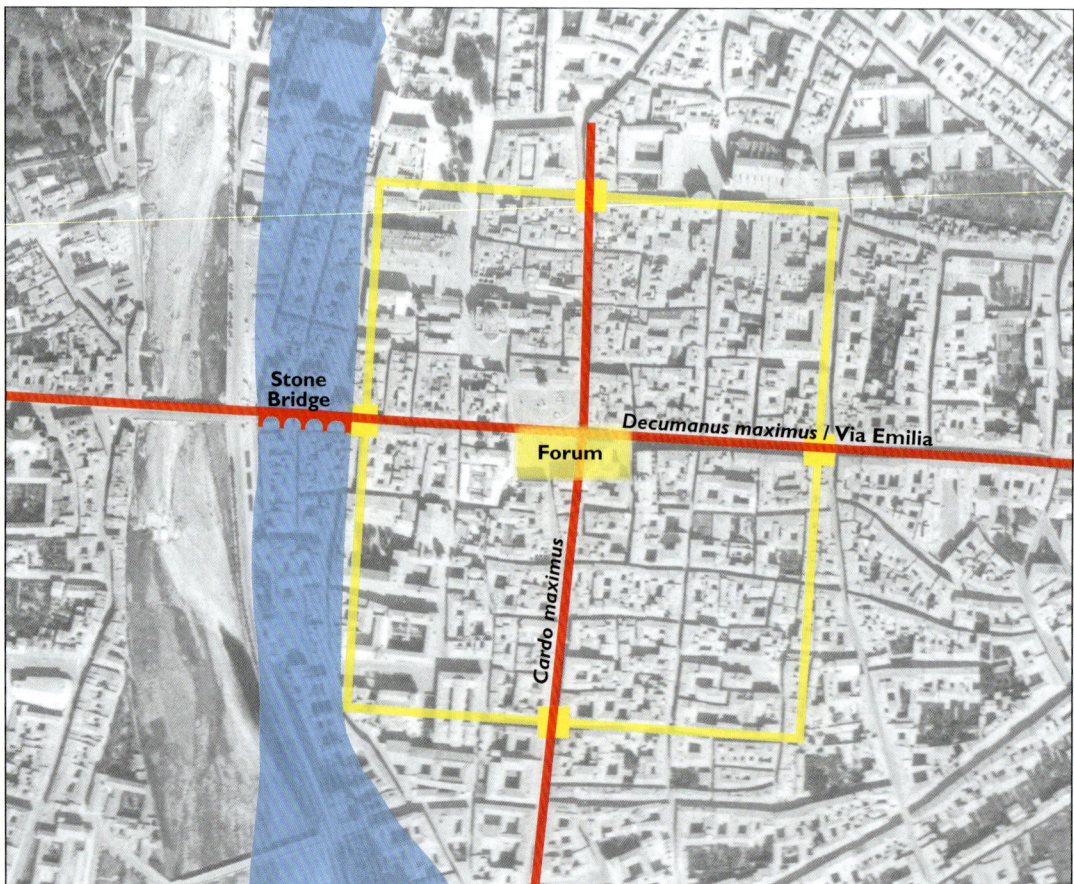

Stone Bridge

Decumanus maximus / Via Emilia

Forum

Cardo maximus

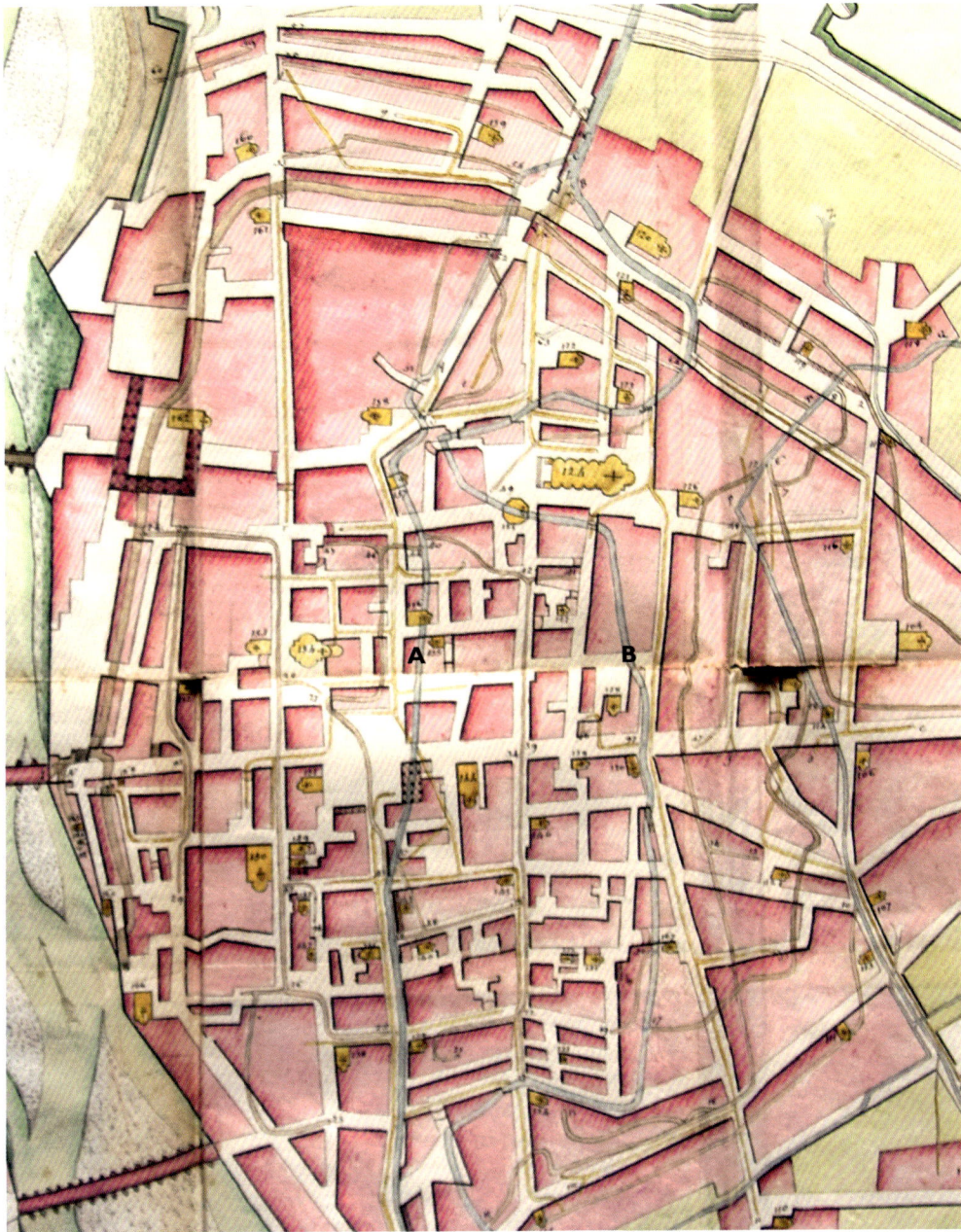

than masonry walls until late antiquity, when a proper enceinte was built.[26] By late antiquity, four fortified gates pierced the masonry walls built along the city's Roman perimeter, one at each end of the intramural paths of the via Emilia and *cardo maximus*. When the city grew beyond them, these fortifications were not systematically dismantled but rather incorporated into surrounding structures.[27]

When the medieval city eventually expanded beyond its Roman boundaries, the colony's orthogonal grid and major thoroughfares remained the backdrop against which later nodes and landmarks were established, although the city's original Roman pavements and buildings were long buried, minor Roman streets were overtaken by expanding city blocks, and diagonal or serpentine paths cut across former Roman *insulae*.[28] By the eleventh century, two major canals traditionally attributed to Theodoric's patronage carried water into the city from the Apennine foothills—the

Canale Maggiore traveled along the city's eastern Roman boundary, while the Canale Comune flanked the *cardo maximus* (fig. 6). An additional navigable waterway, the Naviglio, connected the city to the Taro River, about 7 kilometers west.[29] When a terrible flood in 1177 deviated the course of the Parma westward, leaving the Roman bridge high and dry, another soon replaced it nearby (first in wood, again in stone after 1207–10) (fig. 7). The pebbly former riverbed, or *glarea,* was repurposed as a marketplace, and merchants appropriated the ancient stone structure, turning it into shops (and eventually adopting its image as the seal of their guild). Upstream, an additional wooden bridge supplemented the via Emilia traverse.[30] At the southeastern edge of town, another Roman survival enjoyed a prestigious afterlife. By 1162, an imperial palace for Frederick I Barbarossa occupied part of the city's former amphitheater (fig. 8); it was known as the Palazzo dell'Arena.[31] Although by the twelfth century the city had

sprouted suburbs to the north, east, and west and new, more expansive fortifications to defend them, by 1169 only ecclesiastical buildings challenged the still-standing earlier circuit of walls, bridges, and imperial palace for prominence in the cityscape.[32]

The most significant among these were the cathedral, canonry, and bishop's residence constituting the episcopal compound and located along the northern boundary of the Roman city. Regardless of the precise positions of predecessor structures, most scholars agree that by the late twelfth century the present cathedral church dedicated to the Virgin of the Assumption faced a turreted bishop's palace whose footprint coincides with part of the larger, extant Palazzo del Vescovado.[33] Several important monasteries anchored the newly enclosed suburbs. The powerful Benedictine abbey of San Giovanni (founded 980) and convent of San Paolo (by 1000) occupied large tracts of land to the north; another group of

Fig. 7 Diagram of Parma c. 1190. The solid yellow line represents the path of the city walls. The dotted yellow quadrangle corresponds to the hypothetical placement of the city's Roman fortifications, which partly survived in this period. The small yellow squares represent the principal city gates.

Fig. 8 Traces of the arcade of the imperial Palazzo dell'Arena, built into part of the city's Roman amphitheater, remain engulfed in the later masonry of the Collegio Maria Luigia on borgo Lalatta, Parma.

Benedictines established the convent of Sant'Uldarico (c. 1000), which stood near the city's southernmost gate. But smaller religious foundations could also be found in the heart of Parma, such as the convent of Sant'Alessandro (by 835), sited near the pre-1177 eastern bank of the torrent, and the churches of San Pietro (955) and San Vitale (972), located respectively near the western and eastern edges of the former forum.[34] The most important families and institutions clustered opportunistically around the major morphological elements of the ancient city and the newer Christian institutions: near the city gates, around the cathedral and important monasteries, and along the busiest streets. Extant Roman building materials both commonplace (recycled bricks) and exalted (sculpted and colored marbles) were reused by Parma's medieval inhabitants. Similarly, the surviving remains of Roman law and political and literary thought were mined by Italy's late medieval population to produce a distinctive social and political urban culture. As Philip Jones has observed: "In Italy as nowhere else city and city-commune were seen and felt to re-embody the ancient *civitas* . . . because here, as nowhere else, by force of ancient custom . . . all races and classes had preserved the Latin habit of urbanity."[35]

The Patrons

Despite their common Roman heritage, the Lombard plain in the High Middle Ages was a markedly different world from the late medieval Tuscan environment more familiar to Anglophone art historians.[36] Since Jones's trenchant 1978 article on the "legend of the bourgeoisie," a preponderance of historians have accepted that the engine driving political and economic change in twelfth- and thirteenth-century northern Italy was not some imaginary burgeoning merchant class but rather the increasingly independent and affluent landed nobility. However, the elegant model proposed by Henri Pirenne fifty years earlier, in which political and social privilege are acquired by international merchants who then transform the cities, continues to haunt the *art-historical* literature on Italian urbanism. While this model is valid for some northern European cities and perhaps even a few of the Tuscan and maritime cities of Italy, it does not fit Parma's circumstances or, indeed, those of the dense network of cities of the Lombard plain. Unlike the Tuscan cities in the thirteenth and fourteenth centuries, Parma was never a mercantile republic; power in medieval Parma was held closely by a small band of aristocrats whose authority derived from military might and whose revenues originated in the region's lavish agricultural resources.[37]

The prosopographical investigations undertaken by political historians and antiquarians for Parma reveal that although the urban elite continually fractured into new political alliances throughout the twelfth and thirteenth centuries, it was nonetheless ideologically and socially homogeneous. It had its origins in the region's imperial and clerical aristocracy. More like their ancient Roman ancestors than the fourteenth-century merchant-princes and burghers to whom they are often compared, Parma's oligarchs were urban dwellers whose economic power originated in the revenues of their lands in the countryside. Their political power emanated from the traditional jurisdictions accompanying those lands, the administrative, diplomatic, and juridical skills associated with their fruitful management, and their individual and collective military prowess. These lords, whether secular or ecclesiastical, resided in the city, although they had jurisdiction over lands of diverse origins—received in association with a particular office, granted to them in exchange for services, inherited from their ancestors, or seized by military conquest.[38]

On the eve of the thirteenth century, Parma's urban elite comprised members of about twenty families, of which three—the Rossi, the da Correggio, and the Sanvitale—towered over the rest in prestige and influence.[39] When the political system that had supported the dominion of the counts and bishops of Parma from the ninth to the twelfth centuries collapsed as part of the erosion of imperial authority in Italy, these families filled the political vacuum, either through the preexisting but evolving offices of the church or by means of new communal societies organized by the elite families themselves.[40] Through coalition, noble clans could gain the strength to effectively challenge the authority of imperial overlords and their local representatives and achieve independence.

In Parma, as throughout northern Italy, these communal associations were headed at first by members of the local urban elite—the so-called consular aristocracy. However, conflicts of interest resulting from a local's administration of the communal government occasioned a change in practice. By the end of the twelfth century, communal councils usually elected as their executive officer a foreigner instead of a neighbor and fellow citizen, in the hope of controlling corruption and civil unrest. The commune's executive office, that of podesta, and later also the offices of rector and military

captain (or *capitano*) demanded men in whom administrative and juridical experience were coupled with substantial personal authority. The persons elected to fill these roles in Parma were typically members of the elites of other north Italian cities, particularly those with whom Parma's ruling class was in political sympathy. For a north Italian male, holding an executive office in a foreign city was both a sign and a source of personal prestige and substantial income.

Members of Parma's top families were distinguished from their peers elsewhere by holding a disproportionate number of offices in other Italian cities, as Olivier Guyotjeannin's groundbreaking investigations show. Only much larger cities such as Bologna and Milan outstripped Parma's high level of "exportations" of citizens to serve as officers elsewhere. This phenomenon demonstrates the exalted social regard in which Parma's elites were held. The Rossi and the da Correggio lineages outdistanced their Parmesan peers: together, they accounted for more than a third of Parma's exported officers and for the largest number of appointments in prestigious cities, such as Bologna, Florence, and Genoa. This renown was also in evidence locally. From the beginning of Parma's communal age, the Rossi were closely involved with the commune's leadership. The clan's founder, Rolando (or Orlando) il Rosso was consul and then podesta of Parma repeatedly in the middle third of the twelfth century; his grandson, another Rolando, served as Parma's podesta in 1180, 1182, and 1201, and rector in 1198. Their relatives Alberto, Bernardo, Gherardo, Orlando, and Sigifredo Rossi likewise occupied many Parmesan communal offices in the twelfth and early thirteenth centuries.[41] Unlike in Florence, aristocratic involvement in the commune survived the brief local heyday of the *popolo,* whose political organization the more politically experienced noble clans promptly took over. Gherardo da Correggio served as podesta of Parma in 1238 and 1247. His son Guido was *capitano del popolo* in 1285. And Guido's son Giberto (or Gilberto) attained lordship over the city in 1303.[42] Although the Sanvitale held Parmesan communal offices from time to time, the clan did not express its political eros principally via communal involvement within Parma. Instead, members chose to exploit church institutions as a springboard for their political aspirations. Alberto and Òbizzo Sanvitale held the office of bishop of Parma from 1243 to 1295; Bishop Òbizzo's brother Anselmo was first canon, then provost of the cathedral chapter. The Sanvitale, Rossi, and Fieschi lineages controlled the bishopric of Parma continuously from 1194 to 1375. Their hold on the cathedral chapter was nearly as strong—for example, in 1280 the canons of the chapter included three Sanvitale, two Rossi, and one Fieschi.[43] It is important to note that every important Parmesan clan had several members who, whether or not they also held religious or communal office, distinguished themselves at feats of arms as well as reading the political winds. Gherardo da Correggio took the field both on behalf of Emperor Frederick II, at Cortenuova in 1237, and against him, at Borghetto di Taro in 1247. Gherardo was on the winning side both times.

The glory of Parma's ruling classes extended beyond the Lombard plain. Members of Parma's elite mingled with the most influential circles of European society. For many years, Bernardo di Rolando Rossi was an intimate of Holy Roman Emperor Frederick II. The Sanvitale and, to a lesser extent, the Rossi were related by kinship ties to Pope Innocent IV (Sinibaldo Fieschi), who had served as canon of Parma's cathedral. Innocent IV's nephew Ottobono Fieschi, also a canon of Parma, was elected Pope Adrian V in 1276, although he died shortly after taking office. Their kin held prebends and bishoprics as far away as Lincoln and Lyon.[44]

Thus, the Parmesan elites who transformed the city's urban core belonged to a broad European class that exercised its talents and privileges well beyond the boundaries of the local territory. They shared the political and social experience of a wider network of individuals who administered the papacy and the church, the Holy Roman Empire, and the increasingly independent city-states of north Italy. The men who made up Parma's ruling class—whether in lay or religious office—had a common heritage, education, and cultural outlook.[45] The clerical, the notarial, and the noble commingled in a single administrative class. As has been demonstrated by Robert Black, Hélène Wieruszowski, Louis Paetow, Ernst Curtius, and others, the administrative class's formal education, whether acquired at a university such as that of Bologna or Padua or locally at Parma's cathedral school, encompassed a legal and literary tradition profoundly steeped in ancient Roman precedents. Whether they studied "the poets" (including Virgil, Ovid, and Horace), prose authors such as Cicero and Sallust, the Justinianic code and its commentaries, or, more commonly, the *ars dictaminis* and *ars concionandi* by means of compendia and florilegia assembled for the purpose, Parma's oligarchs would have been exposed to the Latin authors—and their Roman ideas—from "their grammar-school days." Though little information survives about the contents of the Parma cathedral library in the Middle Ages, one of the texts it owned at the end of the thirteenth century was a book of Cicero's letters.[46]

Rhetoric was at the center of practical education. Above all things, a good administrator had to be able to speak and write effectively. As Lauro Martines has noted, Brunetto Latini (c. 1210–1294) went so far as to assert that "the supreme science of governing a city is rhetoric: that is to say, the science of speaking, for without effective speech the city would not exist and there would be neither justice nor human company." An individual's personal authority and political effectiveness depended not only on his military and administrative skills but upon his eloquence, as Enrico Artifoni has documented. An official must have "sapientia, nobilitate, moribus et eloquentia," or, in Salimbene's words, "understanding, eloquence, and virtue"; Salimbene took nobility for granted.[47]

Students learned rhetoric from Latin and vernacular texts that included Cicero's treatises, their glosses by medieval authors, and textbooks that incorporated theory with examples of prose taken from ancient Roman history. Certain school exercises even demanded that students write in the voices of particular ancient figures, such as Cicero and Catiline. "How-to" books helped aspiring administrators to master the art of official communication. Manuals for podestas typically compiled model speeches and letters for various situations, such as taking office or greeting an ambassador.[48] And this grounding in Roman thought was by no means limited to lay education, as surviving glosses in a twelfth-century copy of Sallust's *Bellum Jugurthinum* mentioned by Black indicate.[49]

As Virginia Cox and Stephen Milner have shown, in thirteenth-century Italy abstract knowledge of ancient rhetoric and literature—the Ciceronianism of the classroom—was accompanied by another brand of Ciceronianism, one that was deployed in the piazzas, law courts, and council chambers by speakers who shared his "ideology of republicanism." Medieval political theory and philosophy had, in the precommunal age, sought to exalt the authority of the king, emperor, or pope. Communal governments and their rivals had to devise alternative ways to justify their desire for independence from their overlords, and their claim to exercise regalian rights and jurisdiction. In the campaign to legitimate their form of government, Italy's communal elites repeatedly identified the medieval commune with the Roman state, and its councils with the Roman senate. In the adversarial political and religious environment of the communes in the age of faction, leaders found the persuasive political and juridical speech outlined by Cicero and the republican ideology of Sallust particularly well suited to the need to harness conflict for the public good. These ideas are enthusiastically taken up in the late twelfth and thirteenth centuries by authors concerned with the art of speaking and ruling well, as Quentin Skinner has demonstrated.[50]

If Italy's urban elites were steeped in the remains of ancient Roman culture, they were simultaneously fascinated by the courtly values of their neighbors across the Alps. Chivalric culture, with its exaltation of military prowess, emphasis on virtue, and high regard for honor and status, had been imported to Italy along with French chivalric romances in the twelfth century.[51] The medieval neologism *curialitas*

Fig. 9 In this statue made at the time of Charles of Anjou's appointment as senator of Rome, he is seated on a classicizing curule chair. Arnolfo di Cambio, *Charles of Anjou*, c. 1277–81. Capitoline Museums, Rome.

encompassed the concepts of courtesy and courtliness appropriate to courtly culture while preserving its associations with rule and with the *curia,* or court. It promptly became a useful model of behavior for Italian elites in these unstable times; courtliness in a man was repeatedly noted as worthy of praise through the thirteenth century.[52]

I separate the closely intertwined strands of *romanitas* and *curialitas* to clarify my argument, but not without emphasizing that it is a distinction made in hindsight. In the mid–thirteenth century, not only did *romanitas* and *curialitas* coexist without conflict, but their coexistence was desirable and valued, regardless of how contradictory it may seem to modern eyes. Greco-Roman history and mythology—the Matter of Rome—were as apt subjects for romance literature as Arthurian legend—the Matter of Britain. Hector, Alexander, and Julius Caesar accompanied Arthur and Charlemagne in the pantheon of medieval military heroes.[53] Nor was the synthesis confined to imaginary or historical contexts. In self-conscious evocation of Roman mores, Charles, count of Anjou and Provence, was elected senator of the commune of Rome on the Capitoline Hill in 1265. As Julia Bolton Holloway has noted, his appointment was commemorated by Arnolfo di Cambio's monumental statue of Charles sitting on a curule chair and dressed in classicizing costume, now in Rome's Capitoline Museums (fig. 9).[54] However, Charles's was the epitome of nonrepublican, noble blood. He was a son of King Louis VIII of France, brother of King Louis IX, and he accepted the throne of the Kingdom of Sicily from the pope the same year he became a Roman senator. The royal brothers were renowned for their artistic patronage, and

Charles's military exploits were the stuff of chivalric poetry.[55]

Struggles for Authority in the Communal Age

The great urban building projects of the north Italian thirteenth century did not take place as a result of the calm machinations of increasingly self-assertive merchant-burghers—an insignificant segment of Parma's population—but rather against a backdrop of breathtaking instability. Achieving sustainable order and security was the greatest problem of late medieval society in northern Italy, not the vagaries of trade. As the city-states of northern Italy won their prized independence from the Holy Roman emperor, and as the temporal claims of the papacy weakened in the face of the empire's challenges, the link to authority that legitimated the habitual jurisdictions and privileges of many members of the north Italian elites eroded. Powerful local lords saw an opportunity to seize some of these lands and rights for themselves and their heirs, as there was relatively little effective institutional resistance. The consequence, however, was considerable (and increasing) unrest as individuals and alliances battled for dominance over cities, castles, and regions.[56]

Parma was no exception. In Parma, the bishop had since 1037 held the title of count from the emperor; he was not only the *de facto* ruler of the Parmesan territory but its *de jure* ruler as well. The Parmesan church's relations with the imperial court were close. Most Parmesan bishops since the mid–ninth century had been chosen by the emperors from members of their chancery, and antipopes Honorius II (*reg.* 1061–72) and Clement III (*reg.* 1080–

1100) had been bishops of Parma before their imperial investitures to the pontificate. When, in the aftermath of the investiture controversy, the party led by Countess Matilda of Canossa prevailed in Parma and installed Vallombrosan abbot Bernardo degli Uberti as the city's bishop (*reg.* 1106–33), the local balance of power was destabilized. The saintly Bishop Bernardo not only refused to exercise secular, comital rights over the Parmesan territory but also delegated its military leadership.[57] By the time Aicardo da Cornazzano, the next pro-imperial bishop, took office in 1162, the Parmesan commune was firmly established and had taken over much of the city's administration. His successor, Bernardo II (*reg.* c. 1170–94), asserted his authority as bishop-count and reclaimed some of the bishopric's secular, regalian rights and jurisdictions. However, the privileges granted the communal associations of nobles by Frederick I at the Peace of Constance in 1183—in the hope of retaining nominal, if not actual, control over Lombardy—called into question the temporal jurisdiction accorded to the bishop-counts of Parma by prior emperors. This conflict resulted in an extended period of jockeying for power between several Parmesan clans, played out in part through the existing ecclesiastical and the emerging communal institutions.[58]

Parma's fragmentation into competing factions, or *partes,* was not unusual—it mirrored developments in other northern and central Italian cities at the time. Individual secular and ecclesiastical lords and communal governments resisted Emperor Frederick I Barbarossa's attempts at subjugation, as well as the territorial ambitions of their regional rivals. As did their peers in Bologna, Milan, and Florence, the Parmesan aristocrats pursued all available paths to dominion—including legislation, the establishment of new political institutions, diplomacy, alliance, and violent confrontation—and exploited the weakness of imperial claimants and popes alike to their own advantage. Partisan allegiances among individuals, clans, cities, princes, and even supra-regional entities such as the empire and the papacy fluctuated according to expediency and did not consistently reflect strongly held ideological positions. The 1198 dispute between Philip of Swabia of the Hohenstaufen dynasty and Otto of Brunswick of the Welf dynasty to succeed Henry IV as emperor, and the imperial policies associated with each, lent the enduring nomenclature "Guelph" (for pro-Welf, anti-Hohenstaufen, and hence anti-imperial and pro-papal allegiance) and "Ghibelline" (after the Hohenstaufen castle at Waiblingen, for pro-Hohenstaufen and pro-imperial allegiance) first to Florence's two principal urban factions and eventually to those in other Italian cities. Like communal factionalism itself, the labels "Guelph" and "Ghibelline" (and their Latin counterparts *pars ecclesiae* and *pars imperii*) endured into the fourteenth century. Already by the thirteenth century, neither the phenomenon nor its designations had much to do with papal or imperial sympathies or agendas, but rather with local responses to particular circumstances and conflicts. For example, Bernardo di Rolando Rossi, who had been part of Emperor Frederick II's inner circle, abandoned his support of the imperial party the moment his brother-in-law Sinibaldo Fieschi attained the papal throne in 1244 as Innocent IV.[59]

While the Parmesan nobles vied with each other for power throughout the twelfth century and into the thirteenth, the remainder of the population suffered. War and its consequences disrupted the agricultural production that drove the local economy. Disputes over water rights impeded irrigation and agricultural processing. Roads were not maintained. Travel was impaired, as jurisdiction over roads, passes, and waterways was contested. Public safety was hampered, as vendettas between clans that had originated in the countryside were carried on in the city, and vice versa. There was confusion about who had the right to adjudicate civil and criminal matters. The mismanagement of urban fortifications affected not only their gatekeepers' revenues but also the city's safety from invasion. In sum, the minimum standards of civil conduct that made urban life possible after the decline of Roman imperial administration continued to erode.

In the thirteenth century, Parma's fragmented urban elites attempted to bring the situation under control. The faction that controlled the bishopric and cathedral chapter tried its best to retain the power that remained in its hands. The communal association, led by another elite faction, gradually arrogated many of the duties and privileges of the bishop. It could only keep these privileges and powers over a restless and suspicious population, however, if it could prove that its mode of governance was capable of imposing order on the tumult and maintaining the standards that made civil—and therefore civic—life possible.

Hindsight allows us to see that the power of Parma's bishops was waning irredeemably by the late twelfth century. Bernardo II and his successors would not be able to retrieve their secular authority from lay hands. Nonetheless, clerics were often exempt from the jurisdiction of the new lay government institutions, and clerical offices such as canonries—and especially the bishopric itself—commanded substantial properties, castles, and incomes. Thus, the church and its institutions remained a viable base from which members of the urban elite could struggle with their rivals for power over the city throughout the thirteenth century.[60]

These are the fundamental sociopolitical circumstances in which the civic center of Parma was transformed. One way in which the church faction competed against the growing communal government was by imposing a coherent urbanistic program on the site of the episcopal precinct.[61] This newly ordered piazza could be understood as a metaphor for the orderly society sought by the bishop and his allies. In turn, the factions that controlled the communal government asserted their own growing authority by developing a rival center within the city. Thus, the episcopal and communal squares developed in the course of the Duecento were not only the headquarters for the leaders of their respective rival alliances; they were also beacons for their patrons' political programs, as I discuss in part II. Existing documentation indicates how carefully the elites who controlled the communal government affirmed standards of behavior so as to preserve order in their evolving communal compound. Textual records attesting to the desires of the episcopal elites are harder to find, but in both cases the surviving city fabric demonstrates how both factions' will to order was imposed architecturally on the physical city, as both prelude to and symbol of its imposition on the citizens.

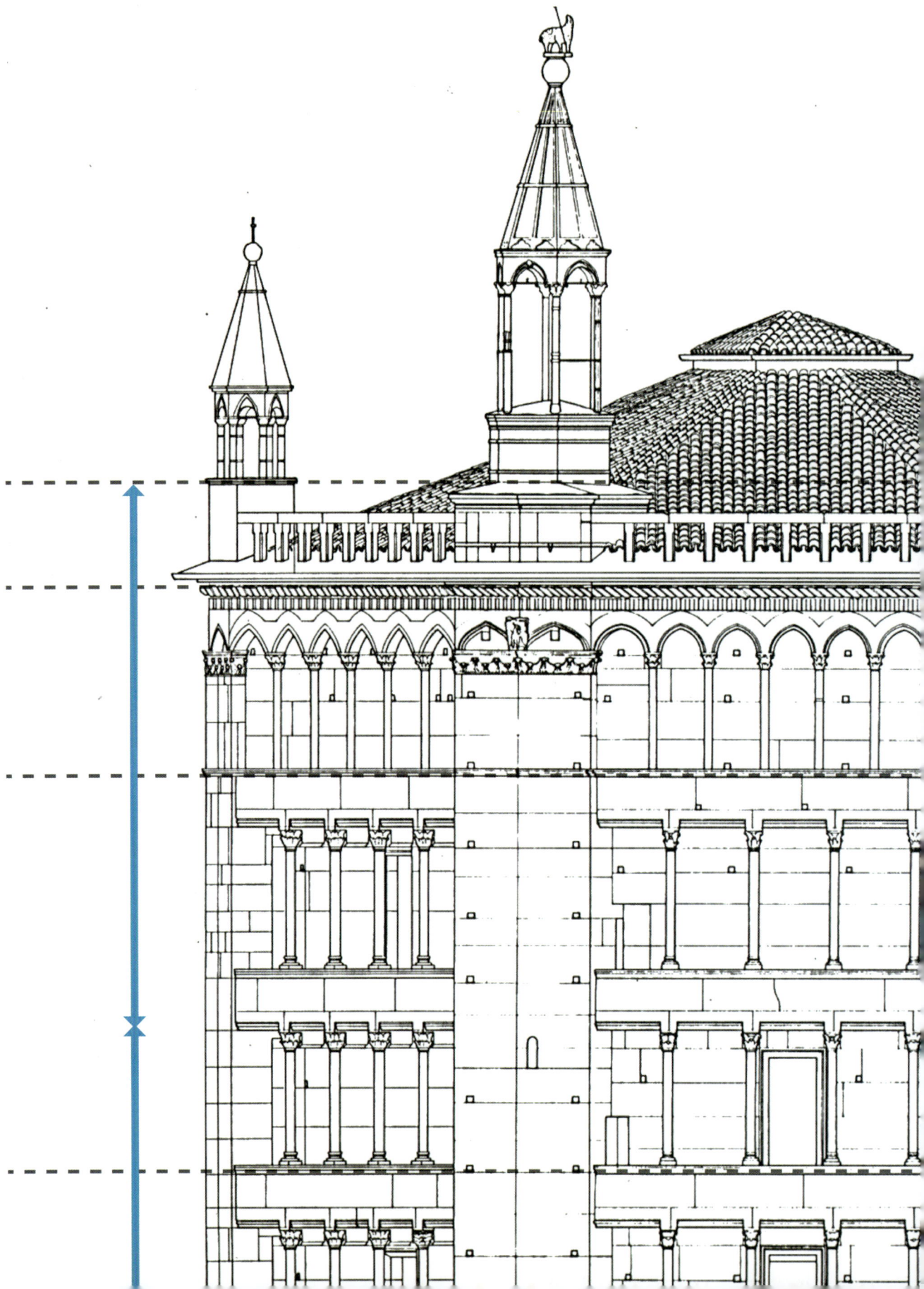

Part I

The Production of Order

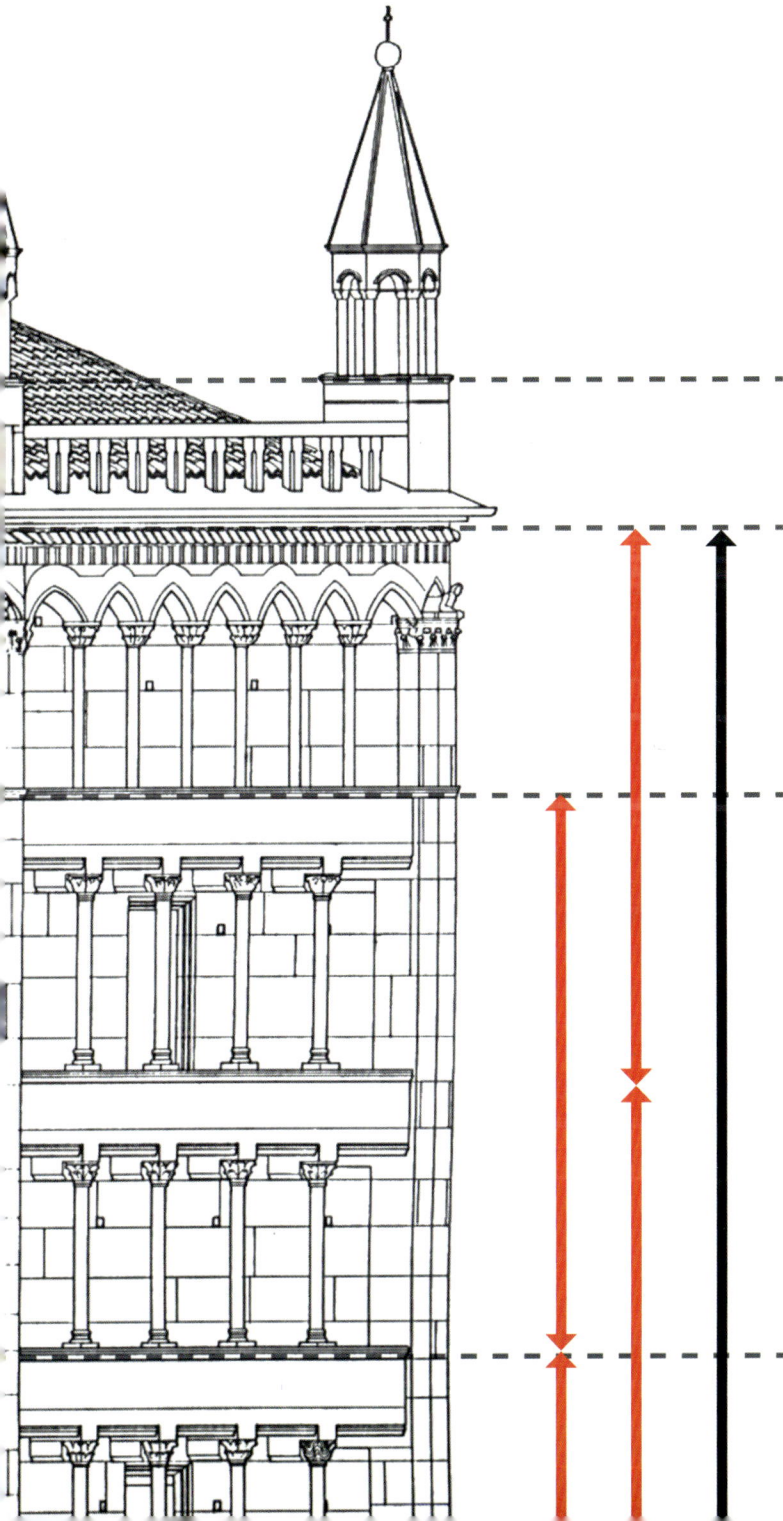

CHAPTER 1

(Re)constructing the Piazza del Duomo

Of Parma's two great medieval piazzas, the Piazza del Duomo has historical precedence (figs. 3 and 10).[1] In 1149, when the site that was to become the Piazza Comunale functioned as little more than a busy intersection, Parma's episcopal precinct already comprised a bishop's palace, a cathedral, and a chapter house. It had served as the seat of emperors, popes, bishops, counts, and kings. Over the course of the thirteenth century, the leaders of the church faction transformed this prestigious but inchoate site into a coherent urbanistic ensemble. In this chapter, I reconstruct the piazza's transformation and recover its formal program.[2]

The physical qualities of the piazza that delight the eye today—its square shape, the symmetrical arrangement of its buildings, the harmonious repetition of materials and motifs—were all contrived by its thirteenth-century planners. A series of minor, postmedieval interventions in the streets and buildings surrounding the piazza have not changed its essential character. The Piazza del Duomo looks much as it did in 1300, despite the periodic updates to the bishop's palace facade, the insertion of a new street to the south of the cathedral in the sixteenth century, the addition of private chapels along the cathedral's flanks,

the initiation of a never-completed new tower in the seventeenth century, and the replacement of the chapter house with the Seminario Maggiore.[3] The Allied bombs that damaged a third of the city center and demolished buildings on the piazza's northern edge in the spring of 1944 spared (some say miraculously) the medieval cathedral, campanile, baptistery, and bishop's palace.[4]

To reconstruct the piazza's building history, I worked backward, using close examination of the surviving fabric and the pertinent textual evidence to conceptually peel off the layers of change undergone by the site and arrive at the piazza's likely state in the mid–twelfth century. Rather than encumber the reader with an account of this tangled research, I present my reconstruction—and the evidence supporting it—chronologically, testing my method in the process.

The Episcopal Precinct in the Late Twelfth Century

In the late twelfth century, the episcopal center of Parma was located just inside the northern perimeter of the city's late antique walls, on a site known as the *curtis regia,* or the royal court (fig. 7), which was given to the bishops by King

Carloman of Italy (*reg.* 877–80) in 877.[5] In the episcopal precinct, the reconstruction of the cathedral—which had been severely damaged by an earthquake in 1117—was nearly complete. The newly finished church, dedicated to the Virgin of the Assumption, was the most imposing structure on the site (figs. 11 and 12). Like other cathedrals in the region, it was a three-aisled basilica with a projecting transept and three apses, though its greater scale and architectural massing evoked the grand imperial basilicas at Speyer and Limburg an der Haardt.[6] Three portals and a series of galleries pierced its sandstone-revetted, "Lombard" screen facade.[7] A heterogeneous cluster of smaller structures, including the chapel of Sant'Agata, assorted tomb monuments, a portico, and the canonical complex, occupied the space immediately to the basilica's south.[8] A bell tower of uncertain date stood southwest of the cathedral facade, approximately on the site of the current campanile.

After the cathedral, the next largest structure in the *curtis regia* was the bishop's palace to its west.[9] Like the church, it was founded in the eleventh century and expanded in the late twelfth century under Bishop-Count Bernardo II. In 1194, the palace was most likely an L-shaped brick structure with at least two towers, one to the northwest and another to the northeast (fig. 13).[10] The northern wing of today's palace contains substantial passages of eleventh- and twelfth-century fabric, as do portions of its eastern wing (fig. 14; note the remains of a tower projecting above the palace's northwestern corner). The irregularly shaped area between the cathedral and the bishop's palace seems to have been unoccupied after the sixth century.[11] Houses owned by powerful Parmesan aristocrats clustered to the north and south of this clear space.[12]

Thus, when Bishop Òbizzo Fieschi (*reg.* 1194–1224) came to power, the episcopal compound consisted of a cathedral, bell tower, chapter house, bishop's palace, and assorted minor structures surrounded by the Canale Maggiore.[13] They bounded a clear but amorphous open space (fig. 11). Òbizzo, a member of the Parmesan branch of the powerful Ligurian Fieschi family and a long-standing member of the cathedral chapter, was elected bishop by his fellow canons.[14] He inherited a complex political situation. Just two years before, his predecessor, Bernardo II, and the commune had become embroiled in a dispute about legal jurisdiction that culminated in podesta Bernardo da Cornazzano's excommunication and his retaliatory sack of the bishop's palace and imprisonment of the bishop.[15] The quarrel, like the bishop's claims to temporal authority over Parma and its *contado* (meaning both countryside and county), had deep roots.

In 962, Emperor Otto I had conceded comital rights over the city and an additional three miles of territory beyond its walls to Bishop Uberto (or Oberto, *reg.* 960–80) and his

Fig. 10 Parma's episcopal square, as represented in the late sixteenth century. Detail from Paolo Ponzoni, *Pianta della città di Parma in prospettiva* (Piacenza: Francesco Conti, 1572), woodcut, after an earlier drawing. ASPr, Raccolta Mappe e Disegni, vol. 2, no. 13. North is at the bottom of the map.

Fig. 11 Reconstruction diagram, the cathedral piazza of Parma c. 1195.

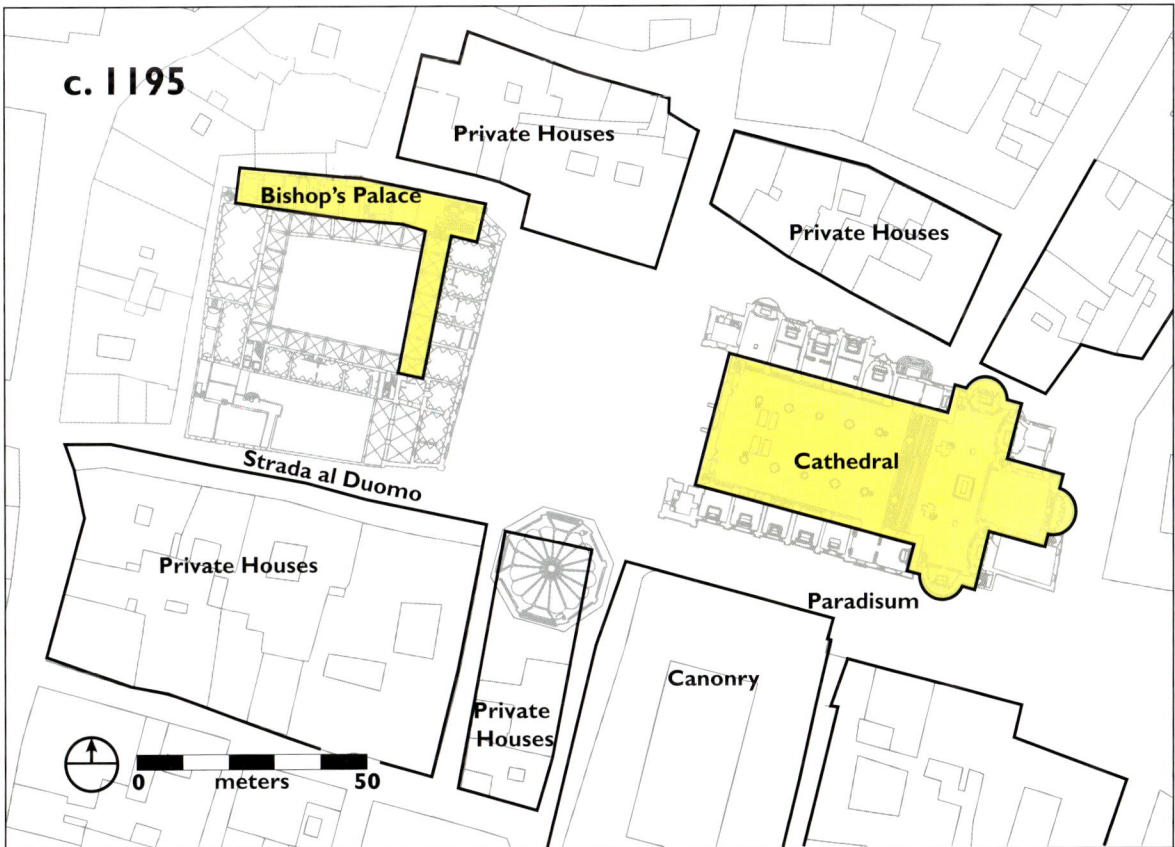

c. 1195

Private Houses

Bishop's Palace

Private Houses

Private Houses

Cathedral

Strada al Duomo

Private Houses

Paradisum

Private
Houses

Canonry

0   meters   50

Fig. 12 Detail of the facade of the Duomo, Parma.

Fig. 13 Plan of the bishop's palace of Parma, with its eleventh- and twelfth-century core indicated in yellow. North is at the top.

Fig. 14 Aerial view of the bishop's palace from the northwest in 1961.

successors. By 1037, the bishops exercised secular dominion throughout the entire diocese.[16] The ecclesiastical and political turmoil of the Gregorian reform, manifested locally by the consecutive appointment of two pro-papal bishops (Bernardo degli Uberti and Lanfranco, *reg.* 1136–63) supported by regional despot Matilda of Canossa, interrupted the Parmesan episcopacy's tradition of secular rule and imperial allegiance. The power vacuum triggered by Matilda's death, in 1115, facilitated the ascendancy of rival claimants to temporal power over the county of Parma, some of whom established the city's first communal government.[17] With the support of Emperor Frederick I, the ambitious Bishop Bernardo II reclaimed for himself and his office the privileges and jurisdictions surrendered by Bernardo I and Lanfranco and arrogated by the commune. However, the contradictory constitutions of the Peace of Constance, which granted regalian rights to the communes while simultaneously claiming to preserve the bishop's comital rights, inevitably led to conflict.[18] Clashes over sovereignty and jurisdiction recurred sporadically for the next century, even in the face of the commune's inexorable ascendancy. Òbizzo, like Bernardo II, boldly insisted on his temporal authority. In 1195, Parmesan politics reached a precarious balance when Emperor Henry VI reconfirmed the political jurisdiction of the bishop and chapter over the county of Parma.[19]

But Bernardo II left Òbizzo another legacy as well: a tradition of using architectural patronage to assert his status and a highly skilled *laborerium,* or cathedral workshop, that included some of the most accomplished artists in the region.[20] Foremost among them was the sculptor who signed the celebrated Deposition

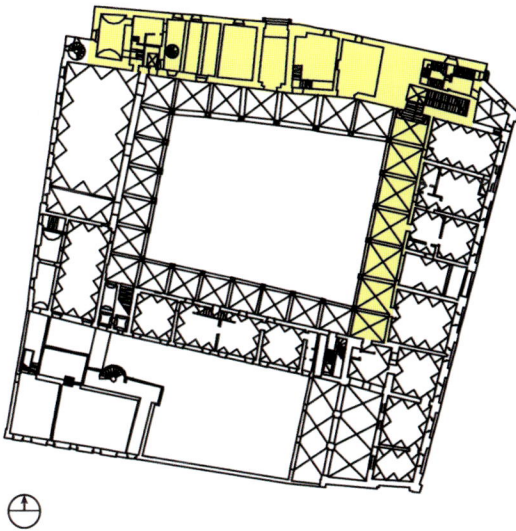

of Christ relief now in the cathedral transept and probably masterminded the now-vanished choir screen of which the relief once was a part: Benezetto Antelami.

The Transformation Begins: The Foundation of the Baptistery

In 1196, the third year of Òbizzo's reign, the cathedral workshop directed by Benezetto Antelami laid the foundations for a new baptistery (fig. 15).[21] This project initiated the century-long transformation of the *platea maioris ecclesia,* as the open space in the middle of the former *curtis regia* was known (fig. 16).[22]

The baptistery begun by Benezetto was made of the typical brick of the Po plain but faced with the pink-and-white limestone known as *rosso di Verona.*[23] Eight polygonal buttresses form the angles of the baptistery's irregular octagonal plan. Three of the building's facets encompass richly sculpted, splayed,

Gothicizing portals on the ground story. The remaining five facets are composed of blind arches supported by classicizing engaged columns. Above the ground story, the exterior of the baptistery is articulated by four tiers of colonnaded galleries, topped by a blind arcade and massive dentil and cable moldings. A balustrade, pinnacles, and a bell cote project from the baptistery's low peaked roof.

The octagonal form chosen for the baptistery's exterior had a long history in Italy. The typology originates in early Christian martyria and baptisteries, but in choosing it, Parma's planners also were participating in a more recent architectural discourse. In the eleventh and twelfth centuries, various communities throughout upper Italy set out to build free-standing baptistery structures that rivaled the peninsula's prestigious early Christian and Byzantine examples.[24] Parma's baptismal building seems closely related to two predecessors, the baptisteries of Florence (by 1059) and

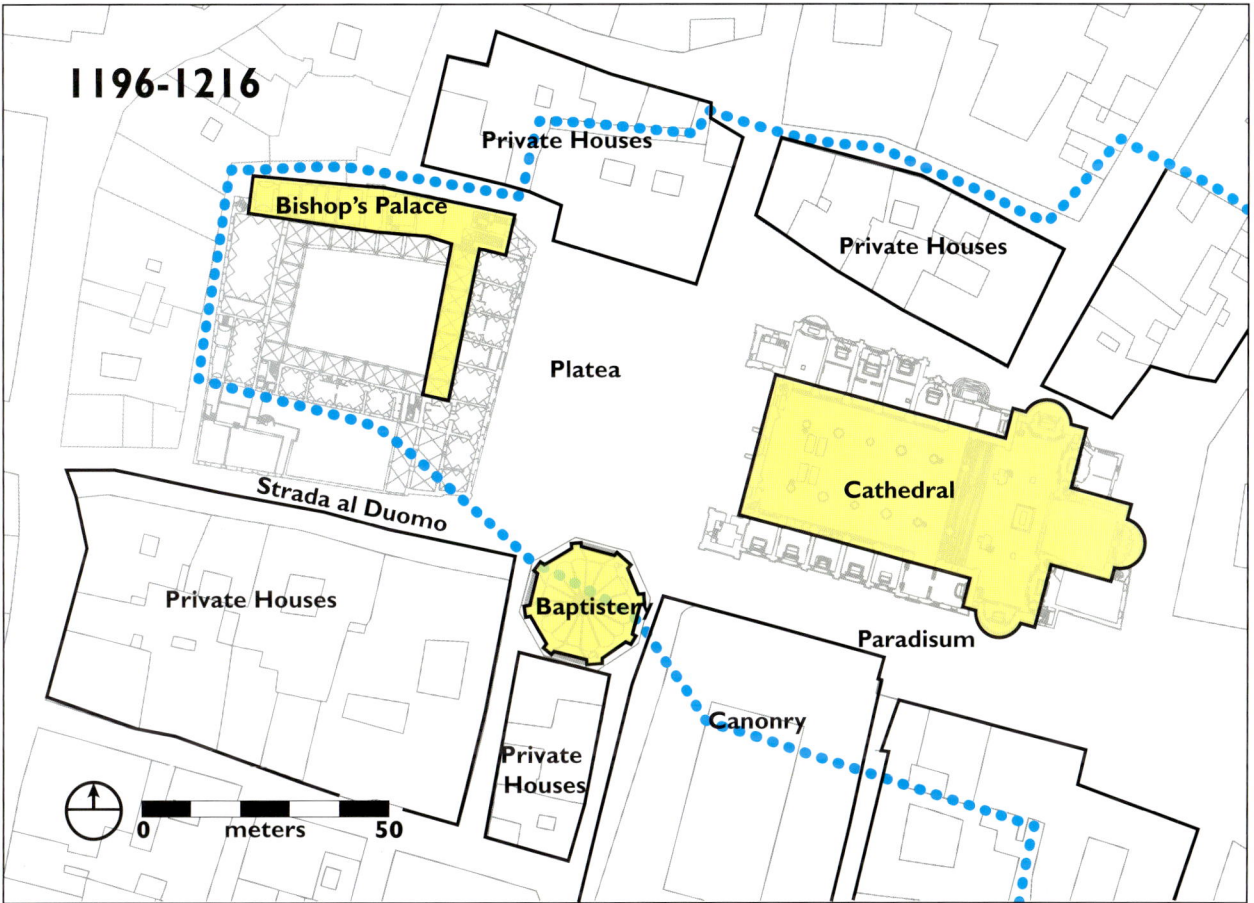

1196-1216

Private Houses

Bishop's Palace

Private Houses

Platea

Private Houses

Strada al Duomo

Cathedral

Baptistery

Private Houses

Paradisum

Canonry

Private Houses

0   meters   50

Cremona (begun 1167), as Saverio Lomartire has remarked. The baptisteries of Florence and Parma share the octagonal plan of Rome's Lateran baptistery, the arcading and double-shelled structure of the Holy Sepulchre rotunda in Jerusalem, and the proportional system and overt classicism of the Pantheon. Cremona's baptistery is structurally and decoratively less ambitious than its Florentine predecessor, but it, too, is an octagonal vaulted building with internal arcaded galleries and polygonal buttresses at its exterior corners (fig. 17).

Fig. 15 Baptistery of Parma from the north.

Fig. 16 Reconstruction diagram, the cathedral piazza of Parma, 1196–1216. The dotted line represents the path of the Canale Maggiore, which was uncovered along the strada al Duomo.

When construction of Parma's baptistery began, Cremona was Parma's staunch ally; their political lives were closely intertwined. Indeed, Parma and nearby Cremona repeatedly exchanged podestas between 1188 and 1246.[25]

Although the baptisteries of other cities inspired its form, Parma's planners made sure to associate their new building with its immediate context. They based the dimensions of their baptistery on those of the cathedral, which in turn derived from a 7-meter module.[26] The cathedral's facade was 27.94 meters wide and 28.67 meters high (four times the 7-meter module).[27] Despite the obvious difficulties in transferring the cathedral's dimensions to a centrally planned structure, the planners of the baptistery nonetheless adapted them for the new building.[28]

The baptistery's elevation is partly based on the 7-meter module, manipulated arithmetically and by means of quadrature (fig. 18). Like the cathedral, the baptistery is four modules high—28.20 meters to the top of the heavy cable molding surmounting its walls. Each pair of its external galleries averages 7.05 meters high (one module), while the height of the baptistery's ground story is 10.05 meters high, a measurement arrived at by the common medieval design practice of rotating by 45 degrees the 7-meter square that served as the base module (fig. 19).[29]

Although the baptistery's facades vary in width, they average 7.01 meters in width as measured between the inner edges of the corner buttresses.[30] Three of the baptistery's eight facets are visible from the center of the piazza: the northeastern, northern, and northwestern facades. When the northeastern and northwestern facades are (in the mind's eye) unfolded and aligned with its northern facade, they measure 28.27 meters (or four 7-meter modules) from the outer edge of the easternmost buttress to the outer edge of the westernmost buttress, closely reflecting the width of the cathedral facade (fig. 20). Understood thus, the baptistery of Parma, like the cathedral, is 28 meters high and 28 meters wide (four modules × four modules).

Fig. 17 Baptistery of Cremona from the north. The stone revetment was added in the sixteenth century in imitation of the baptistery of Parma. The Cremona baptistery's western and southern portals were blinded in the sixteenth century.

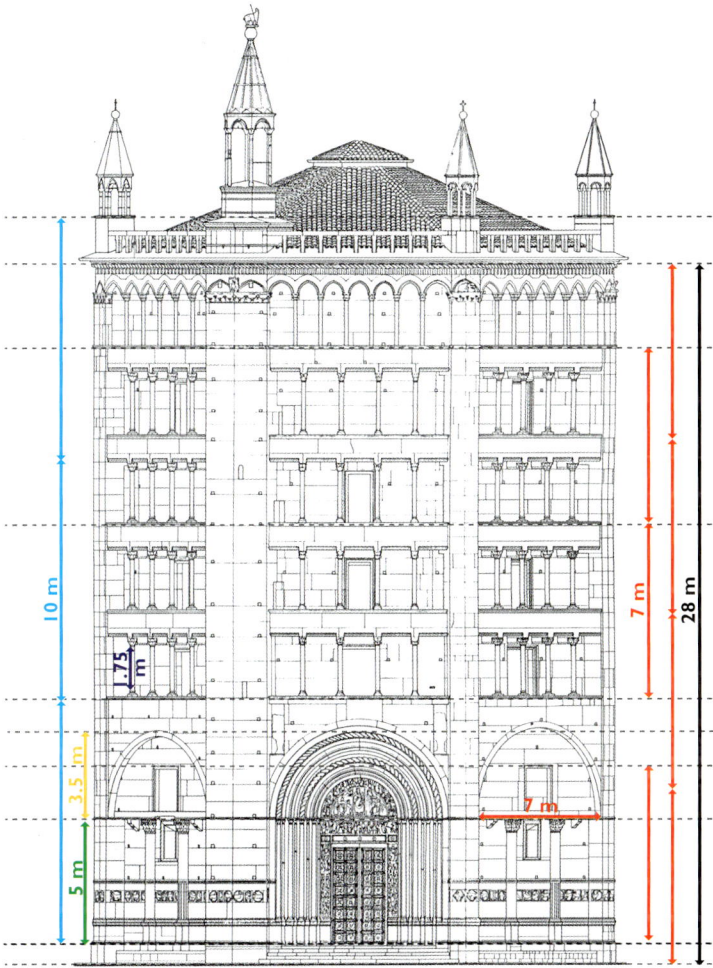

Parma, Baptistery, north façade

Labels on the elevation: 10 m, 1.75 m, 3.5 m, 5 m, 7 m, 28 m, 7 m

Rotation of a 7 m square

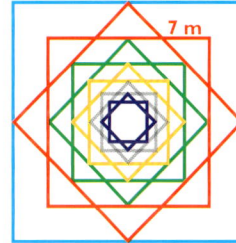

7 m

A B B A B B A B

Fig. 18 Analytical diagram of the north elevation of the baptistery, Parma, illustrating how aspects of the baptistery's design derive from a 7-meter module. From an engraving by Piero Sottili after a drawing by G. Bertoluzzi, in Michele Lopez, *Il Battistero di Parma* (Parma: Giacomo Ferrari, 1864), fig. 4.

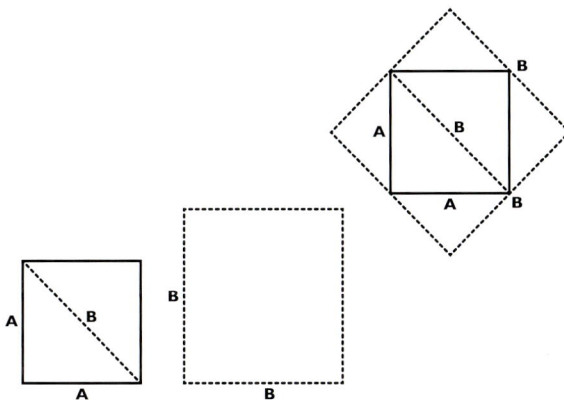

Fig. 19 Rotation of the square by 45 degrees to derive successive measurements from the original base module.

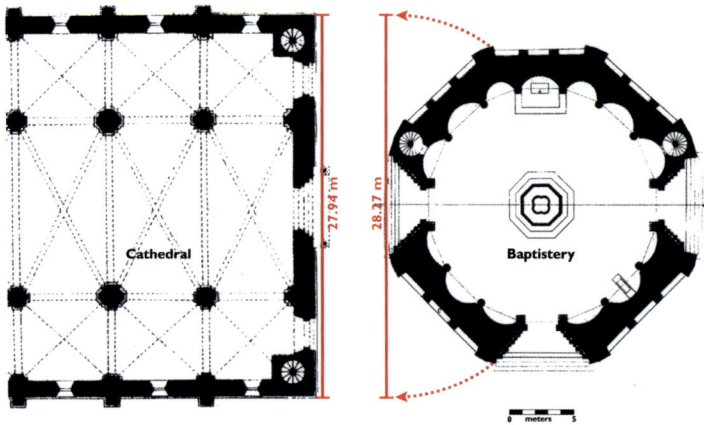

Fig. 20 Analytical diagram illustrating the dimensional correspondence between the baptistery and cathedral facades.

(Intriguingly, the same principle underlies the relationship between the baptistery of Florence and the width of the nave of Florence cathedral, begun a century later, although in Florence, of course, the cathedral's dimensions were derived from those of the baptistery. Parma's baptistery also shares this one-to-one relationship of height to conceptual width with San Giovanni in Florence.)[31]

It is clear that the builders of Parma's baptistery based its proportions and dimensions on those of the cathedral, but what inspired its location? Parma's planners seem to have looked to Cremona, their neighbor and ally, for inspiration (fig. 21).[32] Cremona's baptistery stands to the southwest of the cathedral, with its north portal perpendicular to the cathedral's facade, a placement that keeps the important ceremonial space in front of the cathedral's facade clear.[33] A similar arrangement was followed in Parma, but

it was carefully adjusted to local conditions. Like the Cremonese, the Parmesan planners decided to place the new baptistery to the southwest of the cathedral, with its north portal perpendicular to the cathedral's west facade. I propose that a new urbanistic desire determined the precise location of the baptistery—the desire to establish clear, geometrically derived relationships between the buildings on the site.

Parma's builders appear to have established the distance between the cathedral and the new baptistery by recourse to the 28-meter dimensions of the basilica's facade and Euclidian geometry. They positioned the baptistery about 27 meters west of the cathedral's west facade, and about 28 meters south of its central portal, so that the baptistery's north-south cross axis intersected the cathedral's central longitudinal axis at a 90-degree angle (fig. 22).[34] In this manner, the planners called on the authority of the preexisting fabric on the site to provide the underlying logic for their design process. (The modest, 1-meter eastward displacement of the baptistery relative to the ideal 28-meter distance probably reflects the need to accommodate the site's preexisting street grid and lot lines.)[35] These operations produced the effect of "centering" the cathedral facade between the baptistery and the preexisting buildings to the north of the church.

The planners' desire to impose order on the irregular *platea* did not distract them from ensuring that the baptistery building's design supported its liturgical function. Another factor informing the baptistery site's selection may have been the availability of water for the baptismal font. The spot chosen for the baptistery positioned it atop the Canale Maggiore (indicated by a dotted line in figs. 16 and 22).

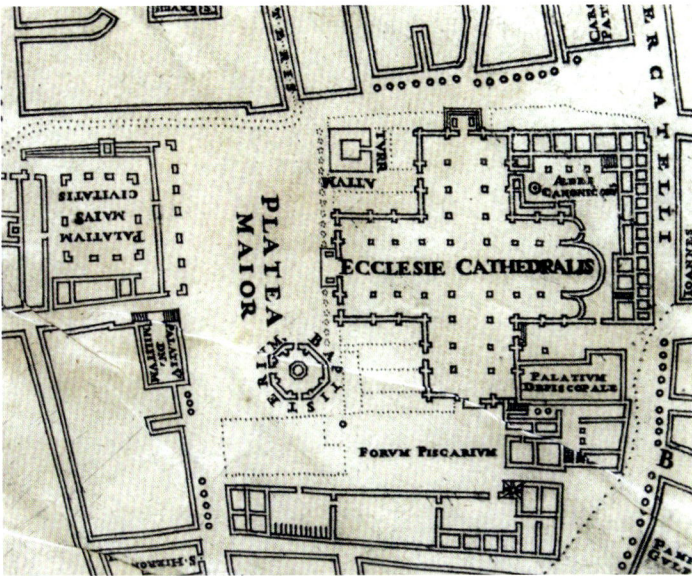

Fig. 21 Platea Maior, Cremona. As in Parma, the baptistery is perpendicular to the cathedral's facade, and its northern portal faces the cathedral square, while its central portal faces west. Detail of the map of Cremona, in Antonio Campi, *Cremona fedelissima città et nobilissima colonia de Romani rappresentata in disegno col suo contado: Et illustrata d'una breve historia delle cose più notabili appartenenti ad essa et dei ritratti naturali de duchi et duchesse di Milano e compendio delle lor vite* (Cremona: Hippolito Tromba & Hercoliano Bartoli, 1585), after p. lxxviii.

Fig. 22 Analytical drawing representing the process used in the siting of the baptistery of Parma. The baptistery is sited to the southwest of the cathedral and perpendicular to its west facade, in such a way that the cathedral seems centered along the piazza's eastern boundary.

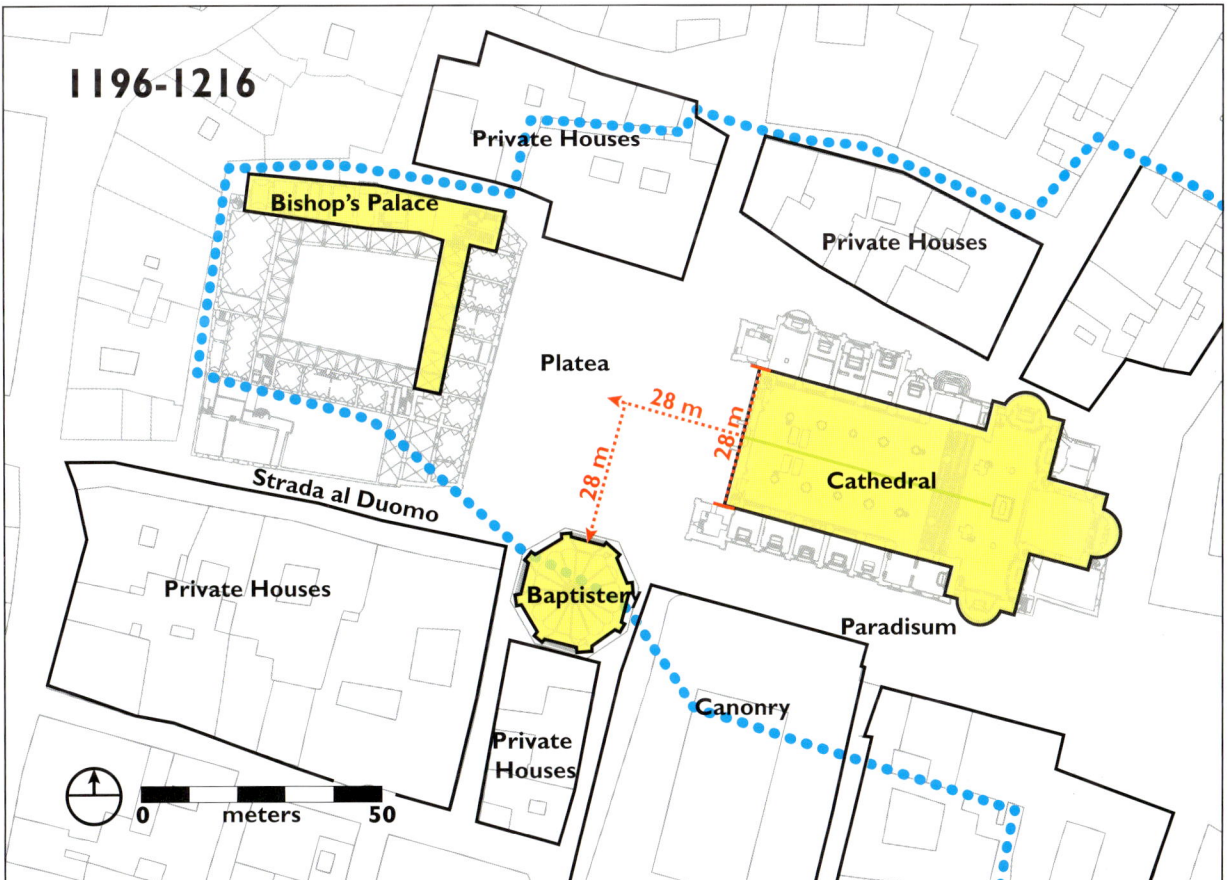

This narrow uncovered canal conducted water underneath the chapter house and the episcopal palace and provided the baptistery with a necessary source of water for baptism.[36]

Liturgical requirements also affected other design decisions. Like their Florentine and Cremonese predecessors, the Parmesans seem to have conceived of their centrally planned baptistery as a church of the more common, longitudinal, basilican form.[37] Liturgical convention dictated that the baptistery's altar had to be placed on its eastern wall and opposite the building's central, western portal. In Parma, however, the baptistery building's western, central portal—the most important liturgically, as it faced the main altar at the east—faced not

the *platea* but a narrow street. The baptistery's north portal was the most important urbanistically, as it faced toward the *platea,* the cathedral, and bishop's palace. Liturgical custom and new urban design imperatives were in conflict with one another.

The building's designers addressed this contradiction iconographically, not urbanistically. They adopted the French convention of marking a church's main doorway with a Last Judgment and used this theme for the tympanum of the baptistery's central, west portal (figs. 23 and 24).[38] The baptistery's north, *platea* portal was decorated instead with an amalgam of several iconographic programs (figs. 25 and 26). On the north tympanum, a large central

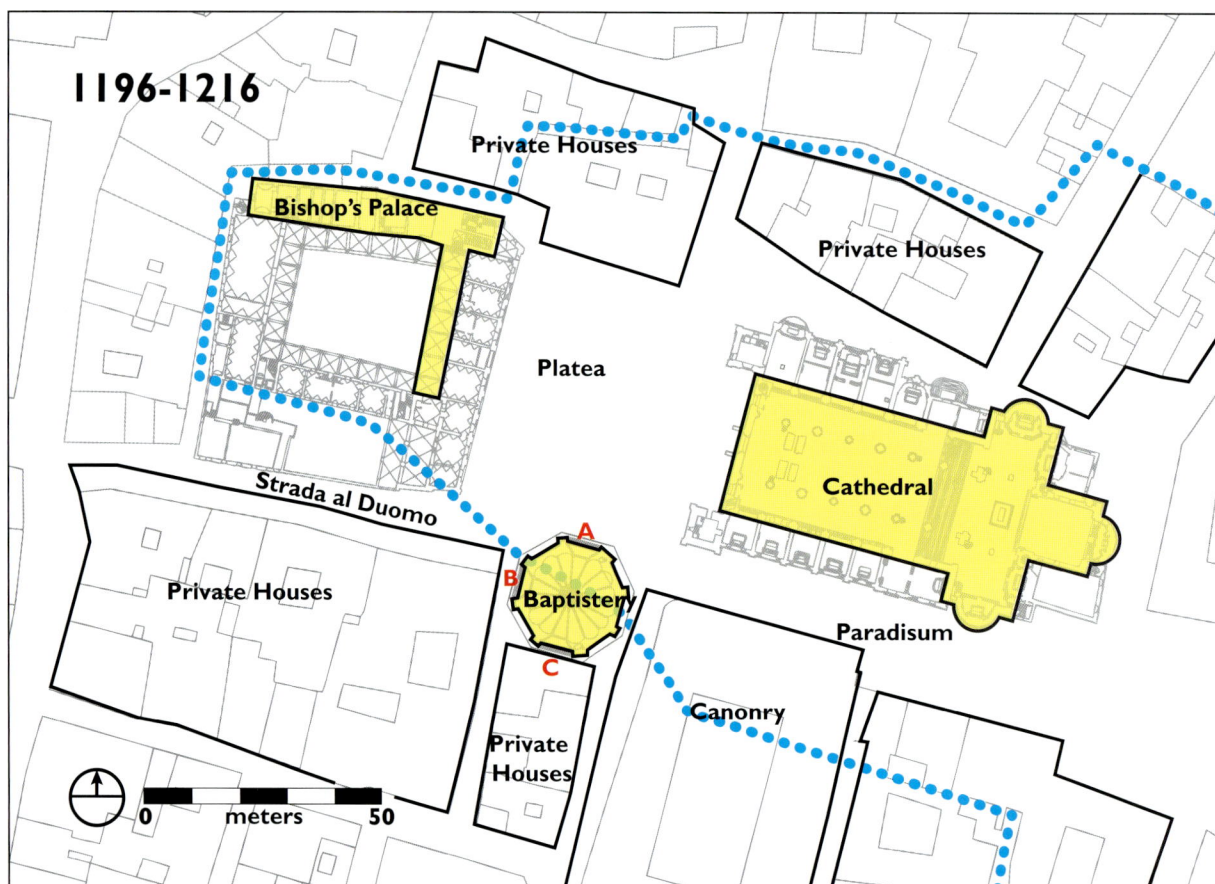

enthroned Virgin (patroness of Parma) and Child receive the adoration of the Magi to her right, while to her left the archangel Gabriel warns Joseph of Herod's impending infanticide. On the lintel below, scenes from the life of John the Baptist are represented, with his baptism of Christ at center left. Thus, the decorative program of the north portal (the baptistery's most important entrance urbanistically) alludes to the building's civic importance by representing the city's patron saint; simultaneously, its representation of the Baptist refers to its dedication and liturgical function.

However, the baptistery of Parma—like many basilicas and its Florentine and Cremonese prototypes—had three doorways. As a consequence of the planners' decisions, the baptistery's third, southern portal pressed up against a cluster of privately owned buildings that impeded access to it, rather than open onto a street or *piazzetta* (fig. 23). The solution to this problem awaited a later generation of planners, but its existence reveals resistance to the first designers' urban program. After all of their careful calculations,

Fig. 23 Analytical drawing representing the Parma baptistery portals. (A) The baptistery's north portal was the most important urbanistically. (B) The baptistery's west portal was the most important liturgically, since it faced the altar along the building's eastern wall. (C) The baptistery's south portal remained inaccessible until 1262.

Fig. 24 West portal, baptistery of Parma. The tympanum and lintel are decorated with Last Judgment imagery.

the ideal position chosen for the baptistery was already occupied. In order to build, the baptistery's planners needed to acquire and demolish the houses on the site, which were owned by a branch of the noble Adam family. No documents survive to clarify the circumstances of this acquisition, but the Franciscan chronicler Salimbene de Adam's report of the affair suggests

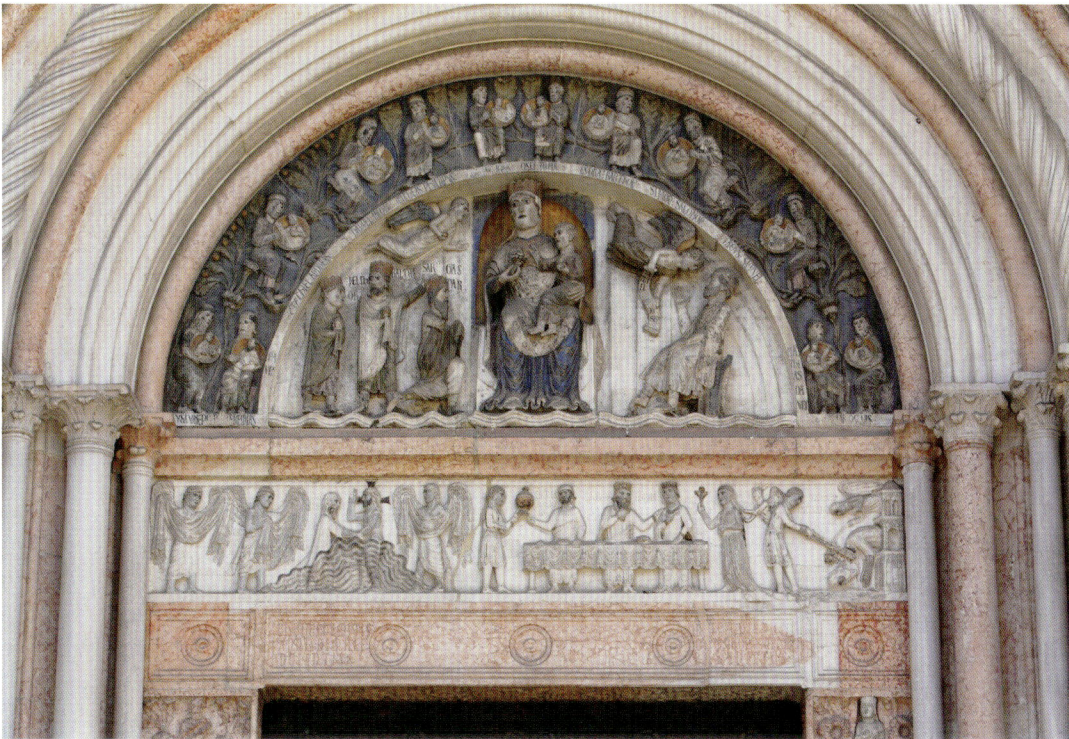

Fig. 25 North (piazza) portal, baptistery of Parma.

Fig. 26 Tympanum and lintel of the north portal, baptistery of Parma. The portal's tympanum depicts the enthroned Virgin, patron saint of the city of Parma. The lintel reflects the baptistery's function and dedication. It shows scenes from the life of Saint John the Baptist, including the baptism of Christ.

that his kinsmen were coerced to give up their homes.[39] That houses still pressed up against the baptistery's southern walls and remained there for over fifty years indicates that this resistance was not easily overcome.

The position of the baptistery, together with its octagonal plan and its ornamentation, rendered it the most distinctive building visible to persons traveling to the episcopal complex from the city's northern gate or on the principal access road into the *platea* from the center of town, the strada al Duomo. One of the baptistery's eight facets can be seen from the intersection where the strada al Duomo meets medieval Parma's most important north-south artery, the Roman *cardo*, today named strada Cavour (fig. 27).[40]

Far from being a casual choice, the site selected for the baptistery of Parma preserved the prestigious, open, usable space of the *platea*. Furthermore, it took advantage of the Canale Maggiore, which provided water for the baptistery's rites. And, finally, it provided an impressive preview of churchly magnificence to

persons traveling toward the episcopal complex from the *platea*'s principal approaches. As baptistery construction continued throughout the thirteenth century, the urbanistic decisions made by the baptistery's planners would have long-lasting effects.

Squaring the Piazza del Duomo

As the baptistery's construction continued, Bishop Òbizzo and the canons undertook no new projects on or around the cathedral precinct for the remainder of his reign. In the first decades of the thirteenth century, the focus of new building activity in Parma shifted away from the episcopal square. The burgeoning communal government reinforced and expanded the city's infrastructure and fortifications. As I show in chapter 2, in 1221 the commune responded to the baptistery's defiant expression of episcopal might by initiating construction of the city's first communal palace a few blocks from the cathedral. Throughout the thirteenth century, both the communal and episcopal factions repeatedly used architectural one-upmanship as a complement to the diplomatic and military tools deployed in their recurrent contests for power in Parma.

Like his predecessor Òbizzo, Bishop Grazia (*reg.* 1224–36) responded to the commune's persistent challenges by further transforming the episcopal precinct. Pope Gregory IX, not the cathedral chapter, appointed the Florentine Grazia

after the canons wasted several months following Òbizzo's death feuding with the Visdomini episcopal vassal family over control of the episcopal palace and benefices. The pope may have hoped that Grazia, as an eminent jurist who had led the *studium* in Bologna and assisted three popes in resolving thorny regional and international legal and diplomatic problems, would assert the rights of the church and settle civil unrest among the city's ruling elite. The new bishop spent the first years of his rule engaged in local politics, winning the canons to his side and trying—with mixed success—to get the commune to fulfill the legal agreements about division of powers it had made with Òbizzo. Like other prelates in crisis, Grazia turned to architecture to express his authority.[41] In 1233, Bishop Grazia added a dramatic extension to the episcopal palace (figs. 28 and 29).[42] This construction gave the imposing, fortresslike earlier building a truly palatial appearance. With its new arcaded portico on the ground floor—sealed in the fifteenth century—and long series of three-light windows on its upper stories, the episcopal palace's exterior matched the iconography of rule of Parma's first communal palace and surpassed it in size.

Grazia was a lawyer and diplomat, not a warrior; his building's expansive openness, painted decoration, colored marble, and ceramic ornament signaled a more refined, courtly affirmation of lordship (fig. 30).[43] The sandstone revetment of the bishop's palace's lower facade set it apart from Parma's usual brick construction and linked it to the cathedral, which was also faced in sandstone, while the *rosso di Verona* colonnettes in its windows tied it to the baptistery too. Yet Grazia and the cathedral workshop did not stop at enlarging the palace and altering its iconography. By the

Fig. 27 View of the baptistery from the strada al Duomo.

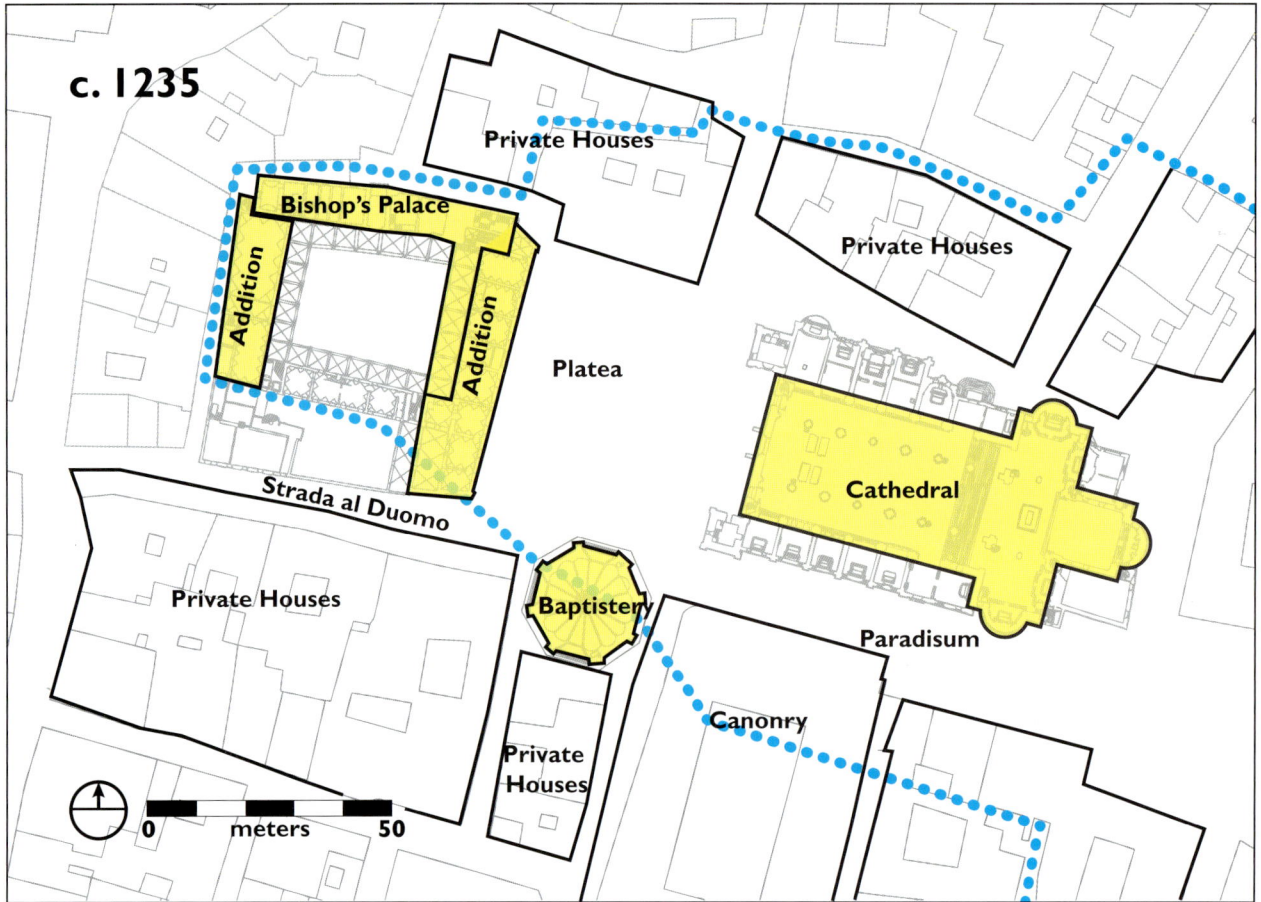

c. 1235

Private Houses

Bishop's Palace

Addition

Addition

Private Houses

Private Houses

Platea

Strada al Duomo

Baptistery

Private Houses

Cathedral

Paradisum

Canonry

Private Houses

0   meters   50

unusual way in which they expanded the palace, they established the piazza's square shape.

Grazia's addition has a highly irregular plan (figs. 13 and 28). It is an asymmetrical structure built against the eastern facade of the preexisting bishop's palace. Rather than make the extension symmetrical and parallel to the old palace's piazza facade, the builders aligned the new facade with that of the cathedral. As a result, the extension is approximately 11.22 meters deep toward the northeastern end of the old facade but only about 7.53 meters deep

Fig. 28 Reconstruction diagram, the cathedral piazza of Parma c. 1235. The palace's extension regularizes the piazza's western boundary, making it parallel to the cathedral's facade.

Fig. 29 Eastern facade, bishop's palace, Parma.

Fig. 30 Detail of painted, ceramic, and masonry ornament on the eastern facade, bishop's palace, Parma.

where it meets the southeastern end of the old facade. Furthermore, the new construction extends southward beyond the old facade by 11.46 meters, or two bays, all the way to the strada al Duomo, and then turns west toward the bishop's orchard. At its northernmost end, the new construction tapers back (westward) at an angle against the preexisting fabric.[44] While irregular in itself, the new addition regularized the piazza. The new facade hid the heterogeneous buildings behind it. As noted above, Grazia's new fabric for the first time made the palace's facade parallel to that of the cathedral. The midpoint of the new facade was the center of the ground story's fifth pier. Although the palace's facade is not strictly symmetrical—the fenestration of the *piano nobile* is not in vertical alignment with the arcade below it—this midpoint coincides exactly with center of the cathedral facade. Thus, the southward expansion of the palace seems to have been designed to align and harmonize its facade with that of the cathedral.

The expansion of the bishop's palace drastically altered the western boundary of the *platea*. The breadth chosen for the new facade of the bishop's palace (51.81 meters) nearly equaled the distance between the baptistery and the buildings bounding the *platea* on the north (56.25 meters), minus a small 4.44-meter margin to facilitate circulation. The modern appearance of the piazza's north side merits an explanation (fig. 31). Although the buildings along the north edge of the piazza were damaged during World War II and do not appear to be medieval structures at first glance, they were rebuilt on the preexisting foundations and encompass some passages of medieval masonry. Their original alignment was at least in part quite close to today's, as evinced by the fragment of a medieval two-light window visible within the facade of the building now occupying the piazza's northwest border; it is set back about five centimeters from the postwar facade (fig. 32). The current alignment also seems to coincide with that noted by Sardi in his eighteenth-century atlas of the city. Together, this evidence suggests that the line of buildings to the piazza's north in the thirteenth century was quite similar to the present one.

The depth of Grazia's new facade was determined not only by the desire to make the bishop's palace facade parallel to that of the cathedral but also by the desire to impose even greater geometric order in the piazza (fig. 33). The expansion's unusual footprint resulted in the transformation of the asymmetrical space into an almost perfectly square piazza with sides of 56.25 meters and 53.90 meters (a variance of less than 5 percent), or about two times the width of the cathedral facade, bounded on the south by the line of the baptistery's north portal, on the west by the eastern facade of the bishop's palace, and on the east by the cathedral's western facade (fig. 34). Notably, the cross axes of the newly reduced, square piazza now coincided with the center of the facades of each

Fig. 31 Northwest corner of the Piazza del Duomo, Parma.

Fig. 32 A building on the north side of the Piazza del Duomo, Parma. The white circle calls attention to a two-light window, an exposed fragment of medieval masonry.

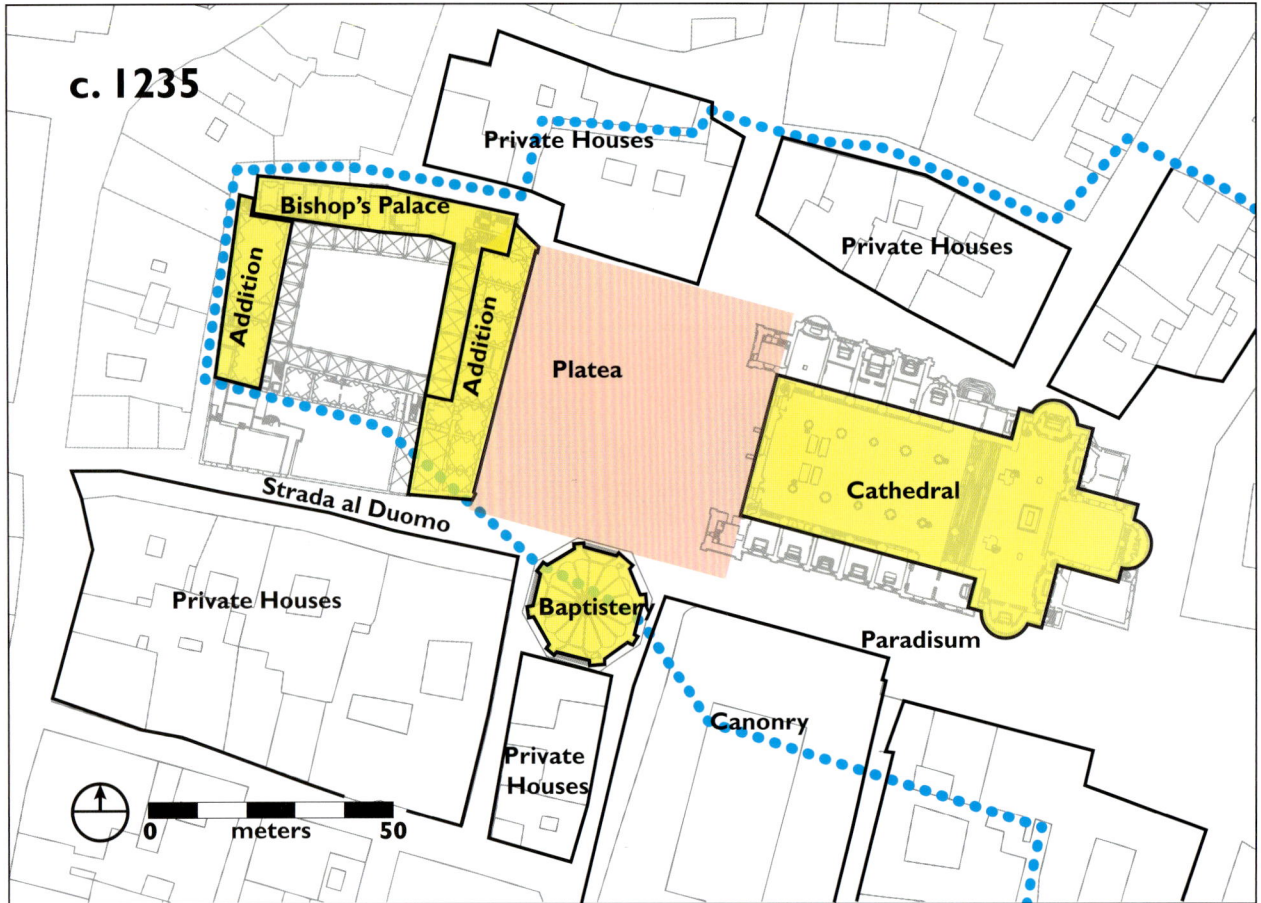

c. 1235

Private Houses

Bishop's Palace

Addition

Addition

Private Houses

Platea

Cathedral

Strada al Duomo

Private Houses

Baptistery

Paradisum

Canonry

Private Houses

0   meters   50

Fig. 33 Reconstruction diagram indicating the ideal square geometry of the cathedral piazza c. 1235.

Fig. 34 Reconstruction diagram indicating the cross axes underlying the design of the cathedral piazza c. 1235. The facades of the cathedral and bishop's palace are parallel and aligned along the same central axis. The baptistery is perpendicular to them and nearly centered between them.

of the three major episcopal buildings, resolving the former problem of the asymmetrical relationship of the bishop's palace to the cathedral facade and the baptistery.[45] These correspondences demonstrate the great likelihood that the planners envisioned a newly regular, square-shaped piazza and attempted to execute it as faithfully as possible given the constraints of preexisting buildings and streets.

A buttress marks the northern limit of the palace's piazza facade (and the piazza's northwestern corner), but the new extension's fabric

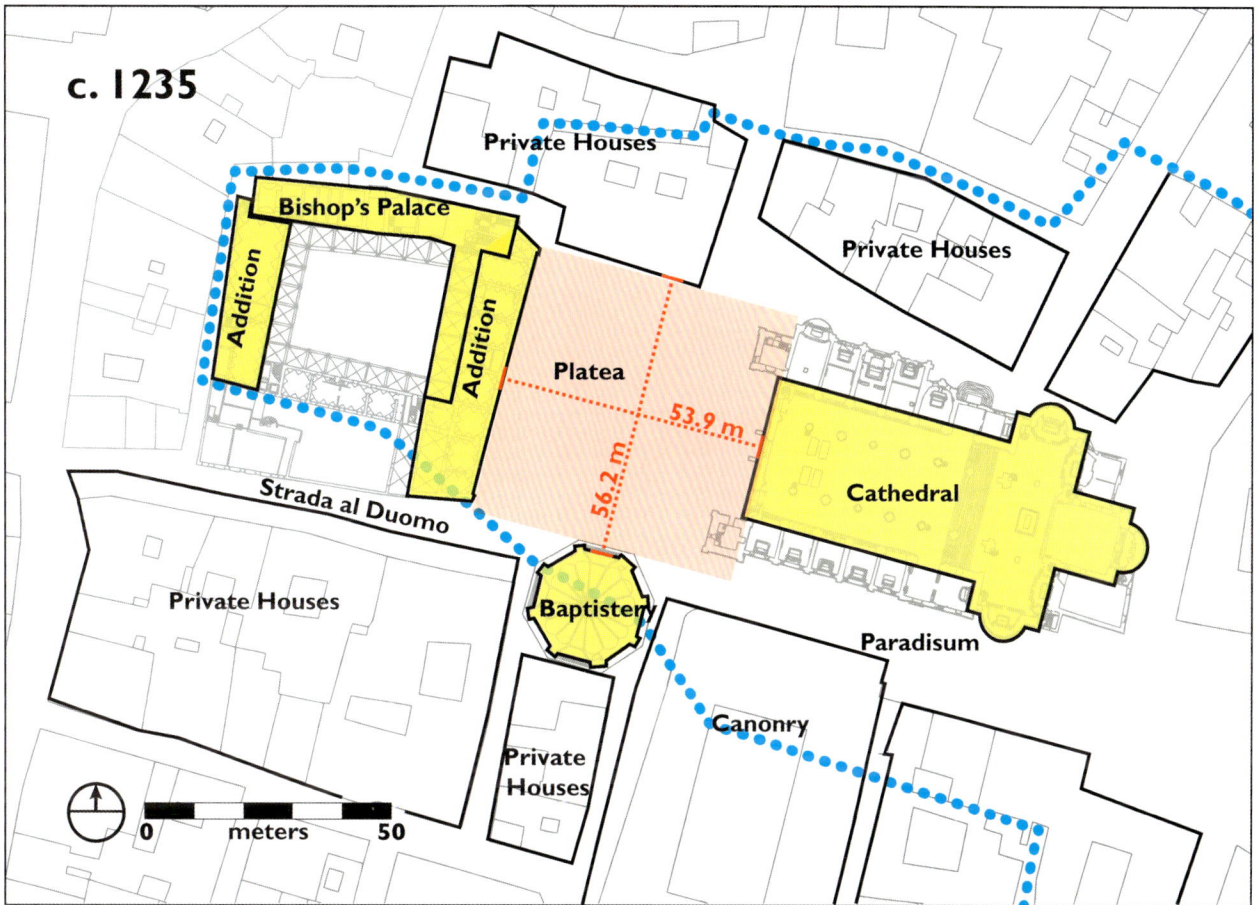

c. 1235

Private Houses

Bishop's Palace

Addition

Addition

Private Houses

Platea

53.9 m

56.2 m

Strada al Duomo

Cathedral

Private Houses

Baptistery

Paradisum

Canonry

Private Houses

0   meters   50

does not actually terminate there. The palace's builders connected the regular new piazza facade of the palace with its preexisting, twelfth-century northern wing by means of a short diagonal wall (fig. 35). The builders' handling of this seemingly minor detail highlights the urbanistic strategies that shaped the piazza. This slanted wall is unquestionably part of the 1233 campaign; its masonry is coursed in with that of the new facade. Although the upper story of this slanted section of the new facade was destroyed in the eigh-

teenth century, traces of the line along which it met the preexisting fabric are still legible on the twelfth-century wall. Indeed, the slanted wall continued the fenestration of the main, east facade of the *piano nobile;* a keen eye can discern the springing of the archivolt for a final three-light window in the masonry to the north of the corner buttress. The extension as a whole reveals some of the principles underlying architectural and urbanistic practice in thirteenth-century Parma. No older fabric was destroyed unnecessarily, the maximum amount

Fig. 35 Northeast corner of the bishop's palace, Parma. A diagonal wall links the 1230s addition to the bishop's palace to the preexisting structure. The truncated arch above indicates that a three-light window extended the elegant fenestration of the piazza facade to the connecting wall.

of the open space of the piazza was preserved, yet order and symmetry were increased.

To summarize, the maximum dimensions of the new square were established when the baptistery was built. The 28-meter ideal measure used to determine the baptistery's siting, multiplied by two, became the unit that determined the ultimate size of the ideal square. The breadth of the new bishop's palace facade derives from that measurement. Nor is the elevation of the bishop's palace arbitrarily determined; it relates to the dimensional system established by the cathedral and continued in the baptistery. For example, the width of the openings of the ground-story loggia, the distance between the top of the ground story arcade and the base of the *piano nobile* windows, and the distance from the intrados of the arch to the base of each *piano nobile* window all measure 3.50 meters (half the 7-meter module). The distance between the molding atop the facade's arcaded corbel table and the molding at the base of the *piano nobile* windows equals 7.01 meters (one module), as does the distance between the top of the *piano nobile* windows and the top of the ground-story arcade.

Although the piazza "reads" visually as a perfect square when experienced personally (instead of via its two-dimensional representation in my reconstruction plan), it does not achieve geometric perfection. It is a virtual, not an actual, square. The church owned the buildings on the eastern, southern, and western borders of the piazza, and therefore it regularized those sides of the square. When the bishop's palace project was begun, the church did not control the structures on the northern border of the piazza and, thus, had to content itself with a less-than-perfect northern boundary. That

Parma's planners might not have been able to fully execute the ideal geometry of the plan does not signify, however, that this geometry was not intended. This accommodation of an ideal plan to the real conditions of a site is not unusual. Even the most famously "ideal" of Renaissance squares, Florence's Piazza della Santissima Annunziata, is not a perfectly regular rectangle, although it is usually characterized as such. Its designers had to inflect their plan to reconcile it to preexisting site conditions. In fact, Parma's Piazza del Duomo is much more regular than Piazza della Santissima Annunziata—the difference in length between Parma's least regular sides is less than 5 percent, compared to the 11 percent variation between the Florentine piazza's northern and southern borders.[46]

The Mid–Thirteenth Century

The extension of the bishop's palace was completed swiftly. While its scale and urbanistic ambitions were great, the means used to express them were relatively simple. Its builders used local brick and sandstone, and its ornamentation was limited: the facade was articulated by the light-and-shadow effects of the series of arched openings and the arcaded corbel tables, the *rosso di Verona* used in the window colonnettes, the ceramic *bacini* set into the sandstone above and between the windows, and red and white checkerboard plaster decoration (fig. 30). The construction of the baptistery, on the other hand, with its steep vaulting, intricate interior elevations, complex architectural sculpture cycle, and extensive use of imported *rosso di Verona,* dragged on for decades.[47] Although the tumultuous middle years of the thirteenth century did not stop urbanistic activity in

Parma—the city's fortifications were expanded, streets were paved and widened, the commune built more palaces and a tower—no new construction was begun in the Piazza del Duomo in this period.[48]

There was, however, some new destruction. In 1262—a moment of singular harmony between Parma's communal and episcopal authorities—the commune enacted a statute commanding the expropriation and demolition of several houses located just south of the baptistery in order to "make the work of the baptistery visible, enable access through that [southern] doorway, and permit circulation around the baptistery" (fig. 36).[49] The space created behind the baptistery allowed its sculpture-decorated south portal to be comfortably seen for the first time (fig. 37). Previously, the buildings next to the baptistery had pressed so closely upon it that its portal sculpture was nearly invisible. The statute precisely prescribes the amount of space demanded: 18 *pedes.* If the *pes* invoked by the statute is the ancient Roman foot still occasionally in use in Italy in this period (29.57 cm), the present irregular setback exceeds the prescribed dimension.[50] The top of the portal's elaborately sculpted lunette is 7.03 meters (one module) above the baptistery pavement. Today, the distance between the baptistery and the closest portion of the small building to its south is 7.20 meters, or 24.34 *pedes.* Notably, this is just far enough to give the viewer a good 45-degree angle of view of the lunette without craning his or her neck. Trachtenberg has demonstrated that this angle of view was normative in Florentine urbanistic practice during the fourteenth century.[51] While the principle seems not to have been consistently

Labels in diagram:
1262
Private Houses
Bishop's Palace
Addition
Addition
Platea
Private Houses
Cathedral
Strada al Duomo
Private Houses
Baptistery
Paradisum
Private Houses
Canonry

0   meters   50

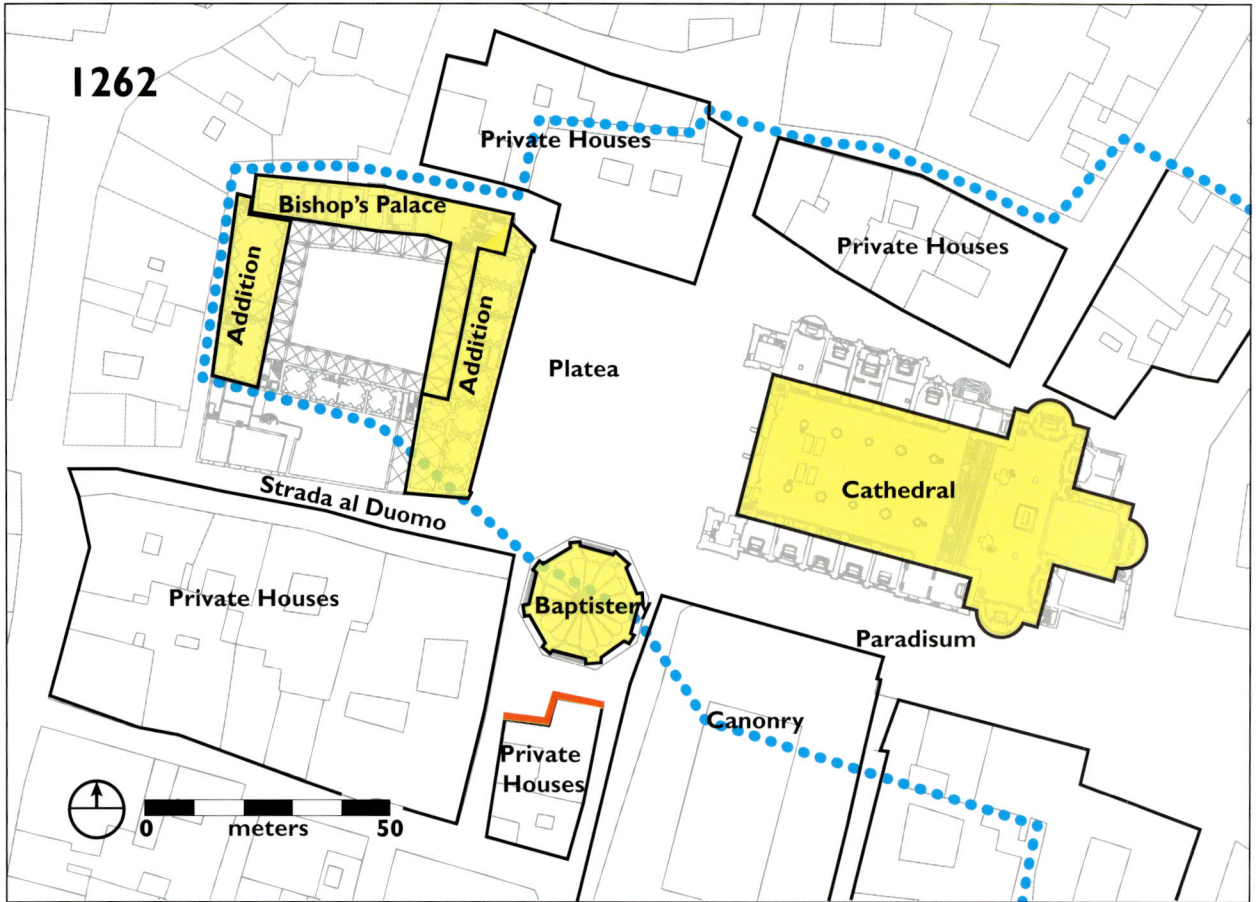

Fig. 36 Reconstruction diagram, the cathedral piazza of Parma in 1262. Buildings south of the baptistery were cut back to facilitate circulation around the baptistery and display the decoration of its south portal.

Fig. 37 South portal, baptistery of Parma.

applied in thirteenth-century Parma, there is nonetheless one more, intriguing example.

The New Campanile and the Last Medieval Works in the Piazza del Duomo

As I show in chapter 2, throughout the middle decades of the thirteenth century, the communal government had repeatedly expanded not only its powers and jurisdiction but also the communal compound on the site of the former Roman forum, a five-minute walk to the southwest of the cathedral square. In addition to erecting houses for communal officials such as the podesta and the *capitano del popolo,* a jail, an impressive bell tower, and even a house for the communal lions, in 1282 the commune doubled the size of its civic square and began construction of a massive new palace alongside the newly enlarged site's northern flank.

As that new communal palace approached completion, Òbizzo Sanvitale, bishop (*reg.* 1258–95) and leader of the *pars episcopi,* or episcopal faction, retaliated by founding a new campanile alongside the cathedral in 1284 (figs. 38 and 39). It replaced an earlier and presumably more modest bell tower of unknown date.[52] Like many of the bell towers built throughout central and north Italy in the late thirteenth century, the bishop's new campanile consists of a square brick tower pierced by multiple-light windows, decorated with blind arches and arcaded corbel tables, and topped by a small balustrade with four corner pinnacles and a large conical central spire. A gilded angel bearing a cross (now in the diocesan museum) danced above its summit.[53] Parma's campanile resembles the bell towers of Pomposa and San Mercuriale at Forlì. To date, all church-spon-

Fig. 38 Campanile, Parma, 1284–1294.

sored construction in the Piazza del Duomo had been covered with expensive stone revetment (at least on part of its piazza facade), even when supply problems delayed its completion for decades. While the new brick campanile did not receive a stone cladding—its brick walls were merely plastered and painted to look like

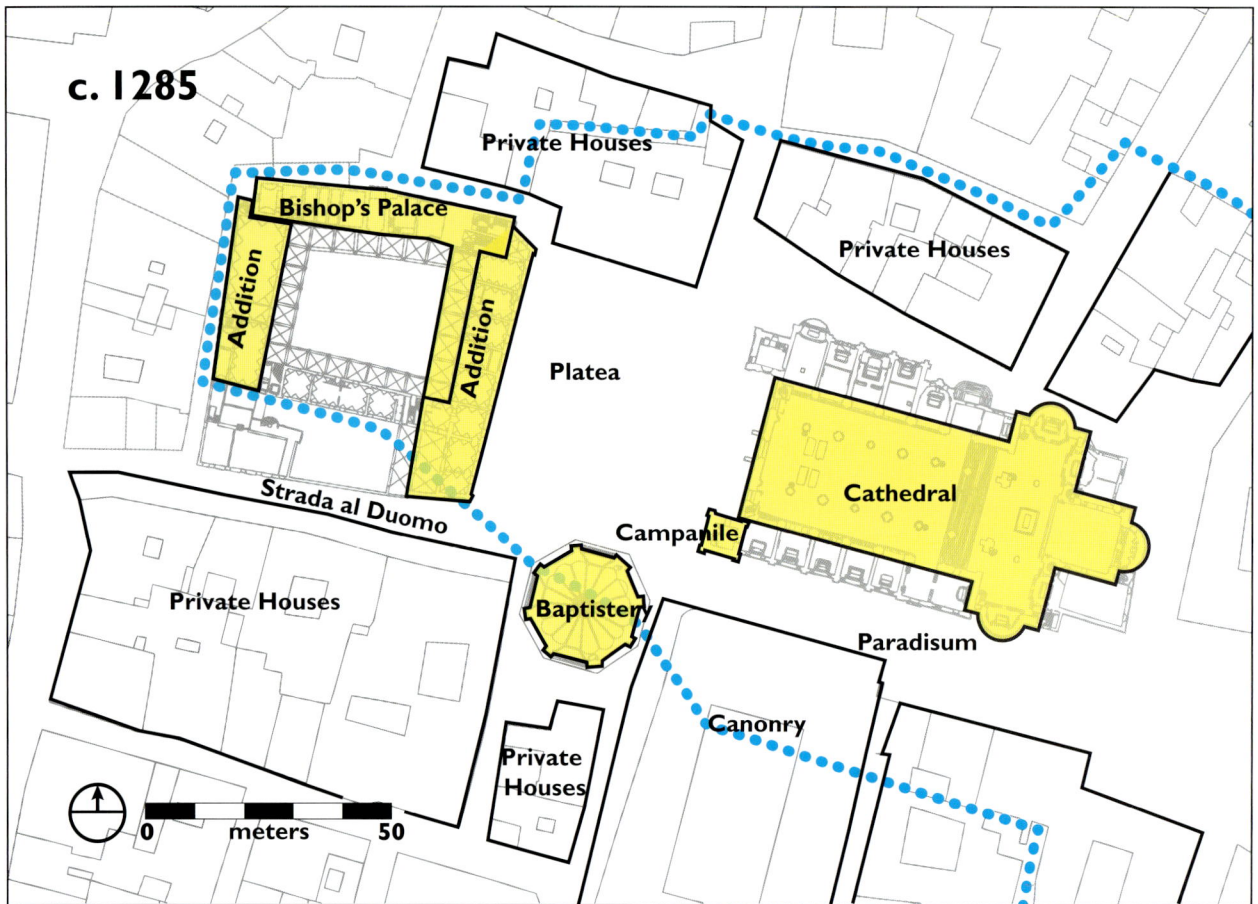

Fig. 39 map labels:

c. 1285

Private Houses

Bishop's Palace

Addition

Addition

Private Houses

Platea

Cathedral

Strada al Duomo

Campanile

Private Houses

Baptistery

Paradisum

Private Houses

Canonry

0   meters   50

stone—it is linked to the greater luxury of the
stone-clad baptistery and the cathedral by the
use of *rosso di Verona* for its corner buttresses.[54]

The church tower was unquestionably
positioned for maximum visual impact (figs. 40
and 41). The most important access road to the
episcopal piazza from the rest of the city was the
strada al Duomo. The view from the strada al
Duomo toward the piazza had featured one facet
of the baptistery. Now the new campanile
dominated this vista. From its position just
slightly southwest of the cathedral's facade, the
bell tower hid the assorted structures between

the cathedral and the canonical complex and
filled the void between the cathedral and baptistery perceived from the strada al Duomo.[55]

At the east end of the strada al Duomo, a
small bridge over the Canale Maggiore marked

Fig. 39 Reconstruction diagram, the
cathedral piazza of Parma c. 1285. The new
bell tower disguises the disorderly space
to the south of the cathedral nave.

Fig. 40 The campanile as seen from the
strada al Duomo, Parma.

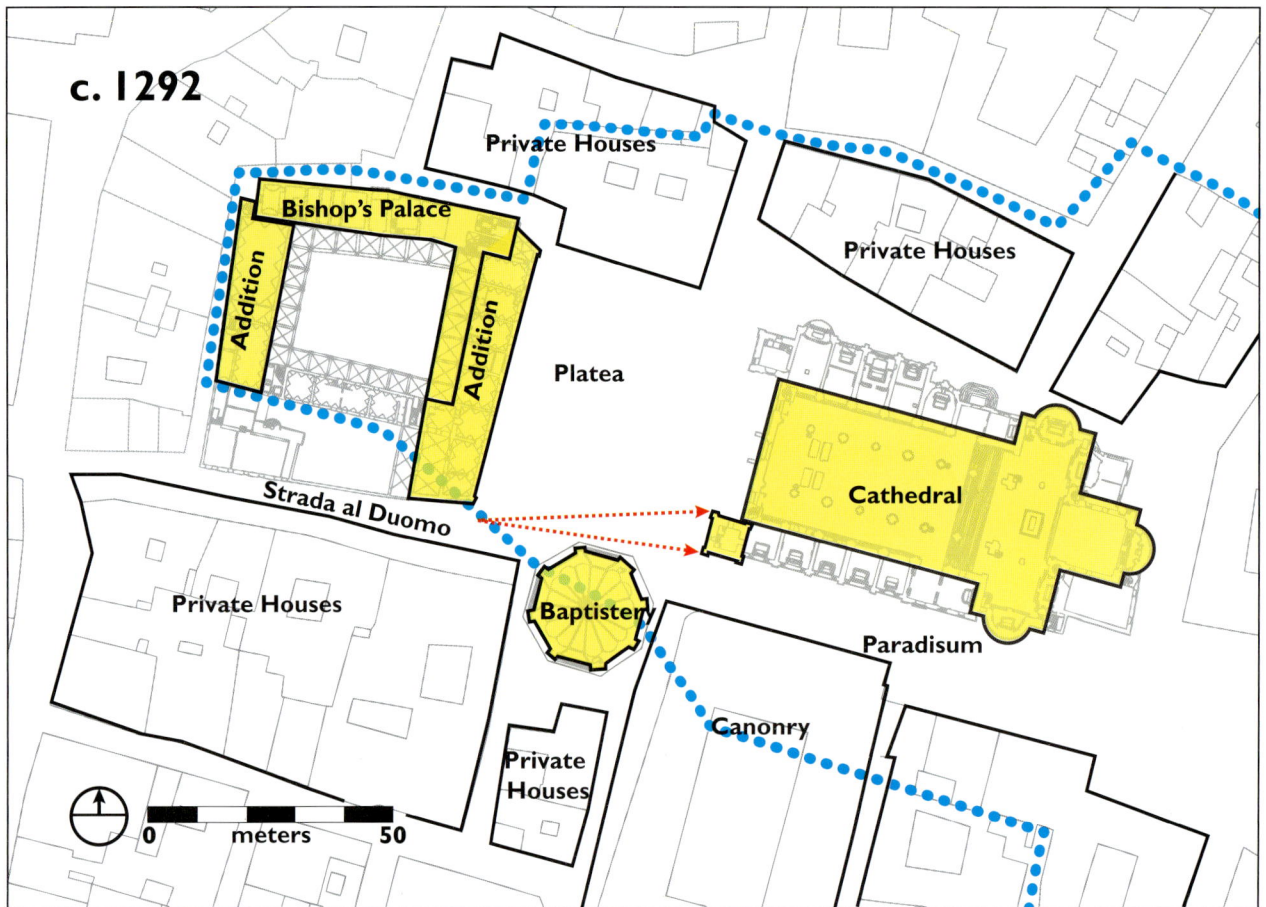

c. 1292

Private Houses

Bishop's Palace

Addition

Addition

Private Houses

Platea

Cathedral

Private Houses

Strada al Duomo

Baptistery

Private Houses

Paradisum

Canonry

Private Houses

0   meters   50

the entrance to the cathedral square. (Now the canal is underground, but in the early thirteenth century the canal had not yet been covered by pavement.)[56] To maximize the tower's visual effect, its builders seem to have used the distance between the bridge and the site of the tower to determine the tower's height (48.65 meters to the top of its surmounting balustrade), rather than the 7-meter module of earlier campaigns on the site. That distance was in turn used to derive other dimensions for the tower. For example, its square base measures 8.61 meters per side, five rotations along a

quadrature series from 48.65 meters.[57] The viewer entering the piazza from the strada al Duomo would see the tower at the same ideal 45-degree angle of view that seems to have determined the area cleared to improve the visibility of and circulation around the baptistery after 1262 (fig. 42).

A person traveling north along the via Cavour was drawn eastward up the strada al Duomo first by a glimpse of the campanile in the distance (fig. 27) and then by the glistening, pink-and-white northwestern facet of the baptistery (fig. 40). Soon, the traveler would see

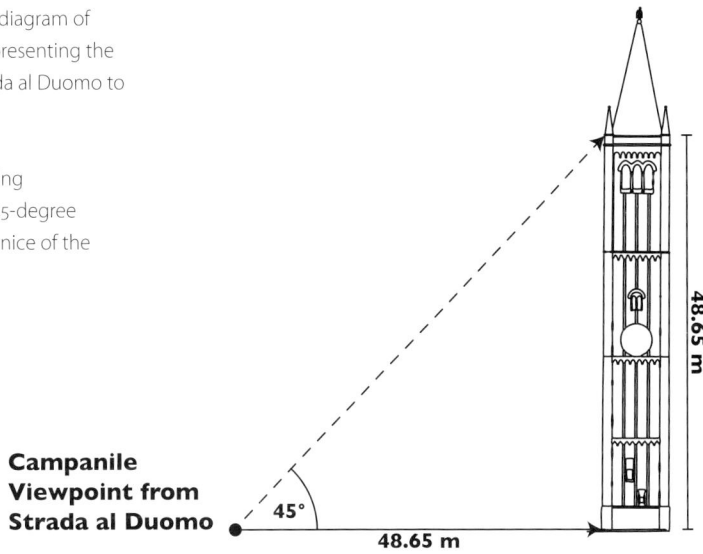

Fig. 41 Reconstruction diagram of the cathedral piazza representing the sightlines from the strada al Duomo to the campanile c. 1292.

Fig. 42 Analytical drawing representing the ideal 45-degree angle of view to the cornice of the campanile, Parma.

Campanile Viewpoint from Strada al Duomo

45°

48.65 m

48.65 m

the cathedral facade through the open loggia of the bishop's palace, take in the extent of the campanile, and cross the bridge to enter the piazza itself (fig. 43). Upon entering the piazza, the visitor's journey east was blocked by the northward projection of the baptistery, forcing a change of course. The desire to enter the cathedral, or merely to better view its facade, among other possible factors, could then draw the visitor to the center of the piazza.

From that vantage point, a person could admire the baptistery and its sculpted north portal, as well as the cathedral facade, and see into the expansive portico of the bishop's palace (fig. 44). In that same position, the visitor was approximately 27 to 28 meters away from each of the major episcopal buildings: cathedral, palace, and baptistery (fig. 45). The baptistery and cathedral facades, each 28 meters high, are virtually at the conventional 45-degree angle of view. The top cornice of the bishop's palace facade is 18.4 meters high (one-third the width

of the piazza); it is at a 35-degree angle of view. But the angles of view are not the most crucial issue here; the Piazza del Duomo of Parma does not have, nor did it intend, the rigor of Florence's Piazza della Signoria, which privileges the perspectival view of a single monument, the Palazzo Vecchio.[58]

What is most significant to note, without forcing the reading, is the distinctive proportional relationships between the buildings and the piazza's open space. The relationship of the height of the baptistery and cathedral facades to the width of the piazza is 1:2. The ratio between the maximum height of the bishop's palace and the width of the piazza is 1:3. The ratio between the maximum height of the bishop's palace and the height of the cathedral is nearly 2:3. And so on. Even though these three buildings went up in three distinct phases, their proportional systems are in careful harmony across the open space of the piazza. Indeed, the ideal 56-meter square formed by the piazza can be derived by

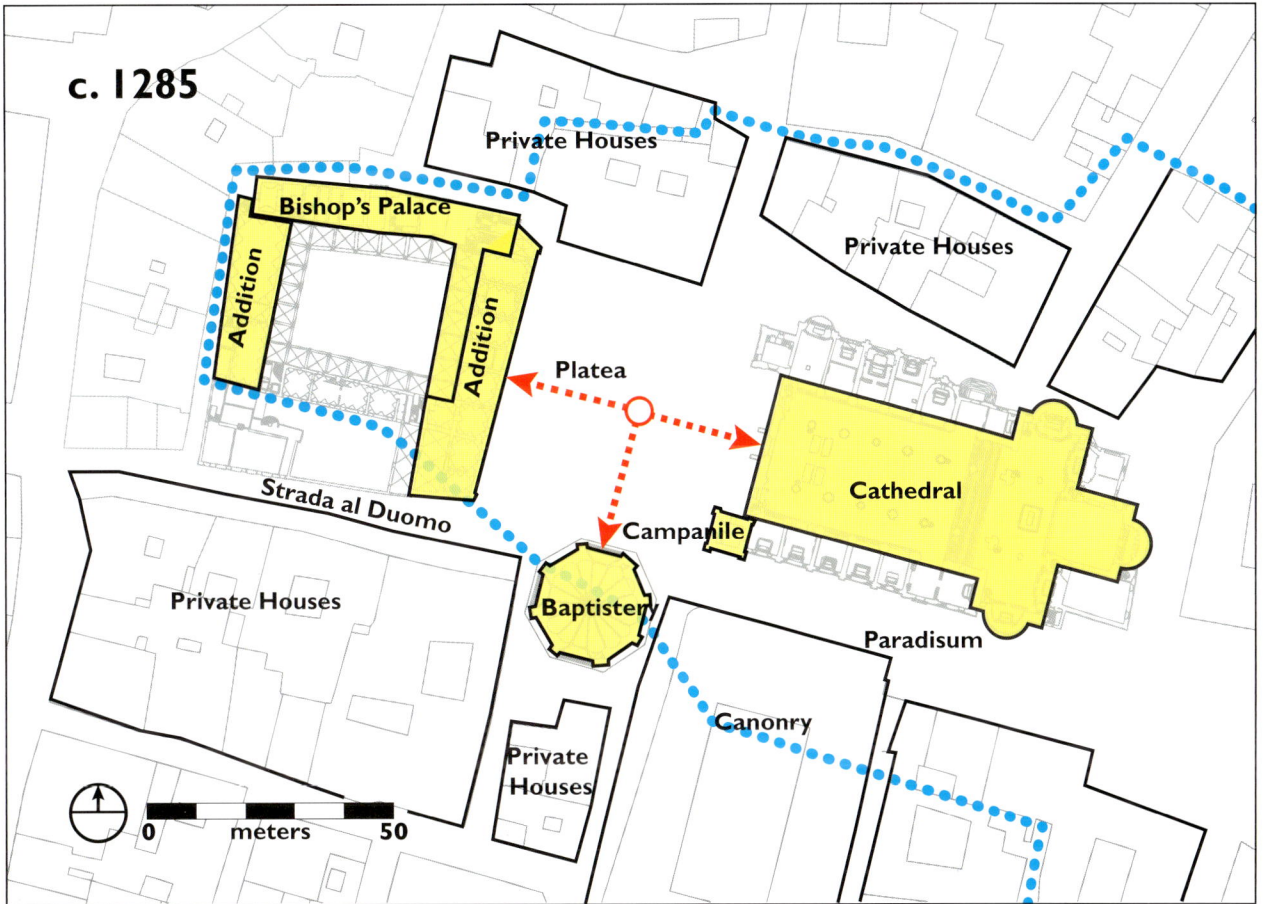

c. 1285

Private Houses

Bishop's Palace

Addition

Addition

Private Houses

Private Houses

Platea

Strada al Duomo

Cathedral

Campanile

Baptistery

Private Houses

Paradisum

Canonry

Private Houses

0   meters   50

rotating the original 7-meter square module six times. These overall mathematical relationships do not have the trigonometric precision uncovered by Friedman in his investigation of the design of the new towns founded by Florence in the fourteenth century;[59] nonetheless, they are so pervasive—extending from structure to structure and across the generations—that they cannot be coincidental.

Nor was the concerted and repeated use of Romanizing and courtly motifs and materials throughout the piazza accidental (fig. 46). The

Fig. 43 View of the entrance to Parma's episcopal square from the strada al Duomo. Before the loggia of the bishop's palace was closed in the fifteenth century, visitors could see through it to the cathedral facade.

Fig. 44 The episcopal square seen from its center, looking south.

Fig. 45 Reconstruction diagram of the cathedral piazza representing the axial relationships between its major buildings c. 1285.

baptistery's Corinthian capitals, engaged Doric column fragments, and trabeated galleries evoked imperial and Roman papal authority, as did the cathedral's sculpted porch supported by *stylophore* lions, added to the facade in 1281.[60] The massive ground-story arcade of the bishop's palace recalled arched Roman monuments and imperial palace architecture, while the elegant three-light windows of its *piano nobile* invoked the galleries and triforia of prestigious French and German churches, as did the *trifore* of the cathedral facade and bell tower. Indeed, the baptistery's splayed portals and elaborate sculptural decoration were among the first examples in Italy of a northern European architectural style closely associated with the French, Burgundian, and imperial courts.

Parma's builders repeatedly used expensive, imported *rosso di Verona* on all four of the piazza's major buildings even though it was sometimes difficult to obtain. The ancient Romans had used this pink-and-white limestone in their Parmesan architecture, and the Parmesans seem to have self-consciously exploited this association. When seen in combination with the orthogonality and monumentality of the site, these elements unmistakably embodied the claims to political authority of the piazza's patrons—power derived from their Romanizing, imperial heritage and noble mores, as I explore in chapter 4.

The Panoptic Piazza

In addition to its newly regular form and the harmonious reiteration of motifs and materials throughout the site, the Piazza del Duomo had another distinctive quality relating to the production of power. The visitor to the site, whether standing at any of the best vantage points—atop the Canale Maggiore bridge or in the center of the piazza—or simply wandering about the square, found him- or herself surrounded by monumental episcopal buildings on three sides. The piazza and the church-controlled buildings establishing its perimeter were deliberately crafted to fill the visitor's vision. These monumental and symbolically charged structures presented themselves as a panoptic, panoramic three-sided ensemble when viewed from the square's northern side, or embraced the viewer partly or fully when viewed from any other point within the piazza.

Although no further major construction projects were initiated in the Piazza del Duomo during the waning years of the thirteenth century, its builders increased the ornamentation of the structures already on the site of the old piazza (fig. 46). In addition to building the new campanile, the cathedral workshop added a new, sculpted prothyrum porch and another gallery in *rosso di Verona* (parallel to the church's gable) to the cathedral's screen facade in 1281.[61] A blind arcade above the baptistery's four galleries and a balustrade on its roof were installed by 1302 (fig. 15).[62] But for a few minor refinements to the baptistery's decoration, the transformation of Parma's episcopal *platea* was complete.[63] The Parmesan church would never again reach the height of temporal power achieved in the late Middle Ages. Its most important representational space, the Piazza del Duomo, underwent few significant alterations in succeeding centuries.[64]

To summarize, the planners of Parma's episcopal square and complex—the cathedral's *laborerium* and its cohort of administrators and

Fig. 46 Cathedral, campanile, and baptistery from the northwest corner of the Piazza del Duomo, Parma.

masons—systematically created this orderly piazza via a series of interconnected projects. Their transformation of the piazza began with the insertion and integration of the new baptistery into the existing episcopal center of the city, introducing order and symmetry into the formerly irregular piazza. Then the cathedral workshop's planners continued to pursue this new aesthetic with the expansion of the bishop's palace and the consequent regularization of the piazza's plan. The addition of the new campanile reaffirmed the church faction's desire for prominence within Parma's cityscape.

By imposing order on the disorderly features of the former imperial compound, the church faction asserted both the legitimacy of its claim and its ability to impose order on the city as a collective body as well as a physical body. The orderly, harmonious, and square Piazza del Duomo was an architectural and urbanistic metaphor for the orderly rule of the *pars episcopi* and the harmonious society it would establish. The dense web of formal relationships that bound the encircling buildings to each other, to the site, and to the city fabric as a whole also bound the visitor, engulfing him in the church faction's architectural political program.

CHAPTER 2

(Re)constructing the Communal Piazza

While the Piazza del Duomo is now at the margins of modern Parma's political and economic life, the site of the communal piazza remains its center (figs. 4 and 47). The town hall, most local and regional government offices, the most important banks, the city's greatest concentration of cafes, its primary commercial artery, and its chicest promenade—all surround or converge upon the enormous square-shaped site, which has been renamed Piazza Garibaldi. Despite the changes wrought by the intervening centuries on the buildings and streets that form the communal piazza's perimeter, the piazza retains the vitality, grandeur, and essential form it had at the beginning of the fourteenth century, if not its medieval ornamentation.[1]

Today, the piazza extends to either side of the via Emilia. The site looked very different at the end of the twelfth century (fig. 7). In 1200, the via Emilia (the ancient *decumanus maximus*) demarcated its northern boundary; buildings occupied the land to the north of that road. The perimeter of the long rectangular clearing to the south of the via Emilia had been established in antiquity (fig. 5)—it constituted Parma's forum and was the heart of the Roman colony's political, religious, and economic life.

The site's importance had declined in the early Middle Ages, as the political and religious foci of the city moved elsewhere, but it remained a significant nexus of communications traversed by two important thoroughfares. The via Emilia (called strata Claudia or Clodia in the thirteenth century) was the major regional east-west axis and bore much of the region's commercial land traffic, as it had since Roman imperial times. It linked the medieval city's eastern and western gates and intersected the city's *cardo maximus,* the north-south axis that connected the former colony's northern and southern gates.[2]

In the thirteenth century, the long rectangular space to the south of that intersection remained mostly unencumbered (fig. 48); it was all that survived of Roman Parma's forum. Two churches, dedicated to San Vitale and San Pietro, respectively, flanked this space on the east and the west.[3] Both churches were conventionally oriented in the Middle Ages. San Vitale's main entrance facade faced west; San Pietro had a portico along its northern flank, turning its apse toward the forum. The site's illustrious past endured merely in the appellation routinely given the church of Peter, "Sancti Petri quae est constructa prope forum."[4] Passersby could take

Fig. 47 Parma's communal square, as represented in the late sixteenth century. Detail from Paolo Ponzoni, *Pianta della città di Parma in prospettiva* (Piacenza: Francesco Conti, 1572), woodcut, after an earlier drawing. ASPr, Raccolta Mappe e Disegni, vol. 2, no. 13. North is at the bottom of the map.

Fig. 48 Reconstruction diagram, the communal piazza of Parma c. 1220. The open space of the former Roman forum extended south from the *decumanus maximus*.

shelter in San Pietro's portico, and families could bury their dead in its cemetery, but otherwise the site that was to become the city's most important public space was architecturally and urbanistically undistinguished.[5]

In this chapter, I reconstruct the events that transformed this space into a monumental showcase for Parma's burgeoning communal government. The redevelopment of Piazza Garibaldi in the thirteenth century took place in four stages. In the first, the commune established a meeting site away from the episcopal compound and built the first communal palace. In the second, the commune built a compound modeled on the urban complexes of the aristocratic clans. In the third, the commune expanded beyond the communal compound by acquiring property around the communal piazza. And, finally, in the fourth stage, the commune radically altered the character of the site by doubling the piazza's size and building a monumental new palace to assert its dominion.

Reconstructing the communal square is a greater challenge than reconstructing the cathedral square. The centuries have been kind to the Piazza del Duomo—medieval facades survive on three of its four sides. Only fragments of Piazza Garibaldi's medieval past are evident at first glance (fig. 49). Beginning in the middle of the fourteenth century, a succession of rulers altered the square to suit their new political and iconographic programs—the Visconti walled it, the Farnese and the Bourbons renovated it in the latest classicizing styles, the republicans renamed it, the fascists monumentalized its entrances, and the postwar governments updated its town hall and installed the piazza's eighteenth-century-style street furniture. The site has suffered further misfor-

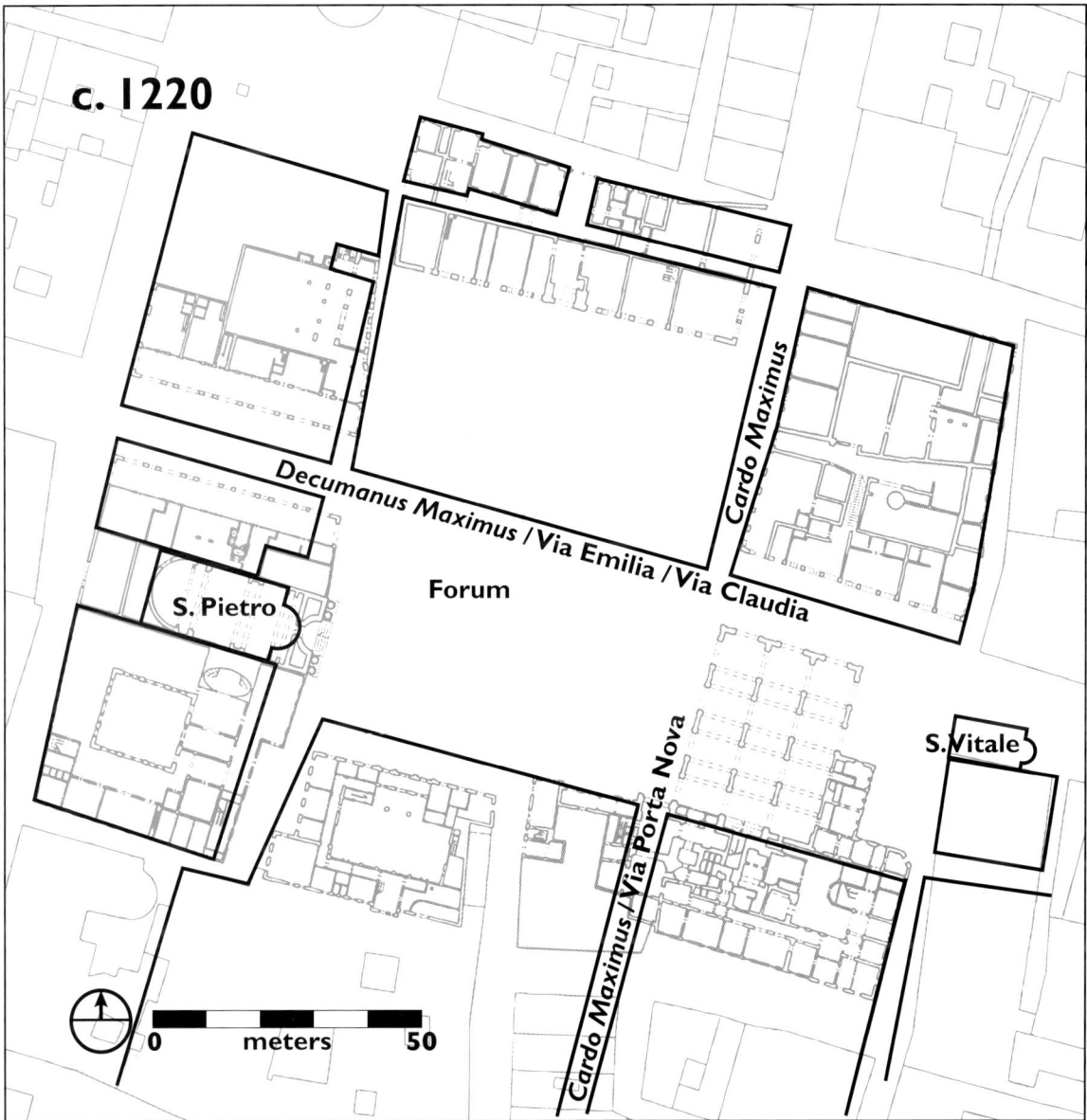

c. 1220

Decumanus Maximus / Via Emilia / Via Claudia

Cardo Maximus

Forum

S. Pietro

Cardo Maximus / Via Porta Nova

S. Vitale

0   meters   50

tunes. In 1606, the communal tower collapsed, and its debris demolished the first communal palace and surrounding buildings. In 1943, Allied bombing destroyed part of the piazza's western boundary. So while much of the perimeter of the piazza is medieval in origin, only three medieval facades are visible today. Modern plaster obscures most of what remains of the piazza's thirteenth-century fabric, and building interiors have been altered beyond recognition.[6]

The fragmentary condition of the site is only the first of two factors hampering successful reconstruction of Parma's communal piazza.

Fig. 49 Medieval facades visible on Piazza Garibaldi, Parma.

The second is the lack of scholarly consensus about the identity and chronology of the buildings that make up its perimeter. Since so little of the piazza's medieval fabric is evident, scholars have concentrated on the relatively abundant documentary record. The thirteenth- and fourteenth-century statutes of the commune of Parma frequently address the communal piazza and buildings, and they are also mentioned repeatedly in the *Chronicon Parmense.* However, Parma's chroniclers, notaries, and legislators were writing not on behalf of modern historians but rather for their own purposes and to an audience intimately familiar with the spaces and monuments named in the texts. Consequently, even the most thorough scholar must contend with ambiguities and apparent contradictions in the textual record. As I have done in the case of the Piazza del Duomo, I here harness physical and textual evidence together to reconstruct the history of the communal piazza throughout the thirteenth and early fourteenth centuries.

The study of a piazza inevitably must account for the buildings that define its perimeter. While the communal square's perimeter buildings also have rich and complicated histories, this text foregrounds the space of the piazza. I have consigned detailed discussion of the identity and history of the communal buildings making up its borders to appendix II.

The First Stage: New Communal Space

Before the thirteenth century, Parma's communal consuls, podestas, council members, and officers did not have a permanent palace to house them and their records. Surviving documents tell us that the officers of the commune performed their duties in assorted venues around town, often (but not always) in some part of the episcopal complex and in a place or places called *porticus communis.*[7] None of the extant twelfth-century documents provides further information regarding the location of that portico or, indeed, any reason to assume that there was only one or that it was on, or near, the forum.

By 1219, the already tense relations between the commune and the church became intolerably strained. The communal government had gradually usurped many of the legal rights traditionally exercised by the bishop; both bishop and commune turned to such authorities as they could muster to bolster their claims. In 1219, the commune extracted from Emperor Frederick II a sentence confirming its extensive

rights over Parma and its territory in exchange for the commune's loyalty and support of his claims to dominion over north Italy. Shortly thereafter, Bishop Òbizzo Fieschi obtained a contrasting imperial diploma stating that any rights the emperor had granted the commune could not supersede the traditional rights of the bishop as count of Parma and head of the Parmesan church. The commune disregarded this equivocal document, so in 1220 the bishop turned to Pope Honorius III for resolution of the conflict. Although the pope issued an edict confirming the church's rights, the commune ignored that one as well, along with its ensuing excommunication.[8]

Given the animosity between commune and church, the commune could not comfortably conduct its business under the roofs or within the purview of the episcopal authority. In 1221, the commune's podesta, Torello da Strada of Pavia, finally settled the jurisdictional conflict with the bishop, to the church's detriment.[9] He commemorated this victory by spearheading the construction of the first Parmesan communal palace, away from the Piazza del Duomo (figs. 50 and 51).[10]

Torello and the commune elected to build their grand palace at the eastern end of the former Roman forum.[11] This site had several advantages. First, communal officials would have been aware of its Roman origins. Although both of the other sites associated with imperial authority were taken—the bishop controlled the episcopal complex on the former *curtis regia,* and the emperor's own palace occupied the remains of the Roman arena—the forum remained unclaimed. Second, in Parma, as elsewhere in northern Italy, the site of the Roman forum still marked the intersection of

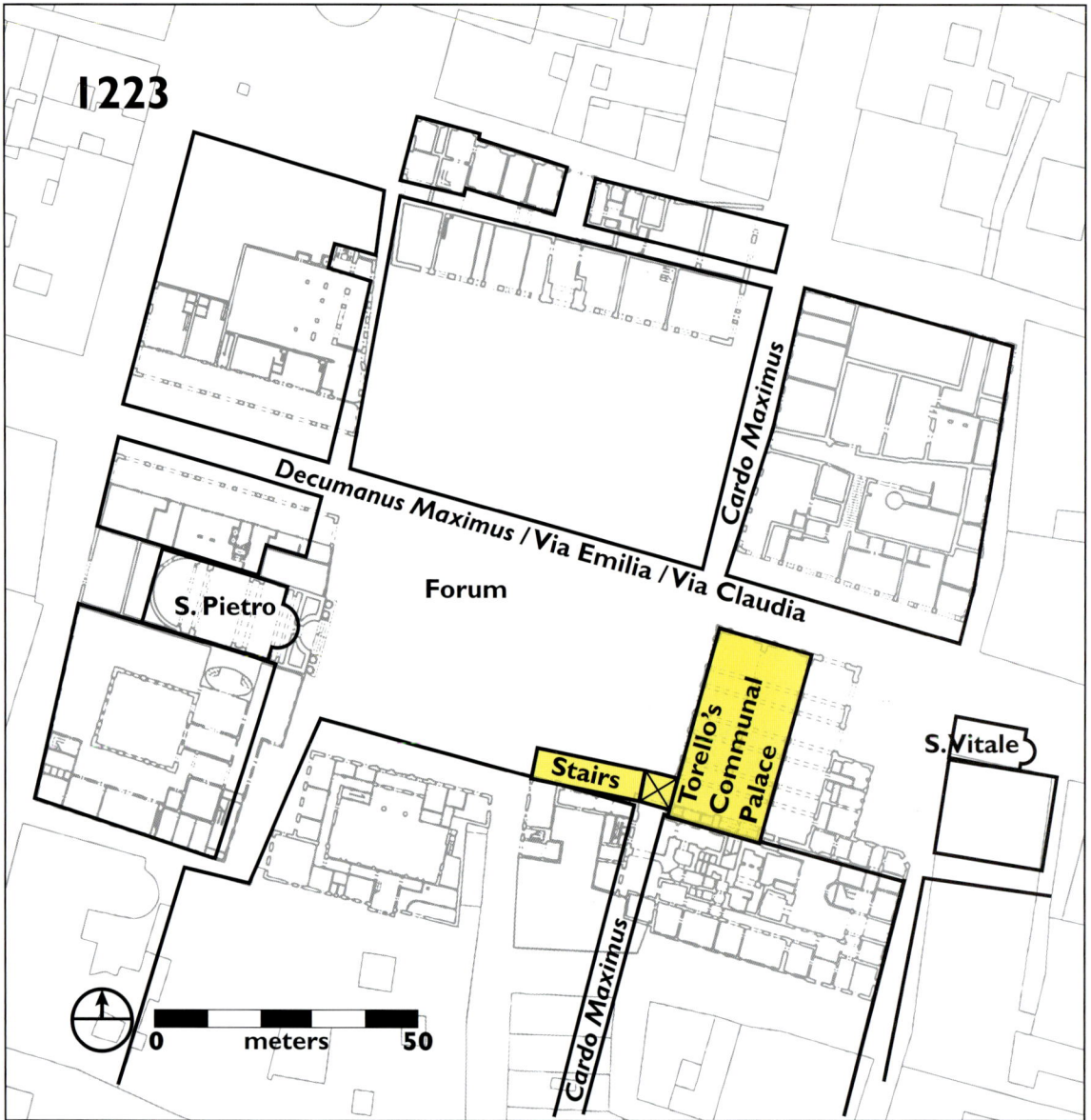

I223

Decumanus Maximus / Via Emilia / Via Claudia

Cardo Maximus

Forum

S. Pietro

Stairs

Torello's Communal Palace

S. Vitale

Cardo Maximus

0   meters   50

the most important commercial streets.[12] Furthermore, the forum already housed another, older political association. The Society of Knights (*societas militum*) met in the portico near San Pietro, on the western side of the forum.[13] Finally, aside from the cathedral square, the forum site was the largest open space within the city walls—few structures, if any, would need to be demolished to build the palace. Extensive demolition and expropriation inevitably would have resulted in resistance and additional expense; here, the commune could build with relative liberty.

Although Torello's palace was destroyed in 1606 by the collapse of the communal tower, we can reconstruct its appearance and location on the basis of textual, graphic, and archaeological evidence. Schulz convincingly argues that the 1221 palace was built on the site of today's Palazzo del Municipio, on the forum's southern boundary (fig. 52). A 1263 statute unmistakably establishes its location. Torello's communal palace, according to the statute, had a square to its east (between the palace and the church and portico of San Vitale) and another square to its west, as can be seen in copies of Smeraldo Smeraldi's plan of the city, which was drawn before 1606 (fig. 53). The only building site with this characteristic is that of the Palazzo del Municipio.[14]

Schulz has reconstructed the form of Torello's building by looking at early maps and views of Parma (figs. 51, 53–55), as well as comparable palaces elsewhere in northern Italy. The palace probably looked much like its representation in a 1572 printed view of the city that probably derived from an earlier drawing (fig. 51). Although schematic, this historic depiction reveals a three-story gabled structure with a loggia on the ground floor, elegant multilight windows on the

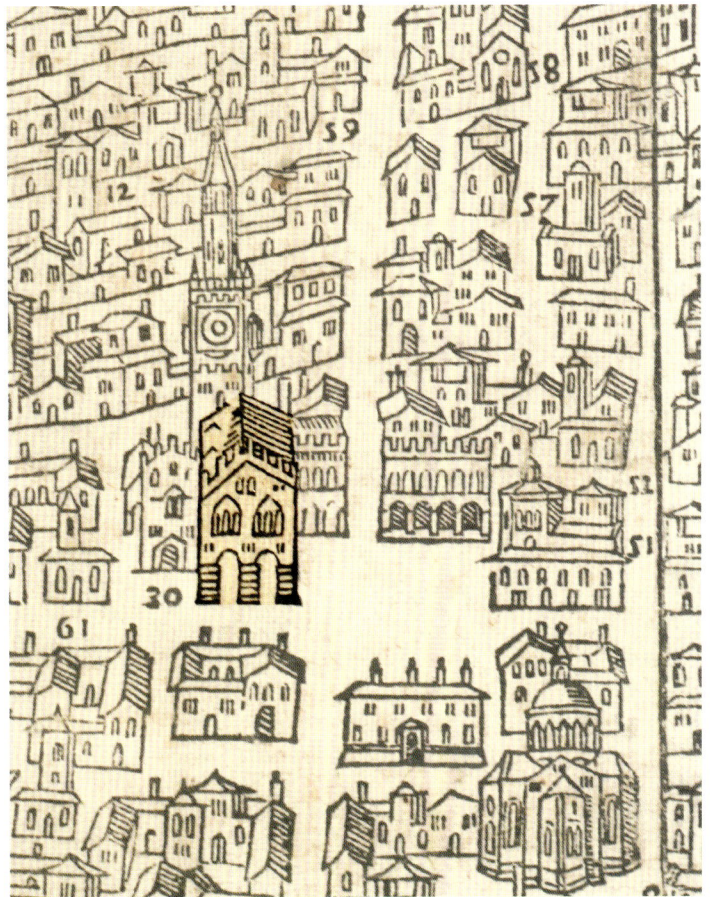

Fig. 50 Reconstruction diagram, the communal piazza of Parma in 1223. The new communal palace, built by Podesta Torello da Strada, is sited to the east of the city's Roman *cardo maximus* and divides the former forum in two.

Fig. 51 Torello's communal palace. Highlighted detail from Paolo Ponzoni, *Pianta della città di Parma in prospettiva* (Piacenza: Francesco Conti, 1572), woodcut, after an earlier drawing. ASPr, Raccolta Mappe e Disegni, vol. 2, no. 13. North is at the bottom of the map.

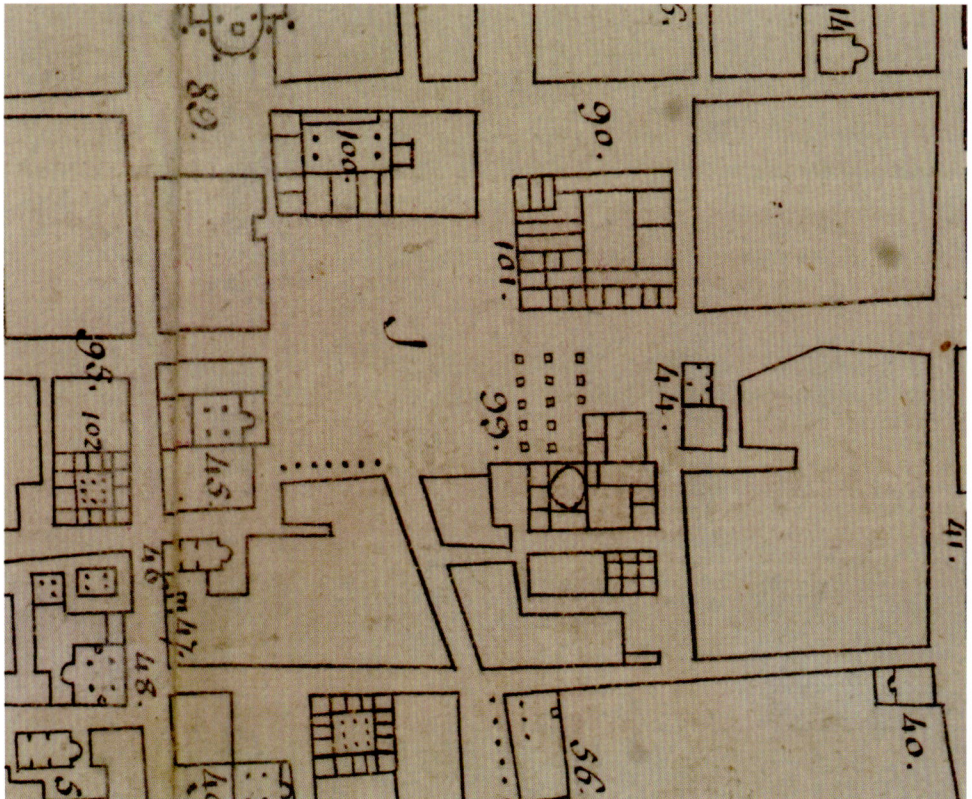

Fig. 52 The Palazzo del Municipio, Parma, which occupies the site of Torello's communal palace. Here it is seen from the west.

Fig. 53 Parma's communal square in the late sixteenth century. Detail from a copy of Smeraldo Smeraldi's 1589–91 map of Parma. ASPr, Raccolta Mappe e Disegni, vol. 2, no. 61. (I have rotated the map to place north at the top.)

Fig. 54 The earliest surviving representation of Parma. Although it is highly schematic, several important buildings are recognizable, including the cathedral, five communal palaces, and the church of San Pietro. The city walls, especially those flanking the Parma torrent, and the bridges across it were given special prominence by the mapmaker. Detail from *Pianta di Parma e del suo territorio con parte di Borghigiano e Reggiano disegnata dopo il 1460*. ASPr, Raccolta Mappe e Disegni, vol. 2, no. 85. North is at the bottom of the map.

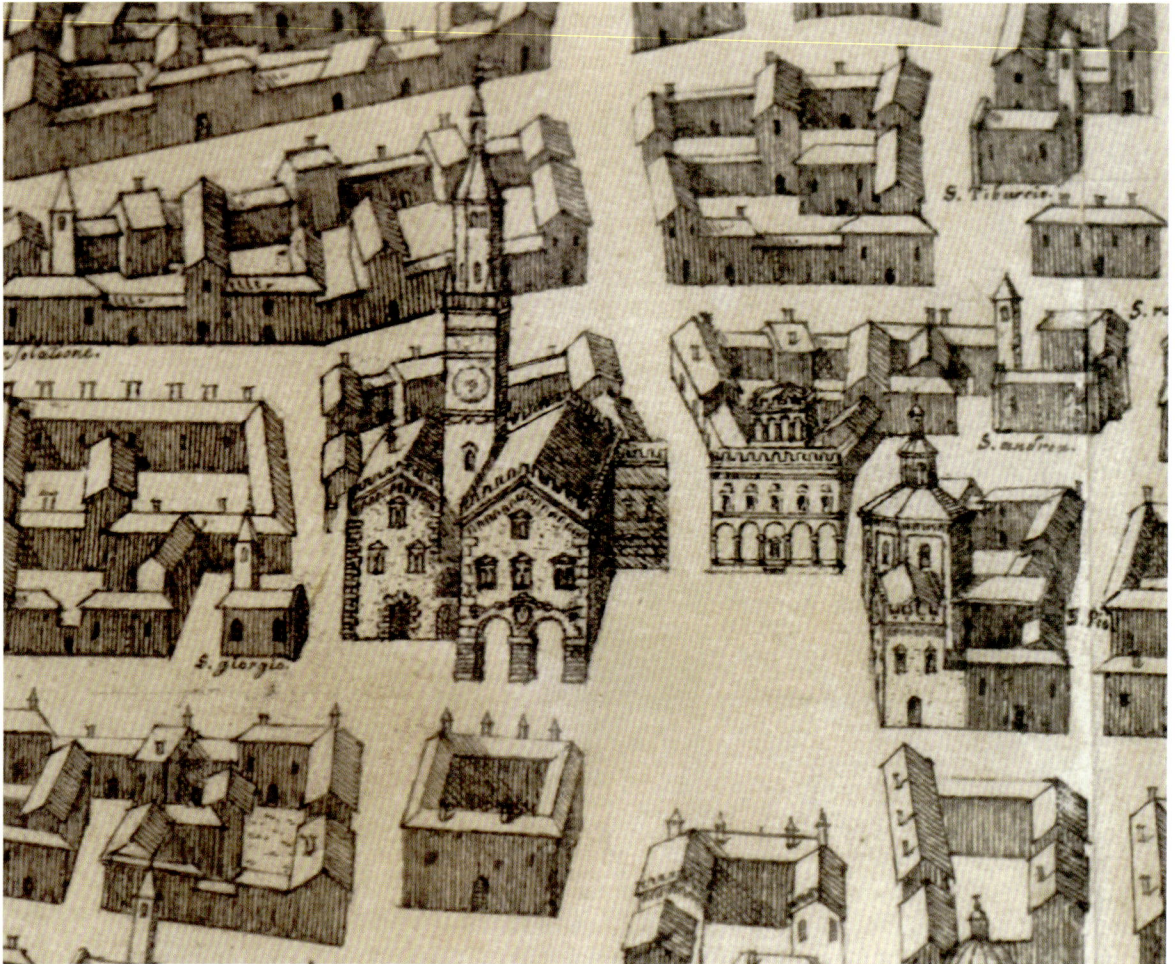

Fig. 55 Piazza Grande (now Piazza Garibaldi). Detail from Pietro Sottili, *Reproduction of Bird's-Eye View of Parma c. 1570*, ink, 1873. Museo Archeologico, Parma. North is at the bottom of the map.

Fig. 56 Sandstone pier and fragmentary arch from Torello's communal palace, Parma, now engulfed in the Volta del Municipio.

main floor, and merlons above, not unlike the extant communal palace of Cremona.[15] A pier and a fragment of one massive arch near the southwest corner of the Palazzo del Municipio, now engulfed by the municipal government's information center, are the only visible surviving remains of Torello's palace (fig. 56).

This civic-building type is found frequently in northern and central Italy in the twelfth and thirteenth centuries; surviving examples include the communal palaces of neighboring

Piacenza and Cremona (fig. 57). The palace type, whose sources include—but are not limited to—the imperial palaces of late antiquity, was successfully adopted by both bishops and communal governments.[16] The open portico sheltered judicial and mercantile activity, while great halls above provided meeting space for the commune's councils.[17] The second story could be reached by means of a monumental external staircase, completed in 1223.[18] The battlements surmounting the palace recalled fortifications and thus emphasized the military strength that backed all aspirations to rule in this period, although the multitude of openings in its walls prevented it from functioning as a true fortress.

Having built a monument worthy of itself, the commune guaranteed its visibility by ensuring it remained surrounded by clean, open space. A statute of 1227 calls for the sweeping out of the *platea communis,* or communal piazza, on a monthly basis (specifying that such waste removal must be performed as cheaply as possible).[19] Another, perhaps earlier statute (amended in 1228) demands on behalf of the commune that the recently acquired land of the *platea nova* be kept clear of obstacles and construction of all types.[20] The building activity and legislation of the 1220s gave the *platea nova* a monumental focus and protected it from the creeping encroachments of medieval urbanization.

Torello's communal palace was magnificently displayed in this carefully defended and well-maintained space. The palace was exposed on three sides. Its long arcaded facades could be seen by people traveling both eastward and westward on the Po valley's most important road, the via Emilia, much in the same way that its successor on the site can be seen today (fig. 58).

Fig. 57 Communal palace, Cremona, 1206–46.

Fig. 58 Like the Palazzo del Municipio now on the site, Torello's communal palace would have been highly visible from the eastern branch of the former via Claudia/Emilia (now via della Repubblica).

The Second Stage: Communal Complex as Aristocratic Clan Compound

In the second stage of the communal piazza's development, the commune built for itself a compound modeled on those assembled within the city by aristocratic clans.[21] This new communal complex was massed around Torello's palace. In the middle third of the thirteenth century, Parma (like much of upper and central Italy) was torn by factional warfare as well as threatened by external forces.[22] The faction that controlled the bishopric and most episcopal offices—which included the Rossi, Sanvitale, and a local branch of the Fieschi clan—had supported the emperor in the hope that he would in turn support the church's authority against the commune's claims. When Parmesan canon Sinibaldo Fieschi (Bishop Òbizzo's nephew) was elected Pope Innocent IV in 1244, part of Parma's imperial party, under the leadership of Innocent IV's nephew Bishop-elect Alberto Sanvitale, promptly switched its allegiance from the emperor to the new pope. Pro-imperial and pro-papal factions fought inside and outside the city walls. In the 1240s, the dominant clans within Parma were allied with, then allied against, and finally besieged by Emperor Frederick II, while opposing Parmesan factions assisted Frederick's forces, first from within the city and later as exiles.[23]

The communal compound began to take shape in these unsettled times. Despite, or perhaps because of, endemic warfare, by 1246 the commune had completed a communal tower next to Torello's communal palace (fig. 59).[24] Maps and views made before its collapse show that the tower was located to the southeast of Torello's palace, and the surviving documents

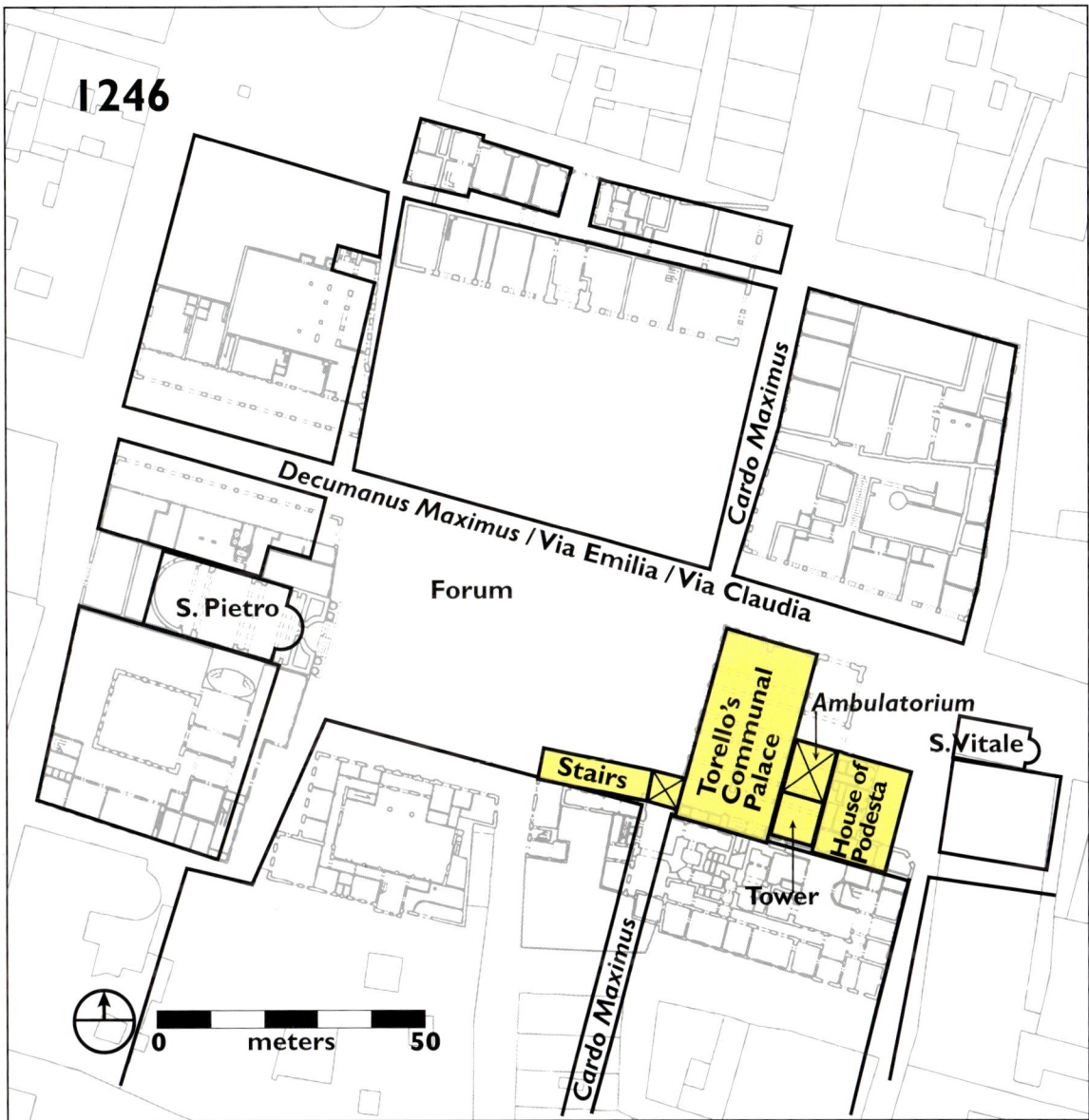

1246

S. Pietro

Decumanus Maximus / Via Emilia / Via Claudia

Forum

Cardo Maximus

Stairs

Torello's Communal Palace

Ambulatorium

House of Podesta

S. Vitale

Tower

Cardo Maximus

0   meters   50

Fig. 59 Reconstruction diagram, the communal piazza of Parma in 1246. The new tower, *ambulatorium,* and House of the Podesta cluster to the east of Torello's communal palace.

73

agree (fig. 60). Sixteenth- and seventeenth-century views depict a tall square tower surmounted by a balustraded and pinnacled parapet and supporting an imposing pierced octagonal superstructure topped with an octagonal spire and lantern—a building worthy of one witness's characterization of it as "sublimis et altissima" (figs. 61 and 62).[25] Several towers of this type survive in northern Italy; close examples include the cathedral bell towers of Cremona and Modena, known as the Torrazzo and the Ghirlandina, respectively (fig. 63).[26] Either Parma's tower lacked the corner pilasters and blind arcading typical of Lombard towers, or perhaps the views are too schematic to include them. Some representations (figs. 55 and 60) also depict crenellations at the tower's midpoint and below the balustrade; these are reminiscent of the battlements buried in the piazza facade of Siena's Torre del Mangia where it meets the masonry of the Palazzo Pubblico, and may reflect a transition between building campaigns.

The medieval tower may not have looked exactly like the one seen in these views, however. Several alterations to the tower were made

Fig. 60 Communal tower. Highlighted detail from Paolo Ponzoni, *Pianta della città di Parma in prospettiva* (Piacenza: Francesco Conti, 1572), woodcut, after an earlier drawing. ASPr, Raccolta Mappe e Disegni, vol. 2, no. 13. North is at the bottom of the map.

Fig. 61 Stucco boss representing the city of Parma as if in a convex mirror, vault of the Sala della Giunta, Palazzo Municipale, Parma, c. 1675. The communal tower (to the right) is represented as taller than the cathedral bell tower (left).

Fig. 62 The communal tower dominates the cityscape in this fresco, *View of Parma*, 1569, by Jacopo Sanguidi, called il Bertoia. Sala d'Ercole, Palazzo Farnese, Caprarola.

in the fifteenth and sixteenth centuries, including the addition of the octagonal upper story and clock discernible in the sixteenth-century images. Some communal towers elsewhere in the Po plain are much simpler in form—the towers of Brescia (Torre del Pégol) and Bologna (Torre dell'Arengo, fig. 64) consist of a square tower block with a pierced upper story surmounted by battlements.[27]

Fig. 63 Torrazzo, Cremona, begun c. 1235, completed up to the four-light window by 1267, and up to the spire by 1309.

Fig. 64 Torre dell'Arengo, Bologna, by 1212.

Whether the towers were ornamented or plain, their construction was the classic urbanistic gesture of the Italian noble classes in the Middle Ages. The tower was the nucleus around which aristocratic clans agglomerated their urban domestic complexes. The tower had both a defensive and an offensive function; clan members could withdraw to it with their valuables if attacked, and they could launch attacks on others from its heights. Furthermore, its prominence within the cityscape asserted the prominence of the clan who owned it.[28] Parma's communal tower shared these two functions with domestic towers, but it also had another purpose. Like a church campanile, the communal tower housed bells. Church bells were rung to mark the passage of time, to call the people to church, to commemorate or announce specific religious or secular events, and to summon the populace in times of danger.[29] When the commune installed a large bell on its tower, as it did in 1246, it appropriated a function formerly monopolized by the church, that of marking time, as well as providing itself with an instrument that had symbolized the church's care for the population.[30] Now that the commune had a bell of its own, the people could be warned of danger by the commune, not the clergy, and summoned to do the commune's bidding.[31] The communal tower and its bell regularly reminded Parma's citizens of their rightful role in the life of the commune. The meeting of a council and the ringing of bells were so strongly linked in the Parmesan imagination that councils were said to be rung, not convened.[32]

The casting of any large bell was expensive, technically challenging, and noteworthy. One chronicler commemorated the completion of Parma's communal bell in 1244 as one of the six memorable events of that year—along with the appointment of a pro-imperial podesta, Lord Ugo Sanvitale's acts of resistance against the imperial party, Pope Innocent IV's flight to Lyon, the passage of new voting rules in the communal council, and the Dominicans' relocation to a new church. Indeed, the installation of a new bell merited a solemn civic procession in 1317.[33]

Although the communal bells could be heard throughout the city and the tower could be seen from the smaller eastern and larger western portions of the communal piazza, the tower did not have a piazza facade. Like Bologna's Torre dell'Arengo, it was, from its inception, attached to another communal building and, in the course of the thirteenth century, it gradually came to be surrounded by others. Although the communal tower's full extent could not be perceived from the communal piazza, its upper stories would have loomed over the lower buildings around it. In sixteenth-century views, it is represented as Parma's tallest structure (fig. 62).

The tower was not the only building added to the communal compound in the 1240s. By 1246, the podesta had acquired an official residence (figs. 59 and 65). In a manner typical of urban noble compounds, the new building was connected to the tower and Torello's palace by means of an *ambulatorium* (also *balatorium,* in Italian, *ballatoio,* an elevated walkway) (fig. 55).[34] The location of the House of the Podesta has been much debated because only traces of it survive and the documentary evidence seems contradictory. The communal tower's collapse in 1606 also destroyed much of the communal complex to its east.[35]

From my analysis of the available evidence, I conclude that the House of the Podesta was part of the now-vanished complex of buildings that extended east-southeast from Torello's communal palace (fig. 59).[36] Early views portray the House of the Podesta as a multistoried building narrower and shorter than Torello's palace. The house, like the palace, was crowned with battlements. Like the communal tower itself, these were loaded with symbolic associations. The rights to fortify and to build towers were traditionally noble privileges, granted on the authority of the emperor. The presence of fortified elements on the communal buildings referred to this privilege, while at the same time reflecting the embattled condition of communal authority. The urban compounds of noble clans consisted of one or more towers and several houses of varying architectural distinction, all connected to each other and often enclosing courtyards and streets controlled by the clan; battlements and defensive gates were not uncommon. In amassing its own magnificent and forbidding complex of buildings, the commune simultaneously identified itself with the values of Parma's aristocracy—by appropriating the traditional urban and architectural forms used by that aristocracy—and challenged the status quo—by inserting its complex into the epicenter of the city, close to the properties of the church-affiliated Sanvitale clan.[37]

Buildings for the *Popolo*

In the mid-1260s, the struggle between supporters of the empire and those of the papacy came to a head once more, with an added complication—the intervention of the *popolo,* Parma's nonnoble property-owning class. Within Parma, imperial supporters banded behind regional lord Oberto Pallavicino. Others, concerned that Parma was going to be subjected to Pallavicino's rule should the imperial party win, rallied behind a tailor. His name was Giovanni Barisello; in 1266 he raised a troop of five hundred *popolari* and rampaged through the city, demanding that noblemen suspected of imperial leanings swear fealty to the church party. This band of *popolari,* under the sponsorship of Charles of Anjou, king of Naples and papal challenger to the imperial forces, mutated into an armed society of a thousand men called the Societatis Croxatorum (Society of Crusaders).[38] By means of this society, and with the implicit sanction of Pope Clement IV and King Charles, the *popolo* infiltrated the patrician communal faction of Parma. The *capitano* of the Society of Crusaders took over from the

podesta the leadership of Parma's militia and became known as the *capitano del popolo.* Like the podesta, the *capitano* had to be a foreigner and was replaced every six months. He also had legislative powers—along with the eight

Fig. 65 House of the Podesta. Highlighted detail from Paolo Ponzoni, *Pianta della città di Parma in prospettiva* (Piacenza: Francesco Conti, 1572), woodcut, after an earlier drawing. ASPr, Raccolta Mappe e Disegni, vol. 2, no. 13. North is at the bottom of the map.

primicerii of the Society of Crusaders, he joined the podesta and the *anziani* in determining which proposals would be presented to the general council of the commune.[39] As the *popolo* extended its juridical and fiscal powers at the expense of the *potentes,* the commune's councils and offices increased in number.[40] The communal complex expanded accordingly (fig. 66).

One of the buildings added to the communal compound to accommodate the commune's expansion was the House or Palace of the Capitano del Popolo, first mentioned in a statute compiled in 1266 (figs. 67 and 68). The *capitano*'s house was erected west of Torello's palace, on the piazza's southern perimeter, as Schulz has proposed. It has one of the few medieval facades that survive on the square (and the modern street address Piazza Garibaldi, no. 1).[41] Alas, the building sheathed by the piazza facade has undergone several radical renovations since the thirteenth century; its ground-story elevation and interior disposition have been altered beyond reconstruction. The house's upper facade was excavated and restored in the 1920s as part of a fascist project to valorize Italy's medieval past. Nonetheless, several distinctive features survive on the house's fragmentary medieval facade. Above the ground story, three round-headed three-light windows stagger across the facade from lower right to upper left, following an 18-degree incline. The windows of the house were built in this seemingly idiosyncratic manner to accommodate the diagonal ascent of the preexisting external staircase of Torello's communal palace.[42] Above them, three more *trifore* pierce the House of the Capitano's walls. The entire structure is surmounted by a series of so-called Ghibelline, swallow-tailed battlements of

uncertain historical accuracy (early views depict conventional flat-topped, or "Guelph," merlons); they have been rendered impracticable by the installation of a pitched tile roof behind them. The crumbling yellowish merlons seem insignificant today; decay, rather than defense and defiance, is all they signal now. The original effect must have been rather different—Salimbene refers to the *capitano*'s building as a palace and reports that he found it "very beautiful."[43] Indeed, although the House of the Capitano was made of local brick, its six elegant *trifore,* with *rosso di Verona* colonnettes, recalled the windows of Parma's most sumptuous palace, that of the bishop. Unfortunately, the monumental staircase fronting the House of the Capitano is now missing. Its existence, however, is not in question. Although it is not represented in any of the site's historic views, it is repeatedly cited by the documents and indicated by the diagonal course of the House of the Capitano's windows.

Today, a three-storied brick structure occupies the gap between the successor to Torello's palace and the *capitano*'s house (fig. 69). This tall, thick-walled, barrel-vaulted structure projects further into the piazza than the house's facade; it appears to be superimposed on the eastern edge of that facade, which suggests that it postdates the house. The structure underwent a restoration at the same time as the House of the Capitano. Its barrel-vaulted ground story and the second-story loggia are medieval in origin. The top, third story is a later addition; its windows were retrofitted with medievalizing frames in the 1920s. Although the precise relationship of Torello's palace, the House of the Capitano, the monumental staircase, and this intermediary

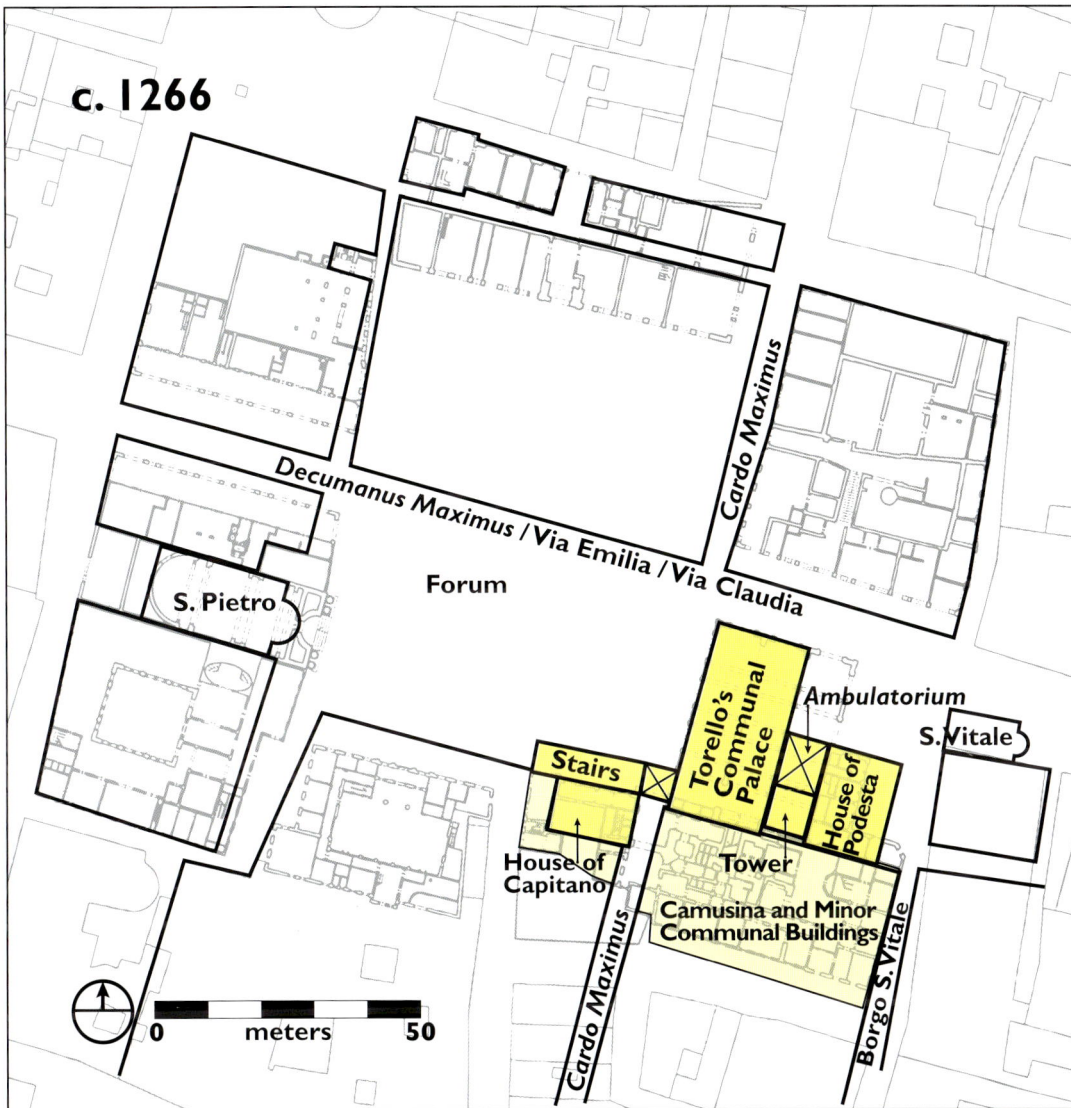

c. 1266

Decumanus Maximus / Via Emilia / Via Claudia

Cardo Maximus

Forum

S. Pietro

Torello's Communal Palace

Ambulatorium

S. Vitale

Stairs

House of Podesta

House of Capitano

Tower

Camusina and Minor Communal Buildings

Cardo Maximus

Borgo S. Vitale

0   meters   50

structure is not completely clear, the architecture of the intermediary structure nonetheless seems to be in harmony with that of the House of the Capitano's facade. Its second-story loggia continues the ascent begun by the three staggered windows of the *capitano*'s house. Its base is aligned along the same 18-degree incline as the bases of the *trifore.* The narrow windows

Fig. 66 Reconstruction diagram, the communal piazza of Parma c. 1266. The communal compound is made up of the communal palace, the House of the Podesta, the new House of the Capitano, Camusina prison, and minor communal buildings. The precise scale and location of the Camusina and minor structures remain uncertain; thus, they are represented by lighter shading on this diagram.

Fig. 67 House of the Capitano. Highlighted detail from Paolo Ponzoni, *Pianta della città di Parma in prospettiva* (Piacenza: Francesco Conti, 1572), woodcut, after an earlier drawing. ASPr, Raccolta Mappe e Disegni, vol. 2, no. 13. North is at the bottom of the map.

Fig. 68 House of the Capitano, Parma. Although the facade has been altered repeatedly, the upper stories preserve their thirteenth-century three-light windows.

Fig. 69 Arched building that connected the House of the Capitano to Torello's communal palace.

of its uppermost story spring from the same height as the upper windows of the House of the Capitano; a string course on the connecting structure marks this height. And the colonnettes of the loggia are made of *rosso di Verona,* just like those of the House of the Capitano.[44] The vaulted, ground-story passageway once bestrode the medieval city's most important north-south street, the ancient *cardo maximus.* (It now leads into an enclosed courtyard housing the city hall's reception desk.) Its distinguished northern facade could be seen by travelers moving south toward the piazza along that street (figs. 66 and 70).[45]

The Communal Piazza and Its Portals

As the commune developed its urban compound, it also improved the network of streets leading into the piazza (fig. 71). By the 1270s the communal compound straddled the city's most important north-south axis (the Roman *cardo maximus;* its northern arm is now called via Cavour, its southern continuation the strada Farini). Perhaps because the traffic that passed through the cluster of communal buildings compromised security, offended against decorum, or flowed inefficiently, the commune rerouted its course around, rather than through, the complex. The *cardo,* which had served well for several centuries, was deviated westward at the height of present-day via Maestri by 1275 (fig. 72).[46]

The commune also addressed the eastern boundary of the communal complex. In a 1264 statute, it demanded the straightening and extension of another north-south street, borgo San Vitale. This newly straight street was between the House of the Podesta and the house of Ugone Sanvitale and extended

northward toward the cathedral (fig. 71).[47] In addition to enhancing the decorum of the communal complex's environs by improving this street, the commune might have felt it opportune to mark more clearly the boundary between itself and the properties of Bishop Òbizzo's Sanvitale clan.

Improvements were not limited to north-south roads. A new street bordering the south side of the communal compound was opened up, straightened, and paved in 1272 (fig. 71). It survives as borgo della Salina.[48] Furthermore, the portion of the via Emilia that extended eastward from the communal piazza to the gate of Santa Cristina (often cited in the sources as the via or strata Claudia, now via della Repubblica), was widened in 1277.[49] The commune had overseen

Fig. 70 The communal vault over the former *cardo maximus* seen from via Cavour.

Fig. 71 Reconstruction diagram, the communal piazza of Parma c. 1277. The upper branch of the Roman *cardo* (now via Cavour) and the eastern branch of the *decumanus* (via Claudia/Emilia, now strada della Repubblica) have been widened. The lower branch of the *cardo* (via di Porta Nova or via Maestri, now via Farini) has been moved to the west, deviating traffic entering the piazza from the south away from the core of the communal compound.

several projects to pave increasing portions of the city. The communal piazza was no exception. Its pavement was ordered repaired and consolidated in 1264 and again in 1266.[50]

Parma's chronicles and statutes mention other communal buildings. These include both large and modest structures, such as two prisons, stables, a customs house, a mint, and a house for the lions of the commune. With the exception of the mint, which was located near the stone bridge (*pons lapidis*) that led across the Parma, these structures seem to have been massed to the east and south of Torello's palace and the communal tower and formed part of

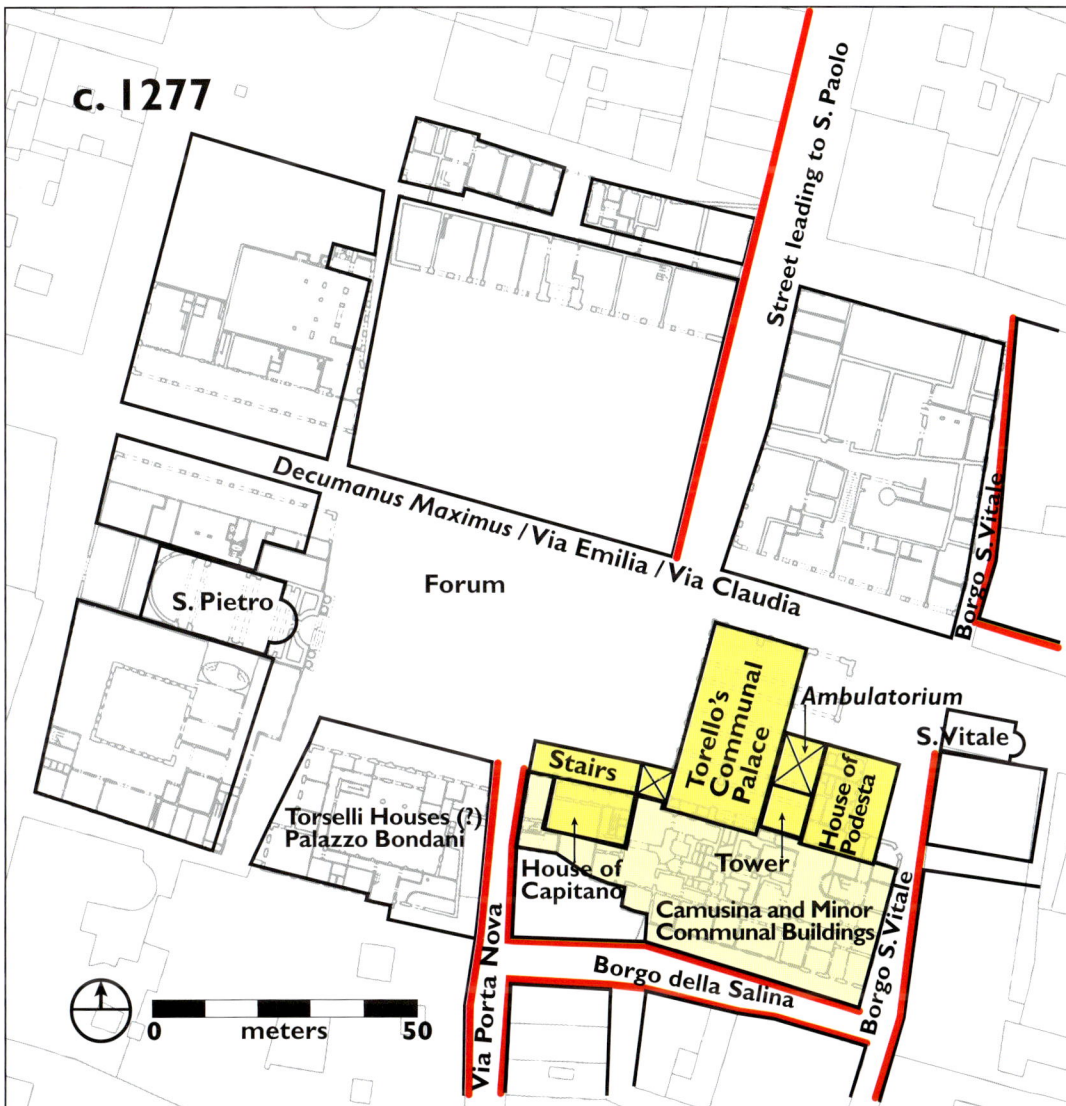

c. 1277

Street leading to S. Paolo

Decumanus Maximus / Via Emilia / Via Claudia

Forum

S. Pietro

Borgo S. Vitale

Torello's Communal Palace

Ambulatorium

S. Vitale

Stairs

House of Podesta

Torselli Houses (?)
Palazzo Bondani

House of Capitano

Tower

Camusina and Minor Communal Buildings

Via Porta Nova

Borgo della Salina

Borgo S. Vitale

0   meters   50

the communal compound (fig. 71). Alas, they, too, were victims of the communal tower's collapse and seventeenth- and twentieth-century construction on the site.[51] Like Torello's tower, none of these structures seems to have faced the piazza. Their primary relationship was to the preexisting communal buildings they adjoined.

By the late 1270s, the commune had established an elaborate, sprawling complex of related buildings near the city's central intersection, although the ensemble manifested little formal order. At this stage, the commune's planners do not appear to have been interested in the panoptic planning principles that animated their episcopal rivals to the north. The

Fig. 72 Aerial photograph from the north showing the westward deviation of the Roman *cardo* just south of the communal piazza.

focus of the communal complex was not on the piazza itself but rather on the buildings of the compound. While the largest portion of the communal piazza was the rectangle of space to the west of Torello's palace, the square's monumental and practical focus lay at the eastern end of the former forum, where Torello's palace, the communal tower, and the houses of the podestà and *capitano* clustered. This is not to say that the commune's designers disregarded the urbanistic effect of their project. As I have

shown, certain values were painstakingly upheld. Communal officials ensured that the communal piazza was paved and that its pavement was zealously maintained.[52] The streets leading into the piazza were improved in keeping with their dignity.[53] And, finally, the communal complex was highly visible from the four main entrances to the piazza.

Torello's palace had the most conspicuous position in town: the city's central intersection. As noted above, visitors from outside the city were most likely to arrive on the via Emilia, as it was the most important regional road. Torello's palace interposed itself in their line of sight from either east or west (figs. 52 and 58). Although no important palace invaded the traveler's view along the *cardo maximus,* the commune was careful to mark its dominion over the thoroughfare by constructing a vaulted building above it and by decorating this structure's facade (at least the one that survives) with a marble-colonnaded loggia. Even today, when the scale of downtown Parma's modern buildings dwarfs it, the communal vault can be seen from several blocks away (fig. 70). Moreover, before the *cardo*'s rerouting, communal buildings bordered the southern arm of that street (fig. 66). The western flank of Torello's palace was aligned with its eastern border, and the House of the Capitano marked its western edge.

Although the communal complex in this period was a highly visible and imposing landmark within Parma's cityscape, it did not seek to reproduce the panoptic effect of the episcopal precinct. The communal buildings were endowed with paved and well-maintained open spaces from which to see them, but the spaces themselves lacked formal coherence and orderly boundaries. The buildings' iconography toyed with their viewers' response—their central location, open porticos, and grand scale and decoration attracted the viewer, while the forbidding battlements that surmounted them and the tower that loomed among them sought to repel any potential desire to challenge the commune's authority. Furthermore, the angles from which Torello's palace and the communal arch are best viewed coincide with those least conducive to lingering—a group of onlookers standing on the *cardo* or the via Emilia would have impaired traffic. This is contrary to the conditions created in the more expansive Piazza del Duomo, where an observer could (and still can) gaze at leisure upon the backdrop installed for his or her benefit by the site's designers.

The communal compound's anxious self-assertiveness is, of course, appropriate for the urbanistic production of a group that needed to proclaim publicly and loudly its importance within the city. The institutions co-opted by the church faction had existed in Parma for centuries; the communal faction needed to announce the arrival of its own political instruments and to emphasize their supremacy. The communal faction inserted its monuments into the urban landscape as it imposed its institutions onto the city's social fabric. But although the piazza successfully showcased the commune's original and principal monument, Torello's communal palace, the commune's designers had not maximized the site's most notable characteristic—the impressive expanse of open space maintained by the commune within the city's densely inhabited heart. This was a situation the commune would eventually act vigorously to remedy.

The Third Stage: The Commune's Acquisition Program

In the 1260s and early 1270s, the commune seems to have launched a deliberate program to buy as much property as possible not only contiguous to the communal compound but also around the perimeter of the communal piazza. From the years 1270 to 1273 alone, twenty-four contracts between the commune and property owners around the piazza survive.[54] Graziella La Ferla Morselli has hypothesized that the contracts attempt to legitimate the commune's politically motivated expropriation of properties around the communal piazza. Since this period coincides with the brief heyday of the *popolo* in communal government,

La Ferla Morselli speculates that the properties' sellers were all of the magnate class.[55] Whether or not La Ferla Morselli's theory is correct, the large number of real-estate transactions indicates that the commune was engaged in a concerted effort to control all the properties circumscribing the piazza.[56] Its intentions for that real estate, however, remain enigmatic.

In a few cases, we know what the commune intended to do with its newly acquired assets, although its objectives changed from time to time. In 1253, the commune determined to acquire three properties near the communal palace. These belonged to Jacobus da Benezeto, Jacobus Preytis, and Ugo and Anselmo Sanvitale. Da Benezeto's and Preytis's properties were to the south and east of Torello's palace, at the foot of the communal tower; the Sanvitales' were next to the communal palace, between the palace and the church of San Vitale. At some point after 1253 but before 1259, the commune decreed that benches for the commune's moneychangers were to be installed on the site of either of these properties. It changed its mind in 1259, ordering that the moneychangers be returned to their original location next to the walls of the House of the Podesta. In 1260, the commune purchased one-half of the Sanvitale lot, which had the via Claudia to its north and the communal palace to its west. Then, in 1262, the commune decreed that two jails and several shops be built on the site of da Benezeto's and Preytis's properties, which had not yet been expropriated. The commune resolved that the lots be expropriated by Lent (which began on 20 February) and that construction be finished by the feast of Saint Peter, on 29 June. The limited time budgeted for the enterprise suggests—in addition to the haste of the commune—that the

buildings intended were relatively modest and were probably adaptations of earlier structures on the site rather than new construction. In the latter instance, the commune's instructions were finally carried out, if perhaps less swiftly than the commune had hoped: the *Chronicon Parmense* reports that the two new jails were completed in 1263.[57]

Most of the transactions for which we have surviving documents involve property on the northern and western halves of the piazza, where the commune did not already own important buildings.[58] Unfortunately, no documentary evidence has come to light to reveal what the commune intended to do with those properties at the time they were purchased. However, several historic views show a large house or palace topped with battlements and fronted by a portico along the western half of the piazza's southern boundary (fig. 73). This is probably the structure known as the Palazzo Bondani (fig. 74); it was replaced by a new building in the 1950s. A close reading of the documents reveals one small trace of the building: in 1270, the Torselli family sold their battlement-topped house to the commune. However, the Torselli house was only one of several properties occupying the land between the southbound street to Porta Nova and the piazza's western boundary. The documents never mention a portico.[59]

As interesting as what the commune's purchase contracts omitted is what they included. Scholars, myself included, had assumed that the entire area of the Roman forum as established—or, at least, as hypothesized—by archaeologists remained clear of construction. Some thirteenth-century documents call that assumption into question. Two

Fig. 73 House with battlements and portico on the southwest border of the communal piazza (Torselli properties, later Palazzo Bondani). Highlighted detail from Paolo Ponzoni, *Pianta della città di Parma in prospettiva* (Piacenza: Francesco Conti, 1572), woodcut, after an earlier drawing. ASPr, Raccolta Mappe e Disegni, vol. 2, no. 13. North is at the bottom of the map.

Fig. 74 House with portico on the southwest border of the communal piazza (Torselli properties, later Palazzo Bondani). Giulio Carmignani, *Piazza Garibaldi,* watercolor, c. 1850. ASCP, Fototeca, Fondo A.P.T., Album Fotografici, 4330/A.

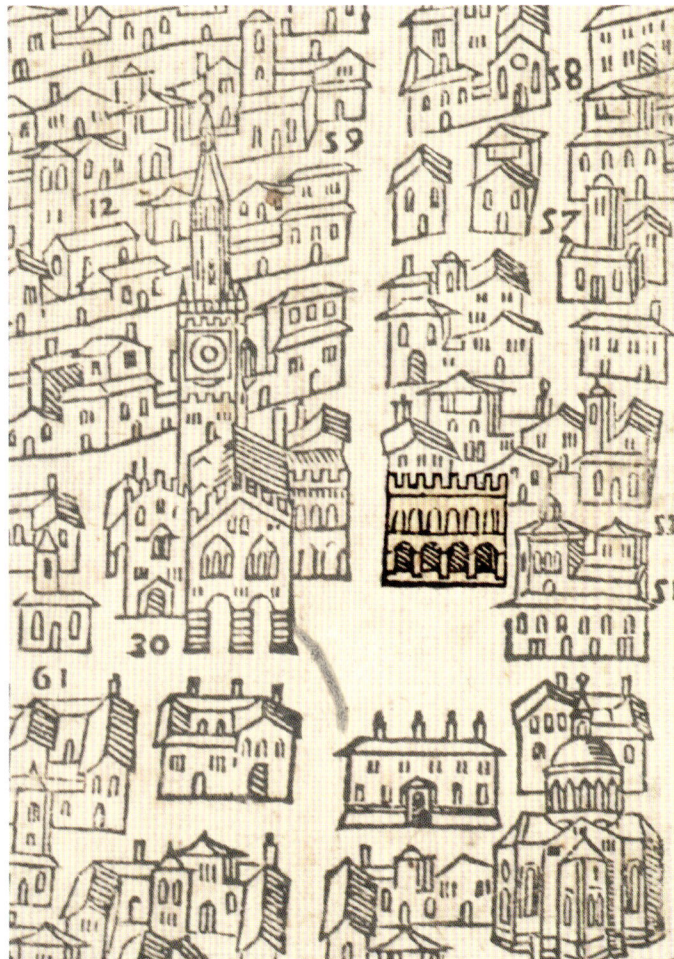

documents specifically refer to the commune's acquisition of a house along the piazza's western boundary but to the east of the church of San Pietro.[60] If the western boundary of the piazza was not straight and crisp in the late thirteenth century, how can one assume that any of the others were? Although no thirteenth-century documents recording the straightening of the piazza's boundaries exist, we know that the commune sought to straighten and order the city's streets. It is possible that the commune's acquisitions of the 1260s and 1270s were meant to enable the piazza's planners to rationalize the perimeter of the commune's most important representational space.

Although the communal compound and the improving condition of the area's infrastructure were the most visible manifestations of the commune's urbanistic policy on the *platea nova,* the acquisitions of the 1260s and 1270s indicate a new outlook on the commune's part. The inward-looking conservatism expressed by the commune's assembly of a compound in the piazza's southeast quadrant began to give way to a new desire to leap across the piazza's open space and bind the entire perimeter to the commune's urbanistic project.

The Fourth Stage: "The Great Square Piazza"

The next stage in the commune's bold emergence beyond the boundaries of the old communal compound and into the space of the piazza did not begin until the following decade. The year 1281 introduced a flurry of communal building that radically reoriented the communal piazza to the north of the via Emilia. The communal faction, I propose, had come to realize that its former urbanistic model, that of the noble urban compound, was no longer the best way of asserting the commune's importance and power. (Although this by no means implies rejection of aristocratic tastes and mores—in fact, nobles rather quickly took over leadership of the so-called government of the *popolo.* By the 1280s, Parma's two principal factions were led by Bishop Òbizzo Sanvitale and Guido da Correggio.) In order to compete urbanistically with the church party and neighboring city-states, the commune needed not simply a cluster of representative buildings but an entire environment in which to deploy its government apparatus.

Through the middle years of the thirteenth century, the commune had become increasingly sensitive to issues of urban decorum. It shifted potentially polluting activities out of the main communal piazza and off its major access roads.[61] The largest market fair—the nine-day market of Sant'Ercolano, in September—had already been transferred to the Parma torrent's eastern bank by 1227 (figs. 75 and 76).[62] Porticos lined the most important streets entering the piazza, and more were being added—the street leading to San Paolo from the piazza acquired porticos on its west side when the commune decreed that the street be widened again in 1281.[63] In that year, the western arm of the via Emilia was improved from the communal piazza to the riverbank and beyond (fig. 77). And the statutes repeatedly call for further improvements to the southbound arm of the *cardo,* from the piazza to the Porta Nova.[64] But the communal faction was no longer content merely to make the environment near its compound more orderly. The major construction projects of the 1280s

Fig. 75 The market space now known as the Ghiaia extended north from the stone bridge, along the east bank of the Parma torrent, on the site of its pre-1177 river bed. Detail from Paolo Ponzoni, *Pianta della città di Parma in prospettiva* (Piacenza: Francesco Conti, 1572), woodcut, after an earlier drawing. ASPr, Raccolta Mappe e Disegni, vol. 2, no. 13. North is at the bottom of the map.

Fig. 76 Aerial photograph showing the Ghiaia from the north in 2004.

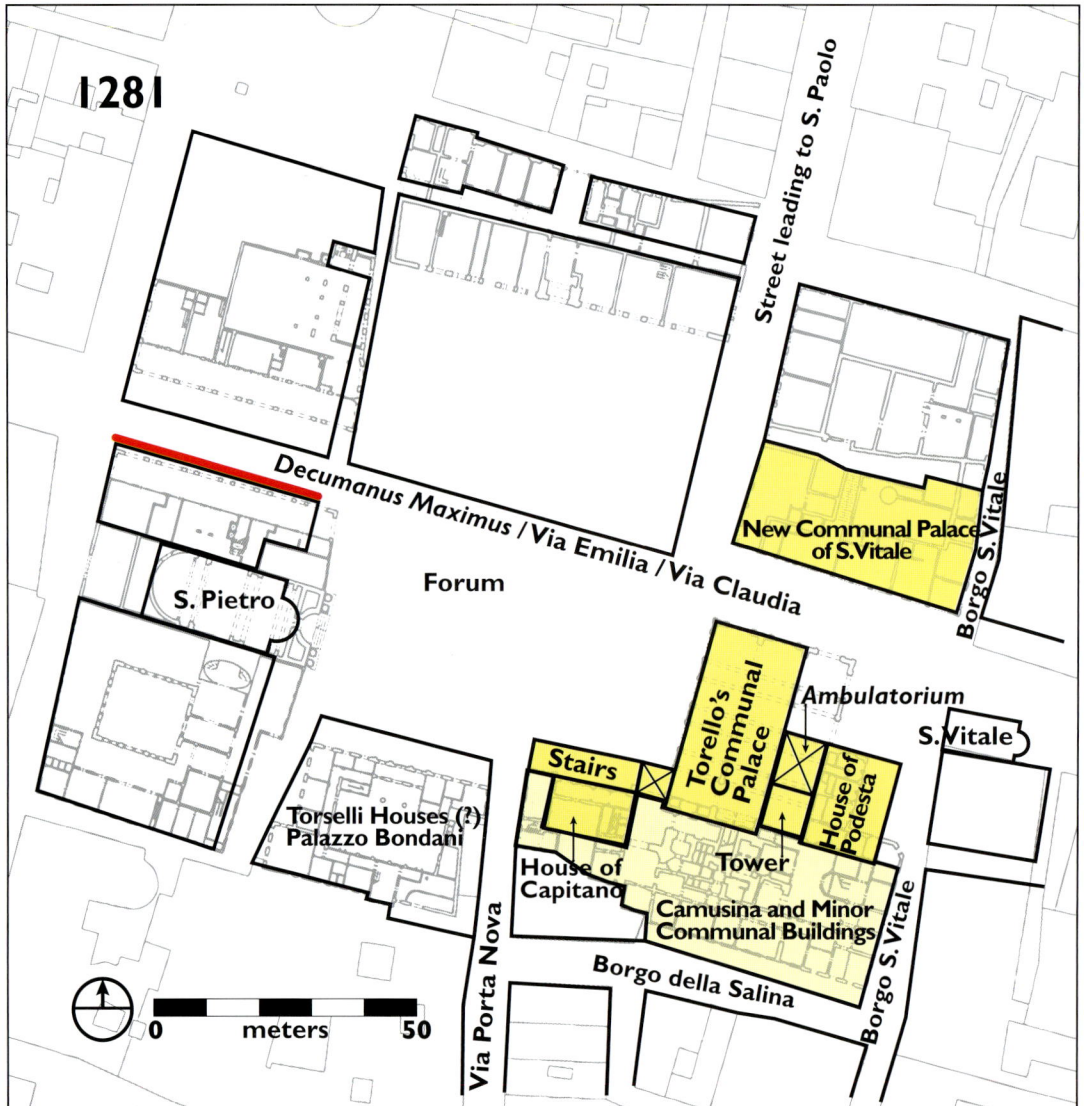

Fig. 77 Reconstruction diagram, the communal piazza of Parma in 1281. The New Communal Palace of San Vitale is sited across the via Claudia, detached from the communal compound.

Fig. 78 The New Communal Palace of San Vitale, now Palazzo Fainardi, from the southeast.

were its next step in rationalizing and exalting the communal space.

In 1281, the commune built a new palace across from the church of San Vitale, along borgo San Vitale on the north side of the via Emilia (figs. 77–79).[65] This vast palazzo, now known as the Palazzo Fainardi, was assembled from preexisting structures and given a monu-

mental, unitary facade. Its medieval facade was buried under modern plaster and only redis-covered in the 1960s. Schulz's reconstruction of the Palazzo Fainardi's upper stories provides a useful notion of its appearance in the thirteenth century: a broad two-story brick structure with three-light windows was flanked by towerlike elements to the west and east of its south facade

(fig. 80).[66] The fortified impression furnished by the towers is reinforced by the battlements that surmounted the palace. Indeed, fenestration aside, the scale and iconography of the upper stories of the palace recall castle architecture as much as, if not more than, palace architecture (compare it to Torrechiara castle, near Casatico in the Parmesan territory, fig. 81). The "New

Communal Palace of San Vitale," as it is called in the documents, sheltered meeting rooms for new communal councils associated with the rise of the *popolo;* the podesta, *capitano, anziani,* and *primicerii* all gathered there to conduct communal business. The new palazzo also housed a debtors' prison (moved here from its former location behind Torello's palace) and a series of ground-story shops.[67] The monumentality and scale of its southern facade could best be appreciated from the recently improved (although secondary) street passing between the church of San Vitale and the House of the Podesta (fig. 78). With its expansive facade along the via Emilia, the New Communal Palace of San Vitale was, to date, the biggest project undertaken by the expanding commu-

nal government for its piazza, yet it was soon to be dwarfed.

In 1282, the commune ordered the construction of a massive extension to the communal piazza (fig. 82).[68] The entire block of houses north of the via Emilia, between the vicolo dei Vernacci to the west and the via Cavour to the east, was expropriated and razed to the ground at the commune's orders.[69] This drastic urbanistic gesture nearly doubled the size of the communal piazza. It grew from a long rectangular space of proportions 5:7—not much larger in footprint than the cathedral—to a gigantic near square with proportions 16:17 (fig. 83). In a single urbanistic stroke, Parma's communal piazza approached the ideal square form of its rival, the Piazza del Duomo, while eclipsing its size (fig. 84). In area, the new square was more than two times larger than the episcopal square. Its size and regular shape were still impressive more than 270 years later, when one writer, reporting to Bishop Guido Ascanio Sforza, described it as a "great square piazza" (*magnam plateam quadratam*).[70] While processions and other civic rituals took place in the communal piazza, there was no significant practical need for a larger space in which to stage them. The commune appears to have transformed its piazza for representational—and not for strictly functional—reasons. But the communal square's transformation did not stop there.

In the same year, the commune deployed a broad new palazzo along the entire northern side of the newly squared piazza (fig. 82).[71] That thirteenth-century structure hides behind the neoclassical veneer of the building now called the Palazzo del Governatore (fig. 85). The *palatium novum de platea* (New Communal Palace of the Piazza), finished in 1285, was a low two-story structure with an arcaded ground story, a painted facade, and battlements.[72] It is evident that the primary function of the commune's newest palace was scenographic. The commune had just recently completed a large palace on the east side of the piazza; its need for space had not increased greatly in the course of a few months. Indeed, the new building, although as broad as the piazza itself, was rather shallow. It housed no important council halls or *spazi di rappresentanza* (ceremonial spaces). The thirteenth-century documents refer more often to the shops along the palace's ground-story portico than to its governmental functions, although it was occasionally used to house the communal grain stores and as a provisional jail.[73] Evidently, what

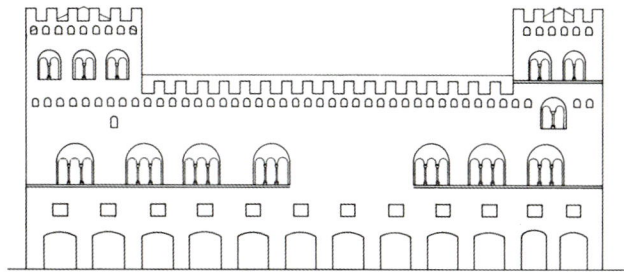

Fig. 79 The communal piazza from the west. *Veduta di Piazza Maggiore di Parma,* in Attilio Zuccagni-Orlandini, ed., *Corografia fisica, storica e statistica dell'Italia e delle sue isole,* vol. 8.1 (Florence: All'insegna di Clio, 1839), Vedute pittoriche, tavola 2.

Fig. 80 Reconstructed medieval south elevation of the Palazzo Fainardi.

Fig. 81 The Rocca di Torrechiara (PR). The New Communal Palace of San Vitale had projecting square towers at its corners, as did castles such as Torrechiara.

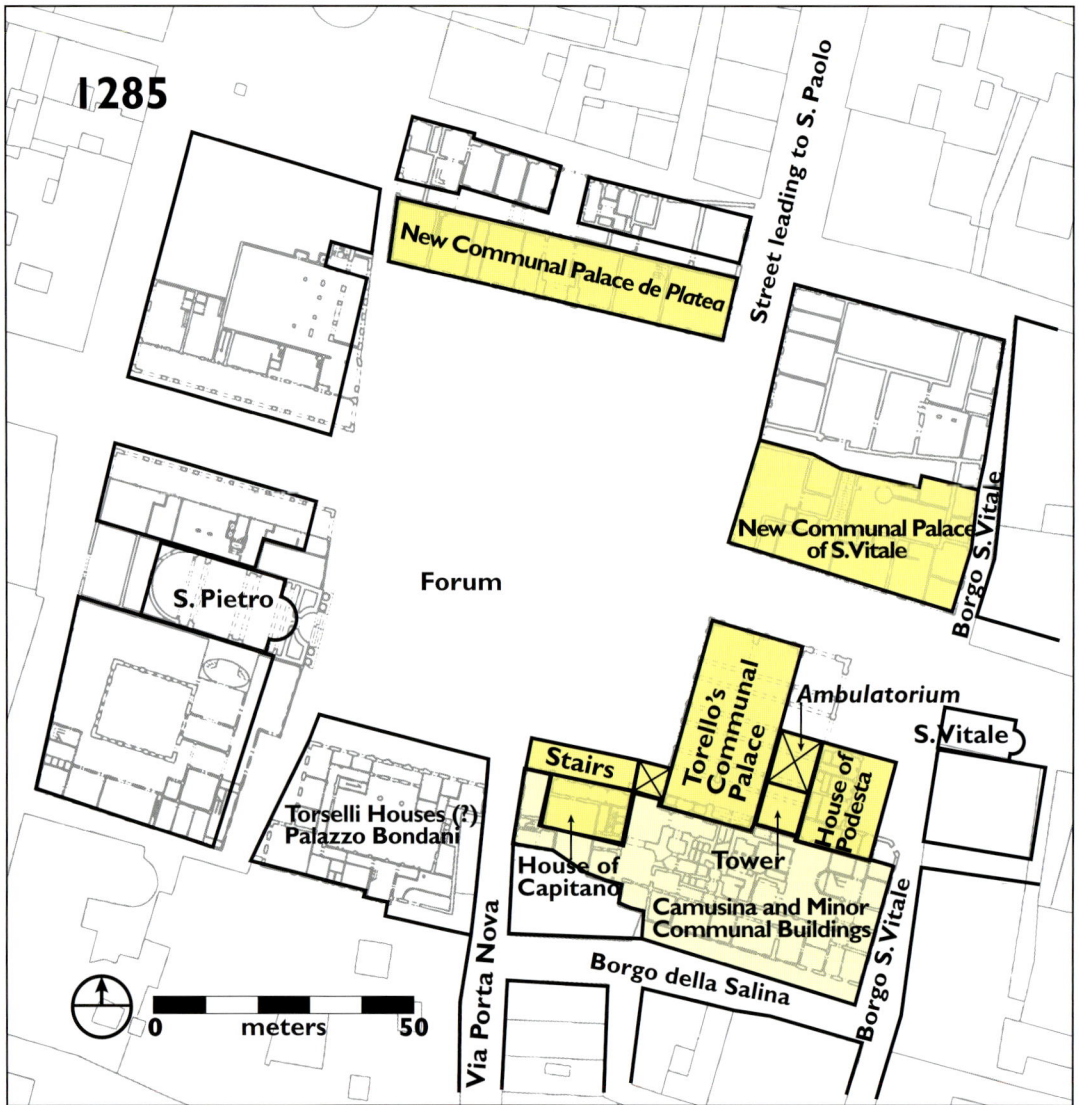

1285

New Communal Palace de Platea

Street leading to S. Paolo

New Communal Palace of S. Vitale

Borgo S. Vitale

Forum

S. Pietro

Ambulatorium

S. Vitale

Stairs

Torello's Communal Palace

House of Podesta

Torselli Houses (?) Palazzo Bondani

House of Capitano

Tower

Camusina and Minor Communal Buildings

Borgo S. Vitale

Via Porta Nova

Borgo della Salina

0 meters 50

Fig. 82 Reconstruction diagram, the communal piazza of Parma in 1285. The commune demolished buildings along the north side of the piazza and erected the New Communal Palace of the Piazza (*de Platea*) along the northern edge of the newly enlarged square.

Fig. 83 Analytical diagram representing the ideal square underlying the communal piazza's design, 1285.

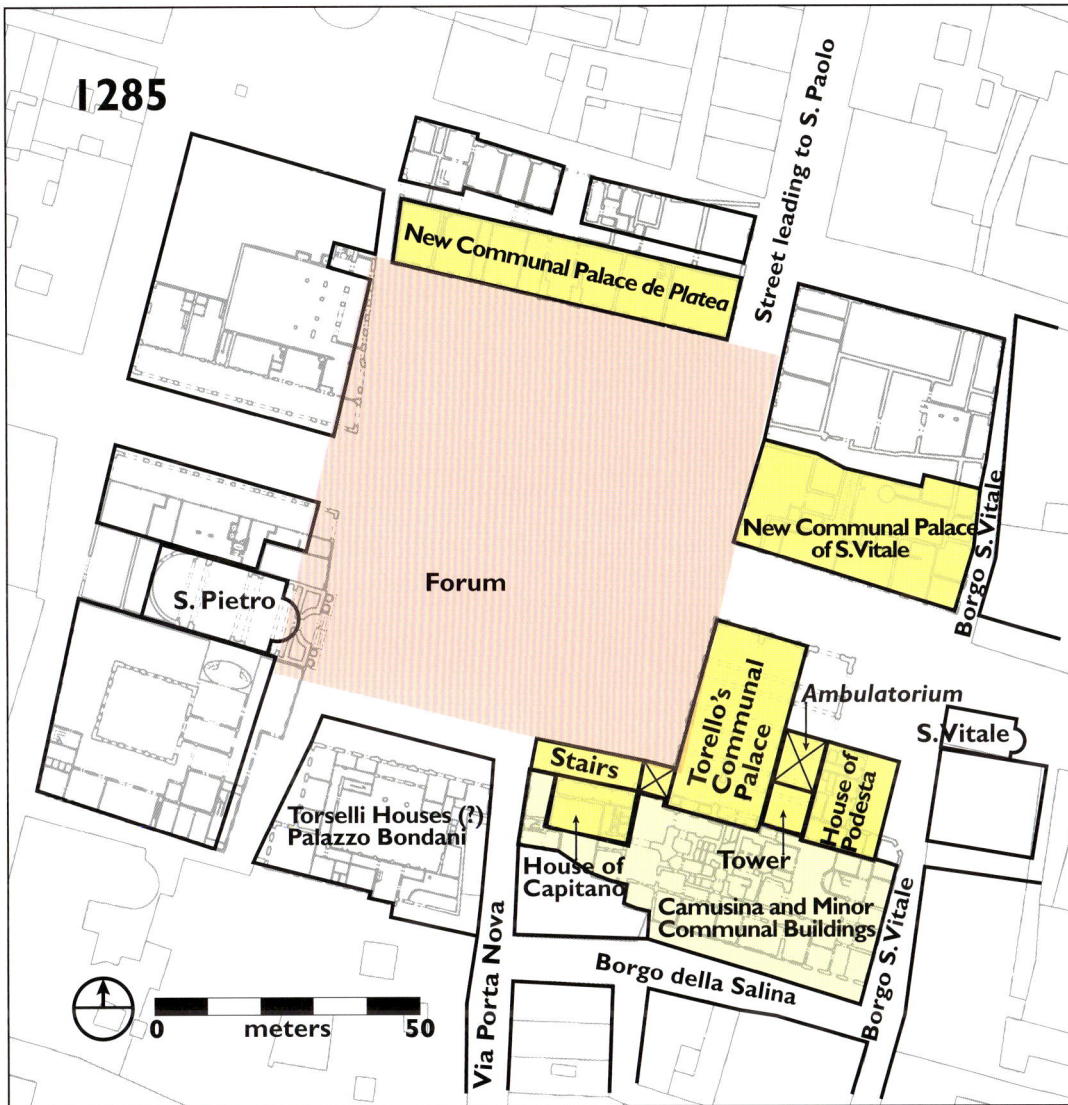

1285

New Communal Palace de Platea

Street leading to S. Paolo

New Communal Palace of S.Vitale

Borgo S. Vitale

Forum

S. Pietro

Ambulatorium

S. Vitale

Torello's Communal Palace

Stairs

House of Podesta

Torselli Houses (?) Palazzo Bondani

House of Capitano

Tower

Camusina and Minor Communal Buildings

Via Porta Nova

Borgo della Salina

Borgo S. Vitale

0   meters   50

mattered most was not what was inside the building but what the building presented to the outside: the new palace established an important monumental backdrop along the new northern boundary of the piazza. It shifted the communal center's spatio-visual (if not functional) focus from the southeast, where Torello's old communal palace was located, to the north.

Palace and piazza were inextricably linked— even the palace's frequent epithet, not only *novum* but specifically *de platea,* emphasizes the connection (fig. 86). The just-completed extension of the communal piazza reconfigured the site as a virtual square. The construction of the *palatium novum* underscored the square's new form. Moreover, the installation of a palace

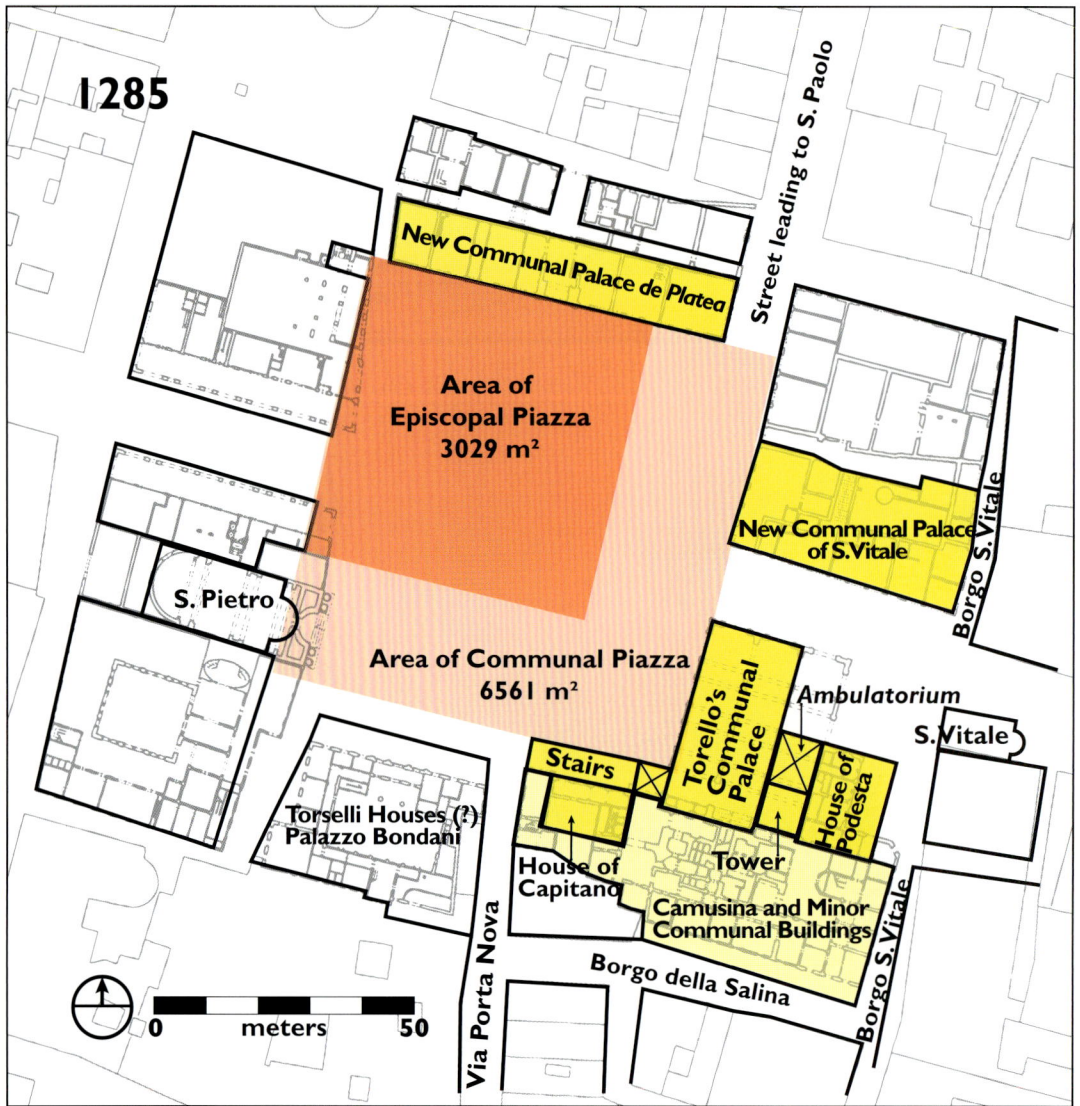

1285

Street leading to S. Paolo

New Communal Palace de Platea

Area of
Episcopal Piazza
3029 m²

New Communal Palace
of S.Vitale

Borgo S.Vitale

S. Pietro

Area of Communal Piazza
6561 m²

Torello's
Communal
Palace

Ambulatorium

S. Vitale

Stairs

House of
Podesta

Torselli Houses (?)
Palazzo Bondani

House of
Capitano

Tower

Camusina and Minor
Communal Buildings

Borgo S.Vitale

Via Porta Nova

Borgo della Salina

0   meters   50

Fig. 84 Analytical diagram comparing the surface area of the communal piazza to that of the episcopal piazza in 1285. The communal piazza is now more than twice as large as the cathedral square.

Fig. 85 The New Communal Palace of the Piazza (*de Platea*), now the Palazzo del Governatore, Parma.

Fig. 86 The communal piazza (now Piazza Garibaldi) from the south.

whose primary facade was notably wider than that of the bishop's palace signified the ascendant claims to power of the communal faction, under the leadership of the da Correggio.[74]

The Panoptic Piazza Revisited

The expansion of the piazza and the completion of the New Communal Palace of the Piazza were the last major communal projects on the site in the thirteenth century. The new piazza challenged the primacy of the old episcopal square in several ways. First, the communal square was twice as large as the cathedral square. Second, a comparable number of magnificent buildings formed its perimeter: Torello's palace, the houses of the podesta and *capitano,* the New Communal Palace of San Vitale, and the New Communal Palace of the Piazza compared favorably with the bishop's palace, chapter house, campanile, cathedral, and baptistery. Third, the streets forming its entrances and egresses were the most monumental and carefully maintained in the city. Finally, with the construction of the last two palaces, the commune broke free of the noble urban-compound model to create a panoramic piazza environment that appropriated for itself the panoptic qualities of the cathedral square.

At the end of the thirteenth century, a citizen approaching the communal square on any of its four major or three minor entrance roads would find himself confronted with at least one and sometimes several of the representational buildings of the commune. A citizen approaching the piazza from the west would first see Torello's palace, then the western facade of the New Communal Palace of San Vitale. As he reached the mouth of the piazza, these two buildings would be complemented by the massive expanse of the New Communal Palace of the Piazza to the north and the House of the Capitano and the grand staircase in front of it to the south (fig. 79). The communal tower would loom from behind the roofline of Torello's palace.

If approaching from the east, the citizen again would initially see Torello's palace in his path (for a similar view of its replacement, the Palazzo del Governatore, see fig. 58). As he got closer, the smaller, eastern piazza extension would open before him, with the expansive New Communal Palace of San Vitale on the right and the House of the Podesta on the left. The communal campanile would again tower before him, from behind the podesta's house. He could choose to stay on the via Claudia and enter the large, square part of the piazza, or he could choose to jostle through the arcades of Torello's palace. The effect on reaching the other side would be the same—the imposing New Communal Palace of the Piazza dominating the square to his right and the House of the Capitano and monumental staircase of the commune on his left, flanking an urban space of unprecedented size.

If approaching from the south, the citizen would see the New Communal Palace of the Piazza ahead of him; then he would be flanked by the House of the Capitano and the communal staircase on the right (for the site as it looks today, see fig. 86). Immediately upon entering the piazza itself, the imposing width of the New Communal Palace of the Piazza would become apparent, and Torello's communal palace, the New Communal Palace of San Vitale, and the inviting breadth of the eastern branch of the via Emilia would attract him eastward, to the older part of the communal complex (for the site as it looks today, see fig. 87).

Not all approaches were equally impressive. If the citizen were approaching the communal square from the north, his experience would be less dramatic, because he would be entering the piazza from its northeastern corner rather than from the middle of one of its sides. His first glimpse of the communal buildings would be of

Fig. 87 The eastern flank of the piazza, with the New Communal Palace of San Vitale, as seen from the opening of the deviated *cardo*, now via Farini.

the vault and loggia connecting Torello's palace to the House of the Capitano (for the site as it looks today, see fig. 70). Upon reaching the mouth of the square, the corner of Torello's palace and the House of the Capitano would be before him, and the short side of the New Communal Palace of San Vitale would be visible to his left, but both the communal tower and the New Communal Palace of the Piazza would not be displayed to good effect from that standpoint.

From every approach, however, visitors would have been struck by the sheer size of the piazza, especially after emerging from the city's narrow secondary streets. This effect would have been intensified by the greater scale of the communal buildings relative to the humbler domestic architecture of the streets around the piazza. The communal piazza was not merely larger in footprint than any other space within the city—twice as large as the cathedral square—it was larger in volume as well. The "negative space" occupied by the piazza extended upward along the facades of the buildings around it. As the statutes made clear, no projecting balconies or permanent or temporary structures were allowed to infringe upon the freedom of communal space. The piazza did, however, encroach outward. The porticos that the commune demanded be built on some of the piazza's access roads extended the arcaded motif of the three communal palaces into the rest of the city.

What about the person standing in the middle of the communal square? Like his or her counterpart in the episcopal square, this viewer would be presented with a three-sided communal panorama. He or she could both see most of the major communal buildings and be seen from them. Panopticism was fundamental to Parma's urbanistic practice in the age of factions, as I explore further in chapter 4. The square's large expanse of open space allowed communal representatives within the communal buildings to surveil any who approached. Communal law enforcement also depended on informants, who could report infractions to the communal authorities, if they dared, and receive part of the fine imposed on the offender. The open and consequently well-lit spaces of the piazza facilitated this informal, ever-present surveillance while simultaneously discouraging potential transgressors. Furthermore, communal legislation regulated behavior in the

communal piazza more closely than that anywhere else in the city, as I show in the next chapter. Citizens were aware of the constraints imposed upon them in this space, and the commune defined the piazza's boundaries and the penalties for breaching the constraints with meticulous precision.

Of course, observation, if not surveillance, works in both directions. The open space of the piazza allowed the citizen to observe the commune's officials at work. As I examine more fully in part II, it provided the stage for the choreographed rituals of communal authority—the office-taking of new officials, the punishment of criminals, the issuing of judgments—and the rituals of defiance by the commune's enemies. Protests, insurrections, and shows of arms often began or ended in the communal piazza and were more potent as a result of this heightened visibility. Communal legislation demonstrates that the civic numinosity of the communal piazza extended beyond its natural confines much as the aura of the episcopal square spilled beyond its boundaries. However, the monumentality of the communal piazza, unlike that of the bishop's square, expanded outward as well, in the improved condition and breadth of its access roads.

The transformation of a busy crossroads into a grand and geometrically regular showcase for Parma's communal government was not a continuous process. The stops and starts in its development reflect the ever-changing complexity of Parma's political life. The same faction did not control the commune uninterruptedly during this period, nor was its composition immutable, but each faction, regardless of its other objectives, seems to have kept in mind one goal: to emphasize the faction's own prestige and authority (and, by extension, the city's) by means of its architectural and urbanistic program. While the creation and evolution of the episcopal piazza took the better part of a century, the elites plotting, planning, and building on the communal square engaged in a series of individual projects whose rewards they reaped within their own uncertain lifetimes—both political and natural. Each of the communal palaces and houses, and even the dramatic expansion of the piazza in 1282, was completed in a few years; the haste of the urbanistic project manifested the urgency of the political emprise.

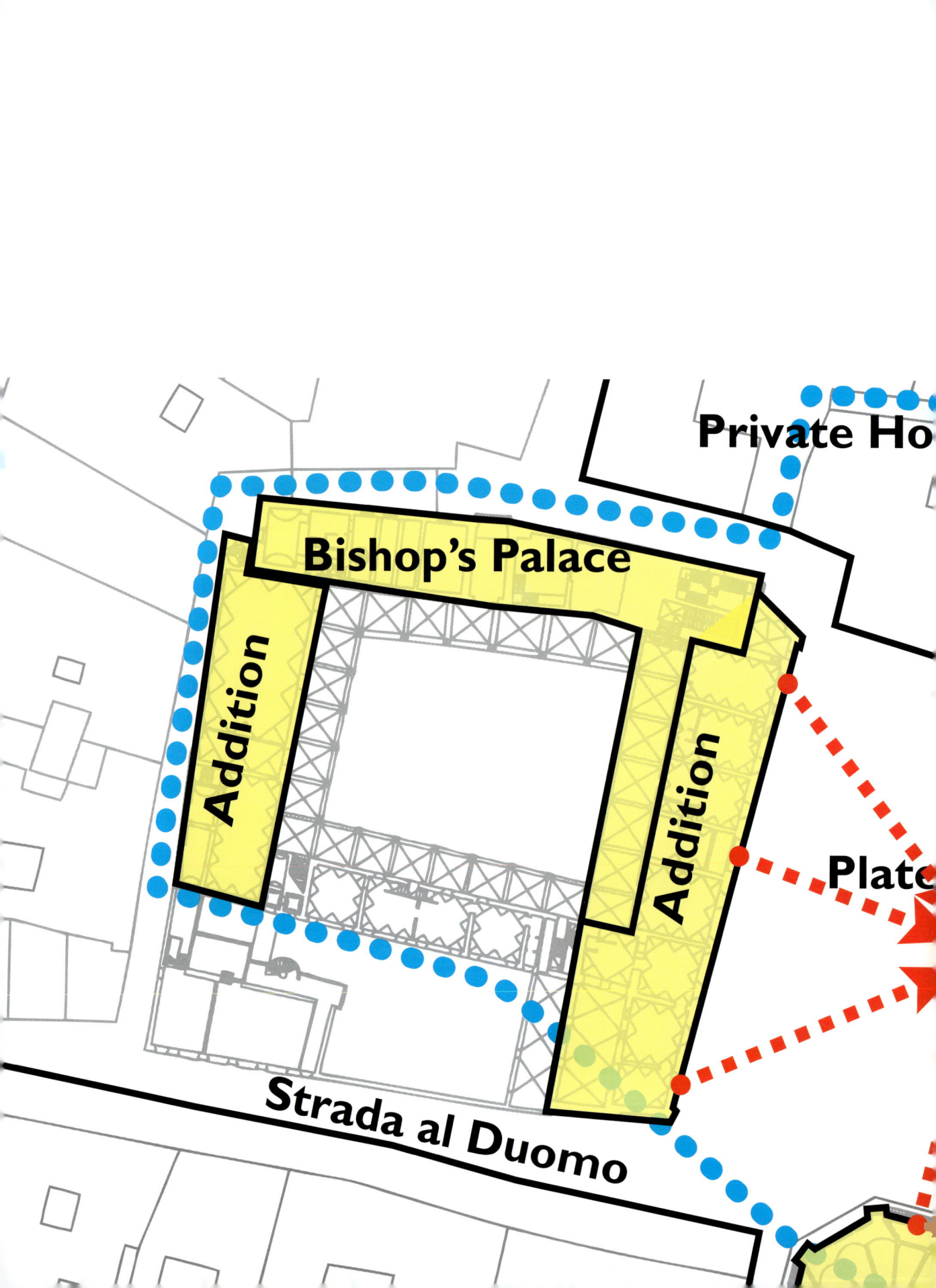

Private Ho

Bishop's Palace

Addition

Addition

Plat

Strada al Duomo

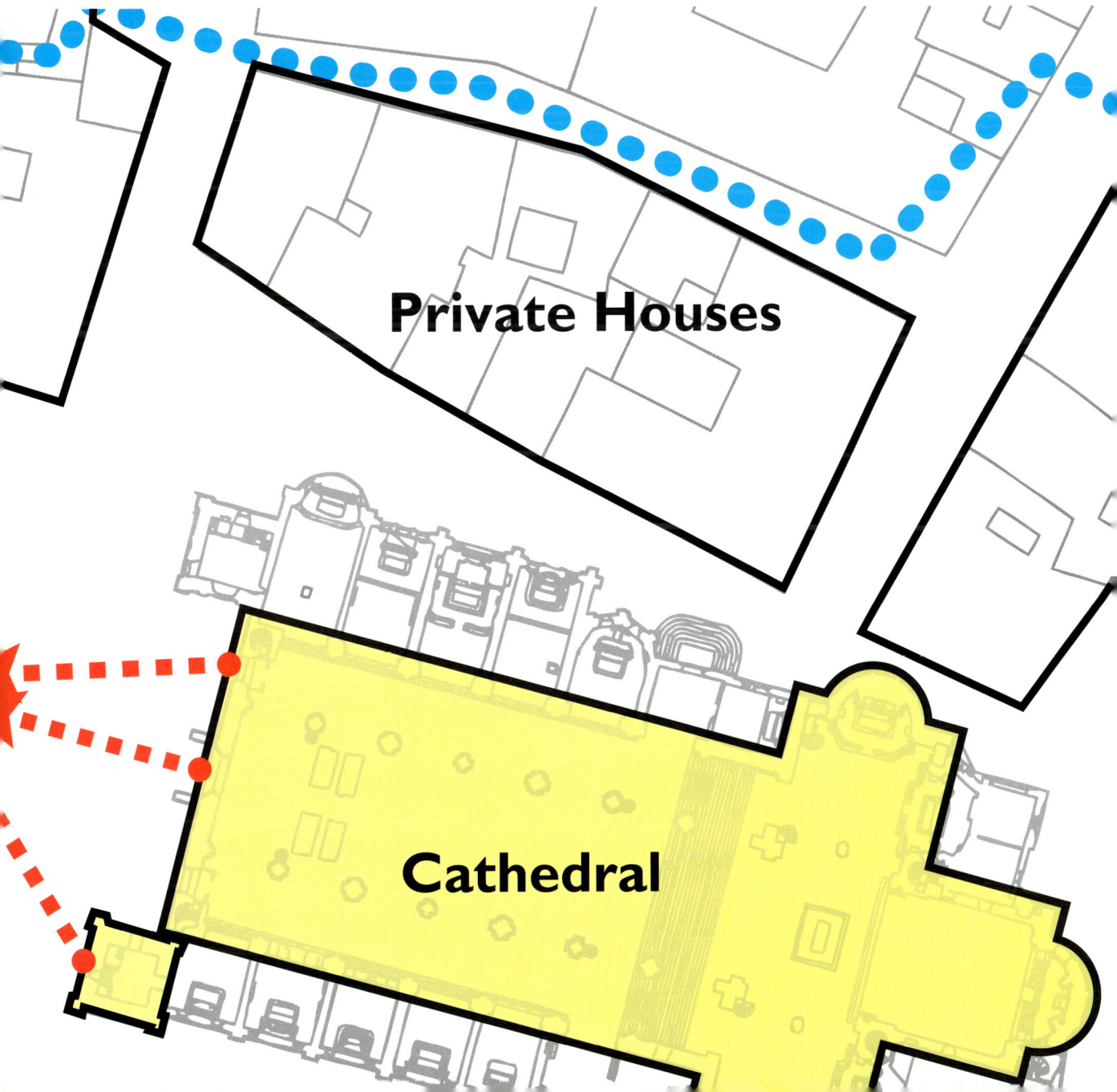

Private Houses

Cathedral

CHAPTER 3

The Legislation of Order

The last two chapters have demonstrated how Parma's administrators and builders transformed two heterogeneous, fragmented sites at the heart of the city into monumental, geometrically ordered squares. The desire for order evinced by the construction of the episcopal and communal piazzas was not limited to these two projects, however. It formed part of a larger urbanistic program encompassing many aspects of urban life, as evidenced by communal legislation ensuring the cleanliness, navigability, defensibility, and decorum of the city as a whole. Parma's program was not unique; the urbanistic "will to order" manifested in the legislation of the city-states of thirteenth-century Italy has been well documented, from Nicola Ottokar's groundbreaking study of the Florentine case in 1948 to the analyses of urbanistic legislation in Italian cities compiled by Michael Stolleis and Ruth Wolff in 2004.[1] I do not examine all of Parma's late medieval urbanistic legislation here, or the other major building projects undertaken in Parma in the thirteenth century (which included the construction of several bridges, the repeated expansion of the city walls, and the establishment of mendicant churches). Instead, I show that the development of Parma's two medieval piazzas intersects, and is inextricably linked to, the contemporary desire to regulate the fabric of the entire city.

The urbanistic will-to-order of Parma's thirteenth-century legislators extended beyond "improving" the quality of the city fabric. Parma's statutes reveal how Parma's political authorities sought to impose order on people's behavior within the piazzas' confines and not only on the form of the two piazzas. Close reading of Parma's statutes uncovers the hierarchy of spaces within the city—actors within the communal and episcopal squares were held to a higher standard of behavior there than elsewhere. The special nature of the two squares—embodied by their breadth, architectural distinction, and ideal form—amplified the importance of gestures performed within their confines.

The Statutes of the Commune of Parma

The statute books of the commune of Parma in the thirteenth and fourteenth centuries are the most useful sources for the study of the commune's desire to order the city. In the laws compiled therein, the communal council codified its aspirations and institutionalized its urbanistic values. (The laws do not necessarily reflect actual practices at any particular historical moment, however. The statute books are palimpsests of laws and amendments composed at different times and alternatively upheld, reinterpreted, or ignored.)[2]

Of the many compilations of the commune's statutes produced in the Middle Ages, four survive: two from the thirteenth century (dating from 1255 and 1266–1304) and two from the fourteenth (dating from 1316–25 and 1347). All of the compilations repeat substantial portions of their predecessors' content.[3] Each of Parma's surviving statute books was originally divided into four parts. The first part addresses laws about the communal offices—how the podesta and other officials are elected and what their duties are. The second deals with lawsuits and civil law. The third part addresses criminal law. The fourth part is devoted entirely to urban infrastructure—to the commune's streets, canals, moats, and walls. The majority of the laws concerning infrastructure address the management of water and waste and therefore prescribe the use and maintenance of the network of canals, sewers, ditches, and drains that crisscrossed the city. Unfortunately, the second oldest compilation—comprising the years between 1266 and 1304—survives only in an incomplete manuscript; its section on urban infrastructure is missing. However, much useful information about the urban fabric can also be found in the other three sections, and the statutes are our best textual source for elucidating the urbanistic agenda of the communal leaders. They reveal much about the physical and social decorum expected in the two piazzas under examination.

Physical Decorum

Just as fallow agricultural land swiftly returns to wilderness, Parma's piazzas would have been invaded by encumbrances and whittled away by encroachments had the commune not zealously defended them. In 1227 and 1228—only a few years after the inception of Parma's first communal palace—the communal statutes already demanded that the new communal piazza be regularly cleared of waste, and forbade anyone to set up any kind of structure in the piazza or throw anything into it—even under cover of darkness.[4] A similar (though undated) statute, located a few rubrics further in the commune's 1255 statute book, provided for the protection of the episcopal square and the porticos around it, which were maintained by the commune.[5] The same statute book included legislation providing for the cleaning and maintenance of all of the principal streets and piazzas of the city.[6] The city's piazzas must be protected not only from waste but from the damage caused by water. In 1259, a portion of the Canale Maggiore was ordered covered by a masonry vault so that the water it carried did not overflow into the cathedral square.[7] Excess water was a concern in the *platea nova* as well: the commune ordered that its pavement be leveled to ensure that water drained away properly and did not accumulate in the piazza.[8] Indeed, the city's legislators paid continual attention to the condition of the communal square's surface—it was repaved or repaired repeatedly through the thirteenth century.[9] This concern with the piazza's pavement paralleled a citywide phenomenon—the commune time and again demanded that all streets, courts, and squares within the city's walls be paved.[10]

What the statutes cannot reveal is that official care for the piazzas was combined with unofficial supervision. In 1233, when the commune posted a guard at the cathedral square to ensure that the walls of the cathedral and baptistery were not "soiled," individual citizens also protected the episcopal monuments on their own initiative.[11] Salimbene reports that while sitting with his neighbors in a portico near the bishop's palace, Guidolino da Enzola prevented boys from throwing stones that might harm the cathedral and baptistery decoration.[12]

Pernicious activities were proscribed not only in the cathedral square, as in the example above, but especially in the communal square, which hosted a weekly market. At various times, fish vendors, armorers, and pepper grinders were enjoined from practicing their trades on the piazza or its access roads.[13] Victuallers were banned from the communal piazza; fires were expressly forbidden.[14] Some practices that seem innocuous to modern eyes were nonetheless prohibited: no one was allowed to bring hay carts to the piazza on Saturdays and Sundays, and babies were not permitted in the piazza market stalls at any time.[15] And the market for unwieldy livestock, such as horses and cattle, took place on the *glarea,* or Ghiaia, on the eastern bank of the Parma torrent, not in the clean and paved communal precinct. After 1227, the Ghiaia—the long, low open space that extended north from the *pons lapidis* along the gravel of the former riverbed—also hosted the annual fair of Sant'Ercolano (figs. 75 and 76).[16]

The commune vigilantly ensured that the commercial activities on the communal piazza did not impair access to the communal buildings. Time and again, vendors were reminded to leave at least two *pertiche* (about 6.5 meters) of space between their stalls and the communal palace and stairs.[17] In addition to straightening and widening the access streets into the piazza (as discussed in chapter 2), the commune

demanded that these, too, be kept free of obstructions and polluting activities. A 1281 statute about the street leading from the piazza northward toward the monastery of San Paolo is explicit: no projecting balconies or impediments of any type may protrude into the street at any height from any of the buildings along its flanks, with a single exception—movable, half-*braccio* benches to be used on feast days. Butchers could not keep animals outside their shops, nor were they allowed to fling blood, offal, or anything else into the street. In time, these proscriptions were extended to all the major streets emerging from the piazza.[18]

Overhead projections in the form of *sporti* and bridges especially concerned the legislators, since they sometimes housed privies that drained onto the streets below. These elevated lavatories were forbidden in certain streets leading to the communal and episcopal squares, so that "the men of Parma could come and go without being subjected to the [human] waste" emerging from drainpipes overhead.[19] The commune also guarded against sewage underfoot. The canal on one street was covered over in order to make the street "beautiful" and preserve the decorum of processions carrying candles to the cathedral on feast days.[20]

Access to the cathedral square and its buildings repeatedly attracted the commune's attention. In 1259, the commune ordered that the opening of a canal at the corner of the piazza adjacent to the bishop's palace be "adjusted" so that "men could freely enter it [the piazza] and come and go." Alas, five years later, the commune's wishes had yet to be fulfilled; in 1264 it resorted to threatening to fine the podesta 10 Parmesan pounds if its orders were not followed.[21] As the 1264 amendment to this 1259 statute reveals, it was easier for the commune to issue legislation affecting the cathedral square than for it to enforce that legislation.

Social Order

The commune regulated more than the cleanliness and navigability of the city's most important public squares. It also sought to exercise tighter social controls within their confines. Gambling, for example, was forbidden.[22] In the case of the *platea nova,* the commune monitored potentially corrupting activities by insisting they be performed within its purview, in prescribed sites within the square. The notaries must perform their duties "sine fraude," during the designated hours, exclusively at their benches in the arcaded ground story of the communal palace.[23] Ad hoc activities with the potential for impropriety were also performed in the communal square. It was the site chosen for the sale of the spoils resulting from *guasti* (demolitions of property, particularly those executed as a criminal penalty); the actual selling was to be performed by clerics as an added safety measure, even though the proceeds would go to the commune.[24]

Two exceptional statutes detail not only the punishments to be suffered by persons who engaged in hostile acts in either of the city's two principal squares but also the exact geographic confines of those squares.[25] The boundaries so precisely described by the legislators uncover another distinctive quality of the piazzas. In both cases, rather than correspond to the piazza's perimeter, as we would define it, they encompass short but discrete portions of the streets leading into the square. The numinous quality of the piazza spills beyond the markers we would consider the site's natural boundaries and extends into the streets leading to it.

The communal and episcopal squares were not the only public places in the city in which ordinary (though undesirable) practices were given extraordinary penalties. On occasion certain sites were awarded special protection—notably, the via Emilia and the stone bridge that carried it across the Parma torrent. Ruffians and prostitutes were banned from the *pons lapidis.*[26] No one was permitted to blaspheme on the via Emilia from the bridge to the gate of Santa Cristina. (At only 100 Parmesan *soldi,* the fine for transgression was not high, but the penalty was harsh for those who could not pay it—they would be stoned all the way from the bridge to the Santa Cristina gate, a distance of about 1 kilometer.)[27] Nonetheless, the special status of the episcopal and communal squares is attested by the statute's painstaking demarcation of the sites' boundaries and the taxonomic precision with which the legislators catalogued potential acts of violence in the piazzas and their corresponding punishments. The severity of the fines imposed even for acts of commonplace violence highlight the exceptional resonance of behavior in these sites. Even pulling another person's hair in the episcopal square carried a fine of 21 Parmesan shillings. Maiming or killing someone there resulted in banishment and confiscation of all property, unless the accused could persuade the victim or all of the deceased victim's heirs to forgive the offense.[28]

The fines also reveal concern that the punishments imposed on the perpetrators befit transgressors of all social orders. Noblemen are penalized more harshly than commoners; their higher authority magnifies the impact of their speech and gestures. The penalty for noblemen who lingered in the episcopal square with their weapons was 3 Parmesan pounds, while an armed commoner would only owe 30 shillings for the same offense. The possession of arms intensified the offense of violent action even if the weapons were not used; the penalties for armed transgressors were correspondingly more severe than for unarmed ones—the fine for a bloodless beating by an armed attacker was 30 Parmesan pounds, but only 21 pounds if the batterer was not armed. Scuffles among unarmed commoners were a much smaller threat to the dignity and honor of the city and to public safety than were bloody entanglements between trained men-at-arms.[29] Yet despite all this legislation, violence persistently contaminated the city's emblematic spaces. Even officially sanctioned rituals, such as the 1268 peace ceremony between Parma's two factions and their counterparts from nearby Borgo San Donnino (modern Fidenza), could end badly. After four days of negotiation, a public announcement of the peace agreement, and the treaty's formal ratification by the city's general council in the communal palace, the joyful celebrations of peace ended in a murderous melee atop the communal staircase.[30]

Agents of Order

All of the legislation adduced above was drafted and enacted by representatives of the commune. In the case of urbanistic legislation, the podesta was initially the official responsible for seeing that it was carried out.[31] As the commune's most senior executive officer, he was ultimately accountable for all that happened (or failed to happen) during his term of office. Occasionally,

he delegated execution of particular tasks to the *massarius* (purser) of the commune.[32]

However, the commune gradually established some communal offices for the oversight of the city's urban fabric. At first, it assigned the men in charge of the city's canals—the *dugaroli*—with the supervision of other aspects of the city's infrastructure, including the paving of the city's streets. One *dugarolus* was appointed for each quarter of the city, and as their duties expanded, each was granted the services of a messenger and a notary.[33] Sometimes, committees were formed ad hoc to oversee particular projects, such as the group convened in 1233 to plan a new canal in the Parmesan territory; it included the podesta, an *inzignerios,* or engineer, and one representative from each of the city's four quarters.[34]

But by 1242, the commune had established the *laborerium communis,* or communal workshop, which was responsible not only for overseeing building activities and supervising the *dugaroli* but even for collecting rents on property belonging to the commune. The commune demanded that the officers of the *laborerium* be churchmen, and literate. In 1261, the statute was amended to specify that they could be "of any religion"—meaning of any religious order—except for penitential brothers.[35] In the second surviving compilation of statutes, the commune again specifies that the two officers of the *laborerium* must be religious, though in this instance one of the two must be a penitent. Literacy is again required.[36] One wonders about the reasons for the insistence on religious overseers. Were they chosen for their literacy, their reputation for probity, or because of their experience serving on the productive cathedral and mendicant church workshops? The *laborerium* of the cathedral also seems to have been overseen by clergy, not laymen. The names of four brothers of the cathedral workshop are inscribed on the portico added to the cathedral in 1282; clerics remained in charge in 1321.[37]

Thus, an expanding array of specialized officials were engaged in the increasingly onerous but important task of establishing and guaranteeing physical and social decorum in Parma's two emblematic public spaces, the communal and episcopal squares. These sites were carefully monitored to ensure that they were fitting stages for the new public life of the thirteenth-century commune.

CHAPTER 4

The Eloquent Piazza

Jacques Le Goff has identified two basic approaches to the study of Europe's urban elites: investigation of their political history and analysis of what he calls the urban imaginary. As Le Goff defines it, the urban imaginary comprises all the fields of "symbolic" production, including literature and the visual arts. (Although imperfect, Le Goff's conception is nonetheless useful because it acknowledges the fundamental role of artistic production in the formation of culture.) In the previous chapter, I have shown how Parma's communal government used its legislative capacity to preserve the form and decorum of the city's new public spaces. Here, I argue that the specific spatio-visual form of the two piazzas developed by Parma's elites performed a constitutive task—it incarnated its patrons' urban imaginary and contributed to its production.[1]

As Le Goff emphasizes, both political history and the urban imaginary share a connection with the history of power. In the medieval Tuscan context, Friedman and Trachtenberg have demonstrated that urbanistic order was an instrument of authority. The same is true of Parma. Architecture and urbanism together were one tool used by Parma's elites to impose themselves on the field of the city.[2] Two factors determined the specific form of the oligarchs' architectural and urbanistic interventions: their conception of what a powerful and well-ruled city should look like and the nature of the patronage expected of its rulers. Both were inextricably tied to the idea of Roman and noble mores.[3]

Romanitas

Throughout *The Italian City-State,* Jones reiterates that the persistence of an urban worldview inherited from the ancient Romans distinguished north Italian cities and their culture from their neighbors across the Alps.[4] Ecclesiastical prelates, secular lords, and professional administrators alike regarded Rome as the paramount model for urbanity, and the Roman state as the ultimate archetype of political authority. Cities boasted of (or invented) Roman origins. Authors across the peninsula wrote urban panegyrics that cast their hometowns in Roman dress, their republican councils as the senate, and their *signori* as emperors.[5]

This urban, Romanizing orientation was self-consciously taken up by Holy Roman Emperor Frederick II, who employed it to advance his claim to rule the Italian peninsula.[6]

In 1247, when Frederick II established a new city not far from the walls of Parma, he used the ancient foundation ritual of the Romans, marking the eventual path of the walls with a plow.[7] As this example shows, certain Roman urbanistic and architectural traditions endured (or were revived) in late medieval Europe. Lengthy passages from Vitruvius and Pliny on the subject of building were subsumed in Isidore of Seville's *Etymologies*. Isidore reports Vitruvius's classification of the architectural orders, the construction methods used by the Romans, the ingredients used in the manufacture of concrete, and even the Roman practice of using colored-marble revetments to face buildings, a technique used in the baptistery of Parma (fig. 15).[8] While Roman ideas about architecture and urban form certainly were communicated verbally—manuscripts of classical texts were, according to Reynolds, "thick on the shelves of libraries"—the peninsula's abundant Roman architectural remains transmitted them visually.[9]

No odes to Parma as the new Rome survive, but the form and materials of the representative buildings and spaces crafted by the city's episcopal and communal factions betray their patrons' desire to appropriate the ancient *urbs*'s authority and status. While no medieval texts specifically link Parma's architectural and urbanistic practice to ancient precedents, a preponderance of circumstantial evidence demonstrates that local patrons, artists, and builders were familiar with, reused, and reinterpreted classical forms and materials in multiple and sophisticated ways.

Beginning with the construction of the baptistery, Parma's builders repeatedly used a building material directly connected to Parma's Roman past, the hard limestone called *rosso di Verona*. The material, which was considered a type of marble in the Middle Ages, literally means "red from Verona," although it ranges in color from a delicate, blushing white to the vivid pink of the best prosciutto. In antiquity, as in the Middle Ages, this stone originated at a single location—the quarries north of Verona now called the Cave di Sant'Ambrogio. The ancient Romans employed this material only in a few places, among them the colonies of Verona and Parma, where Roman *rosso di Verona* remains survived into the Middle Ages and beyond.[10] By applying *rosso di Verona* revetment to the baptistery and cathedral (fig. 46), and by using it to make polished architectural details, such as colonnettes for the windows of official buildings facing the communal and episcopal squares (fig. 68) and the *rinceau*-decorated doorways of the baptistery (fig. 88), Parma's builders imitated the colorism and high degree of finish of ancient Roman architecture and unambiguously connected their new buildings to Roman antiquity. The use of colored "marble" designated the patrons as the heirs of Roman practices and Roman authority.[11]

We have evidence that Parma's builders also used actual ancient Roman materials. The imperial palace built into the remains of the Roman arena joined spoliated column shafts with newly carved capitals (fig. 89). Some have suggested that certain slabs of the baptistery's socle are recovered Roman paving stones. Premodern views of the cathedral reveal sculpted and inscribed Roman tablets of varying sizes inset into its facade, asserting its antiquity and pedigree. Most ancient spoils were used on building interiors, however. Spoliated columns and capitals support the vaults of the cathedral's crypt. The Parmesans lined the inside of the baptistery with as many Roman monolithic columns as they could find (fig. 90). The baptistery's builders used fragments of Roman column shafts not only as parts of new shafts but also as plinths under the columns of the baptistery's ground story. Since they did not have enough pedigreed ancient marble to go around, they manufactured simulated spoils of *rosso di Verona* to use for the same purpose. Sometimes they even carved the counterfeit plinths and the columns' Atticizing bases as a single unit, from the same block of stone (fig. 91).[12]

The builders also adapted spoils to new iconographic needs. In one instance, the baptistery workshop repurposed the body of an ancient Roman statue of a togaed male. As Peter Rockwell notes, the sculptors gave it a new head and feet, added wings, recarved parts of its torso, and installed it proudly in a niche on the baptistery's piazza facade as the archangel Michael (fig. 92). This was not the final exploitation of the ancient statue by the baptistery workshop. It also made a companion piece from scratch, carefully imitating the Roman drapery folds so admired in the original (fig. 93). The new archangel, Gabriel, was installed as a pendant to the Michael statue, on the left side of the baptistery's north portal (fig. 15).[13]

Beyond the pan-European "Romanesque" revival of architectural sculpture in general, Parma's builders repeatedly used Roman ornamental motifs.[14] Romanizing *rinceau* reliefs and dentil and cable moldings survive on the baptistery's exterior (fig. 15). Corinthian and schematic Corinthian capitals remain in place on the facades of the cathedral, bishop's palace, baptistery, and the House of the Capitano (figs.

Fig. 88 *Rinceau* decoration of the north portal, baptistery of Parma.

Fig. 89 Column fragment from the Palazzo dell'Arena, borgo Lalatta, Parma.

Fig. 90 The ground story of the Parma baptistery displays an assortment of spoliated, colored-marble columns.

Fig. 91 Faux spoil fluted plinth and column base carved from a single piece of *rosso di Verona*, baptistery of Parma.

30, 94, 95, and 96). The central portal of the cathedral features a portico whose roof is raised on columns supported by classicizing *rosso di Verona* lions (fig. 97). Segments of Doric column shafts articulate some of the baptistery's blind facades (fig. 98). But most of all, the fundamental antique architectural morphology of arcade and colonnade is repeatedly employed by Parma's builders in both piazzas, outside and inside their perimeter buildings. The stone-revetted trabeated galleries that distinguish the central stories of the baptistery's exterior seem to recall such Roman monuments as the Septizodium in Rome (figs. 99 and 100).[15] They depart from the more common arcaded motifs used in Romanesque architecture elsewhere in Italy in this period and indicate an intention, beyond generic evocation of Rome by the use of "Roman-esque" forms, of self-conscious revival.

The *romanitas* of Parma's two piazzas is not confined to the use of particular forms or materials. Their monumentality and orthogonality are no less Roman in inspiration. The monumental arcades and vaults of Torello's communal palace recall the massive remains of ancient

Fig. 92 Benedetto Antelami (attr.), *Archangel Michael.* Museo Diocesano, Parma (formerly on the baptistery's north facade). This archangel was recarved from a late Roman statue of a togaed male.

Fig. 93 Benedetto Antelami (attr.), *Archangel Gabriel* copied after the *Archangel Michael.* Museo Diocesano, Parma (formerly on the baptistery's north facade).

Fig. 94 Schematic Corinthian capital from the loggia of the cathedral facade.

Fig. 95 Corinthian capitals from the left jamb of the Parma baptistery's north portal.

Fig. 96 Three-light windows from the House of the Capitano, Parma.

Fig. 97 *Protiro,* or prothyrum porch, supported by classicizing *rosso di Verona* lions, central portal, west facade, cathedral of Parma.

Fig. 98 Engaged Doric column shaft, northeast facade, baptistery of Parma.

Fig. 99 Trabeated exterior galleries, baptistery of Parma.

Fig. 100 Trabeated galleries of the ruins of the Septizodium. Giovanni Antonio Dosio (1533–1609), *View of the Septizodium, Palatine Hill, Rome.* Gabinetto Disegni e Stampe, Uffizi, Florence, Italy, n. 2524 A.

public buildings dotting the Italian peninsula. Indeed, the scale of the vast open spaces framed by the monumental perimeter buildings of Parma's two medieval piazzas also aspired to Roman grandeur. Parma's communal piazza was developed on the site of the ancient forum; the surviving footprint of the forum had remained the largest unbuilt space within the city (fig. 5).[16] Contemporaries recognized its large size as a signal feature, describing it as "magna."[17]

The attention to orthogonality and geometric precision used by the planners of the Piazza del Duomo could also have been inspired by the Roman orthogonal street grid that underlay not only Parma's city center but that of many cities of Roman foundation throughout the Lombard plain. Members of Parma's ruling oligarchy were familiar not only with the Roman architectural remains nearby in northern Italy; several had visited Rome and knew that city's ancient remains firsthand—monuments that had already been described by the anonymous author of the *Mirabilia urbis Romae* in the mid–twelfth century and again early in the thirteenth century by Master Gregorius.[18] One powerful Parmesan, Ugolino di Giacomo Rossi, traveled to Rome to take up his office as senator of that city in 1295, attesting to his involvement with yet another aspect of Roman revival on the Italian peninsula.[19]

Magnificence

The vexed question whether the *romanitas* of the architecture we characterize as Romanesque was merely a by-product of local building traditions or a deliberate revival of Roman antiquity will not be settled by my analysis of Parma's squares. In either case, the overall effect produced by buildings of monumental scale, profligate use of "empty" space to frame them, the prevalence of the ancient Roman vocabulary of arch and colonnade, and expensive stone revetments and sculpted architectural ornament is magnificent today and would have seemed even more so against the low-rise brick-and-wood backdrop of the thirteenth-century city.

I use the adjective "magnificent" advisedly. Although the term is commonplace in discussions of medieval art, magnificence as a medieval aesthetic principle has received relatively little analysis.[20] In the context of architectural patronage, the "theory of magnificence" first received prominence forty years ago, in a fundamental article by A. D. Fraser Jenkins that identified arguments in Aristotle's *Nicomachean Ethics* as the justification for lavish Medici spending on building.[21] Although Jenkins focuses on fifteenth-century patronage, the *Ethics* and *Politics* entered the curriculum in the mid–thirteenth century. In its Aristotelian incarnation and later Dominican glosses, magnificence was a moral virtue particular to men of high birth or distinction, as funding substantial projects—especially buildings or "other objects of public-spirited ambition"—demanded considerable wealth. Appropriate expenditure would reward the patron with enhanced honor and prestige and, according to Albertus Magnus's commentary on the *Politics,* also greater political authority.[22] Magnificence and liberal displays of wealth found their thirteenth- and fourteenth-century apologists in moral and theological treatises, such as Thomas Aquinas's *Summa theologica;* encyclopedias and guides for rulers, such as Orfino da Lodi's *De regimine et sapientia potestatis;* and laudatory accounts of the deeds of the *signori* who took advantage of the commune's failure to establish stable governments, such as Galvano Fiamma's *Opusculum de rebus gestis ab Azone, Luchino et Johanne Vicecomitibus.*[23] Corporate and individual patrons alike commissioned grand building projects because this type of patronage legitimized their claims to sovereignty.

If no contemporary commentators explicitly referred to Aristotelian magnificence when Parma's piazza projects were launched, other, well-known sources already emphasized the connection between splendid architectural patronage, personal prestige, and political advantage, starting with Suetonius's *Lives of the Caesars.* His famous remark that the emperor Augustus "could boast that he had found Rome made of brick and left it in marble" followed a statement of Augustus's justification for his building works: "since the city was not adorned as the dignity of the empire demanded."[24] Italy's oligarchs knew that public building projects had been expected of members of the ancient Roman elite, as attested by the inscribed classical remains they saw around them, as well as their familiarity with Roman sources.

Moreover, in the twelfth and thirteenth centuries, architectural patronage was associated with another Aristotelian virtue, liberality, an important attribute of the ideal nobleman.[25] In Italy and beyond, chroniclers and biographers praised secular and ecclesiastical lords alike for their building commissions. Indeed, the notion that men could perform a virtuous public service by erecting public buildings is implicit in Salimbene's discussions of clerical building patrons in Lombardy. The Franciscan friar writes approvingly of episcopal builders, as Miller has observed.[26] Of Bishop Nicholas of Reggio, Salimbene remarks: "He was a Paduan, born of the noble Maltraversa family, a handsome man, generous, courtly, and liberal. He had a great episcopal palace built at Reggio."[27] In Parma, Salimbene makes much of Bishop Grazia's building projects: "In 1233 the episcopal palace of Parma, which faces the cathedral, was being built. At that time Gratia of Florence was bishop of Parma, and he had many palaces built in various places of his bishopric. And therefore, he was considered a good bishop by the Parmese, because, far from being spendthrift of Church property, he had conserved and indeed increased it."[28]

Salimbene links architectural patronage with courtliness, liberality, and virtue. The Italian elites' increasing patronage of secular building projects—neither Grazia nor Nicholas of Reggio are praised for building churches—manifests their growing interest in monumentality as an expression not only of *romanitas* but of courtliness and, ultimately, authority as well.

Curialitas

In addition to their engagement with Roman ideas, Parma's elites were also embedded in the culture of courtliness and chivalry. Rolando Rossi, Oliviero de Adam, Percivallo Fieschi—their very names attest to local familiarity with, and the prestige of, chivalric culture.[29] As Ronald Witt has pointed out, the instability of thirteenth-century Italian society (and the social mobility associated with it) triggered a renewed interest in courtliness. Existing noble families used it as a tool to emphasize their long-standing prestige, while new men could use it to legitimate their new social status.[30]

The theme of courtesy emerges repeatedly, and in many guises, in Parmesan chronicles. In one instance, Salimbene emphasizes the noble virtue of liberality in his chronicle's account of Lord Rolandino of Canossa. A man complains to Lord Rolandino that a thief has stolen his oxen. Lord Rolandino swiftly arranges the cattle's restitution. When the plaintiff adds that the same thief also stole his clothes, Rolandino gives the complainant his own cloak, a gesture the friar calls "extremely courteous."[31]

In another instance, Salimbene foregrounds chivalric pleasures. He writes that during the harsh winter of 1216, ladies danced and knights held tournaments on the Po River's frozen surface.[32] Because jousts and tourneys exalted military prowess in a rarefied environment bound by complex rules and constraints while involving great expense—and thus the opportunity to display magnificence and openhandedness—these contests became the quintessential courtly activities. The *Chronicon Parmense* repeatedly documents courtly rituals in Parma's Piazza del Duomo. On 2 February 1322, Andriasio Rossi and Vanina, daughter of Giovanni Quilico Sanvitale, celebrated their wedding at a banquet held in the bishop's palace. The reigning bishop was the Florentine Simone Saltarelli (*reg.* 1316–22), who orchestrated the marriage in hopes of ending civil strife between the two rival families. In a display of magnificent liberality, the hosts feted sixteen hundred guests. Three hundred and eighty-six ladies were served "well and with honor"—not surprising, given the three hundred servants in attendance. Friends of both the Rossi and Sanvitale lineages engaged in jousting and shows of arms in the episcopal piazza. Another Rossi wedding, this time to a Fieschi, involved tournaments in the piazza in 1328; the ladies watched from the palace's windows.[33]

The Piazza del Duomo's close association with courtliness is confirmed by Salimbene. When Jacopo da Enzola needed to be elevated to knightly status in order to take office as podesta of Modena in 1285, his dubbing took place not in any of the communal palaces or chapels, but rather in the piazza portal of the baptistery of Parma (fig. 25). With its monumental sculpted tympanum and splayed portal embrasures, the doorway of the baptistery was the most architecturally impressive in the city of Parma. It was also the most evocative of a prestigious architectural style that, like the chivalric romances, originated in France.[34] The more violent aspects of chivalric culture also make an appearance in Parma. For example, the capitals of the first major pier on the right (south) side of the cathedral's nave arcade depict knights at war (fig. 101).[35]

The Italian interest in chivalric themes is also expressed in architectural settings elsewhere in the Lombard plain. In nearby Modena, twelfth-century reliefs representing Roland with his iconic horn, Oliphant, and his sword, Durendal, decorate the third story of the Ghirlandina bell tower (fig. 102). And the archivolts of Modena cathedral's Porta della Pescheria depict King Arthur and several other knights attempting to liberate an imprisoned lady (fig. 103).[36] But explicit iconographic references were not necessary in Parma—the lustrous surfaces, lavish materials, decorative profusion, and vast scale of the episcopal and communal squares sufficed to express their patrons' noble liberality and magnificence.

The communal square's connections to courtliness and chivalry are less explicit in the textual record. As attested in the *Chronicon Parmense,* however, and as was normal

Fig. 101 Capital with knights at war, west face of the first major pier on the south side of the nave, cathedral of Parma.

Fig. 102 Roland sounding his horn, Oliphant. Ghirlandina tower, Modena.

Fig. 103 Arthurian reliefs in the archivolts of the Porta della Pescheria, cathedral of Modena.

practice throughout Italy, banners, military standards, and painted and sculpted coats of arms hung from the communal building facades, such as the *balatorium communis* and the New Communal Palace of San Vitale.[37] Such connections between the communal square and courtly conduct also occasionally emerged, unexpectedly, in the statutes, for example, in a law that required that anybody who found an animal used in the noble sport of hunting—dog, falcon, kestrel, or hawk— hold it captive on the stairs of the communal palace until its owner claimed it.[38]

Civic Spirit and Civic Space

Another manifestation of the magnificent syncretism of Roman and courtly values is the repeated emphasis on the good of the urban collective. As noted above, many Roman writers and a handful of Greeks in Latin translation were fundamental parts of late medieval education. Any educated European would have been familiar with Lucan, Virgil, Horace, Ovid, Juvenal, Cicero, and Sallust; they were staples of the medieval liberal arts curriculum. Statius, Terence, Euclid, Ptolemy, Justinian's *Digest,* and Aristotle were also popular.[39] In reading the classics, students would have been exposed to not only the grammar and rhetoric of the sources but also their philosophical and political content. Thus, readers of Cicero's *De officiis* would come away with ideas about public duty and private morality that could in turn impact their own perceptions and experiences of public office. As Skinner observes, medieval commentators repeatedly cite ancient authors on the importance of individuals' setting aside self-interest in order for cities to achieve greatness. One oft-quoted passage from Sallust's *Bellum Jugurthinum* (x.7) stated, "For it is by way of concord that small communities rise to greatness; it is as a result of discord that even the greatest communities fall into collapse." These ideas intersected with noble notions about the importance of the family or lineage and about each member's obligation to promote the interests of the kinship network over his or her own personal interests. Despite continual jockeying for primacy within it, the city was understood as a larger network of which each lineage and each individual formed part. The safety, prosperity, and prestige of the city were the responsibility of each citizen, just as he was responsible for the well-being of his lineage. Factionalism and self-interest coexisted with intense civic pride.[40]

The statutes of the commune of Parma repeatedly refer to improvements to the urban infrastructure done in the name of "honor."[41] Residents identified the social body of the city with its physical form—specifically, with its public buildings. During Frederick II's siege of the city in 1248, the ladies of Parma commissioned a silver simulacrum of the city as a votive offering to the city's patroness, the Virgin Mary. In the sculpture, the city was reduced to its essential components: the communal palace, the bishop's palace, the cathedral, and the baptistery—the structures that symbolized its social organization.[42] In the urbanistic field, the political desires of the factions and the ideology of the common good operated simultaneously. Their interaction resulted in the creation of urban environments that both exalted the status of the city as a whole and codified and imposed the values of the oligarchy.

Visibility and Panopticism

Michel Foucault's investigations into the nature of discipline may help to elucidate the relationships between the form given Parma's communal and episcopal squares, the processes used to shape them, and the production and cementing of power in the city. In Foucault's model, eighteenth-century Europe witnessed the transition between an "ancient" society, in which power is exercised by means of spectacle, and a modern society, in which power is, more economically, exercised by means of surveillance. The result of this development was the production of "disciplinary individuals" who internalized the values of the regime and monitored themselves. I propose that in late medieval Parma spectacle and surveillance were inextricably linked in the production of power and of space. One method did not replace another; the ruling elite exercised power by both means simultaneously.[43]

Parma's medieval piazzas were the stages for civic spectacle. The elaborate ceremonials orchestrated on major church feasts and the carefully choreographed processions associated with the taking or leaving of office by communal officials—the ritualized acceptance and surrender of power—necessitated the large open spaces and opulent backdrops of the new piazzas of the city. In these settings, officials and distinguished citizens could engage in the public speechmaking that marked every important public occasion. This eloquence was most characteristically deployed in public preaching and political ritual such as the (usually) biannual office-taking of the incoming podesta.[44]

In Parma, the new podesta and his entourage of judges, knights, and notaries would march in solemn procession from their lodgings to the cathedral square, accompanied by many "good men" of the city. They would enter the cathedral, where the incoming podesta would make an offering. Then the cortege would exit the cathedral and process along the strada al Duomo toward the communal square.[45] The incoming podesta would ascend the communal palace's stairs in front of the House of the Capitano and make a speech. These orations were usually formulaic; the podesta manuals give many examples. There were speeches for cities at war, for cities at peace, for prosperous times and bad. The speaker typically invoked the honor of the host city, its distinguished reputation, the nobility of its citizens, and the orderly rule the podesta would execute.[46] These concepts were reinforced by the visual cues provided by the monumental architecture and orderly contours of the communal square. The grandeur of the architectural framework, the *all'antica* luxury of the buildings' stone ornament, and their Romanizing architectural vocabulary recalled for the pupils of Cicero and Sallust the ancient Roman halls that housed their masters. It legitimated the communal government by associating it with the Roman republic, much as Cicero himself emphasized the probity of certain clients by reference to the historical associations of important Roman monuments.[47]

Unlike the communal square, the cathedral compound had long-standing associations with political authority. Its use of the Romanizing and courtly architectural language and, in particular, its geometrically idealizing form could be seen to emphasize the church faction's historic associations with Roman imperial authority and its ability to regulate the tumultuous city, even as it hosted "secular" rituals. Similar performances would take place repeatedly throughout the year, as church feasts, the arrival and departure of important visitors and embassies, proclamations, victory processions, weddings, and executions all resulted in further pageantry in the episcopal and communal squares.[48]

The distaste triggered by breaches of protocol demonstrates the importance of this ritual use of urban space. Contemporary chroniclers note with disgust those occasions when traditional protocols were imperfectly observed, referring repeatedly and specifically to the ceremonies' physical settings. The author of the *Chronicon Parmense* characterizes Lord Castellino Beccaria as "intemperate" when he short-circuits his swearing-in ritual as podesta. In 1332, Castellino began the ceremonies appropriately, by visiting the cathedral square to present an oblation in the church, in the customary manner. However, upon proceeding to the communal square, he ascended the staircase of the House of the Capitano to the communal palace unaccompanied by his predecessor and "without further solemnities" began to rule and issue banns immediately.[49] Since Castellino was appointed podesta by King Ludwig of Bavaria (who briefly claimed lordship over Parma) rather than elected by the city's governing council, he may have felt justified in disregarding the niceties of communal custom. The chronicler disagreed.

In another instance, the incoming podesta dispensed with the entire office-taking ritual altogether. Gucius de Malavoltis (*reg.* 1307) was not elected podesta in the customary manner, and he did not follow the traditional processional route in order to take office. Instead, he simply left the house where he was staying in borgo Santa Cristina (a portion of the via Emilia to the east of the communal square) and ascended the communal palace the most convenient way for him, via the stairs in front of the House of the Podesta (instead of those in front of the House of the Capitano), since he was coming from the east. No bells were rung and no council held. Again, this disregard for custom merits commemoration and censure on the part of the chronicler.[50]

In addition to providing a platform from which the members of a civic procession could be seen to advantage and on which a large audience could gather to witness the event, the piazza setting also reiterated its leaders' claims to authority, because it evoked Roman and noble ideas by means of its form. By repeated and simultaneous use of forms and materials associated with Christian, ancient Roman, and contemporary imperial authority, as well as military and chivalric values, the two piazzas reminded and reassured the oligarchs of their own ideology and continually broadcast it to the remainder of the population. By their concerted establishment of geometric order and openness, the planners implied the authorities' probity and capacity to quell disorder. By embodying the political and social virtues of *romanitas* and *curialitas,* Parma's piazzas continually broadcast their patrons' legitimacy and authority, even when the piazzas were momentarily empty of ritual activity. Indeed, the two piazzas functioned as a sort of monumental portrait of the city's ruling citizens, and the sites' ability to express their patrons' political agenda was a mirror of their eloquence.

Surveillance and Subversion

By lining the perimeter of the squares with buildings that filled the field of vision of the square's occupants and whose ornamentation and architectural form proclaimed the ruling oligarch's ideological underpinnings, Parma's planners created a "panoptic modality of power" inverse to that cited by Michel Foucault as present in Jeremy Bentham's model for an ideal prison.[51] Rather than stand at a central viewpoint and monitor the behavior of its subjects, arrayed along a perimeter (as in Bentham's model, fig. 104), Parma's ruling class

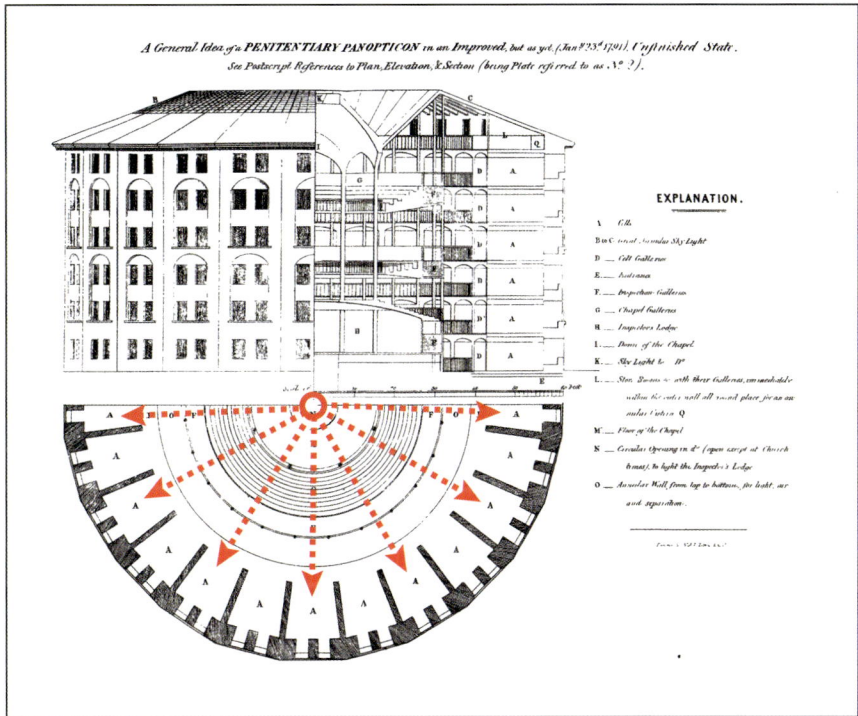

A General Idea of a PENITENTIARY PANOPTICON in an Improved, but as yet (Jan. 23d. 1791), Unfinished State.
See Postscript References to Plan, Elevation, & Section (being Plate referred to as N.° 2).

EXPLANATION.

deployed an architectural representation of itself along the perimeter of the communal and episcopal squares. The subject stood in the middle and was subjected to both the ideological bombardment of the state and its surveillance from a multitude of viewpoints (figs. 105 and 106). Unlike in Foucault's model, in late medieval Parma there was no massive institutionalized police force established to seek out and punish transgression. Each podesta arrived with only a few knights and judges to assist him in enforcing the commune's laws, and only a handful of elected or appointed local guards monitored select activities or sites within the city.[52] Yet despite the absence of a large police force, medieval surveillance was more insidious, because it extended beyond the few officials charged with oversight of a particular site or

project. As in Foucault's model, any citizen could act as informant and betray to the state the transgression of another inhabitant. Repeatedly, the statutes of Parma refer to informers who report offenders to the commune; the accusers usually benefited economically from their

Fig. 104 Analytical diagram showing how in Bentham's panopticon penitentiary, a central observer commanded a view of the prisoners' cells, along the structure's perimeter. Jeremy Bentham, "Panopticon," from *The Works of Jeremy Bentham, Published Under the Superintendence of His Executor, John Bowring,* edited by William Tait (Edinburgh: Simpkin, Marshall & Co., 1843), vol. 4, after p. 172.

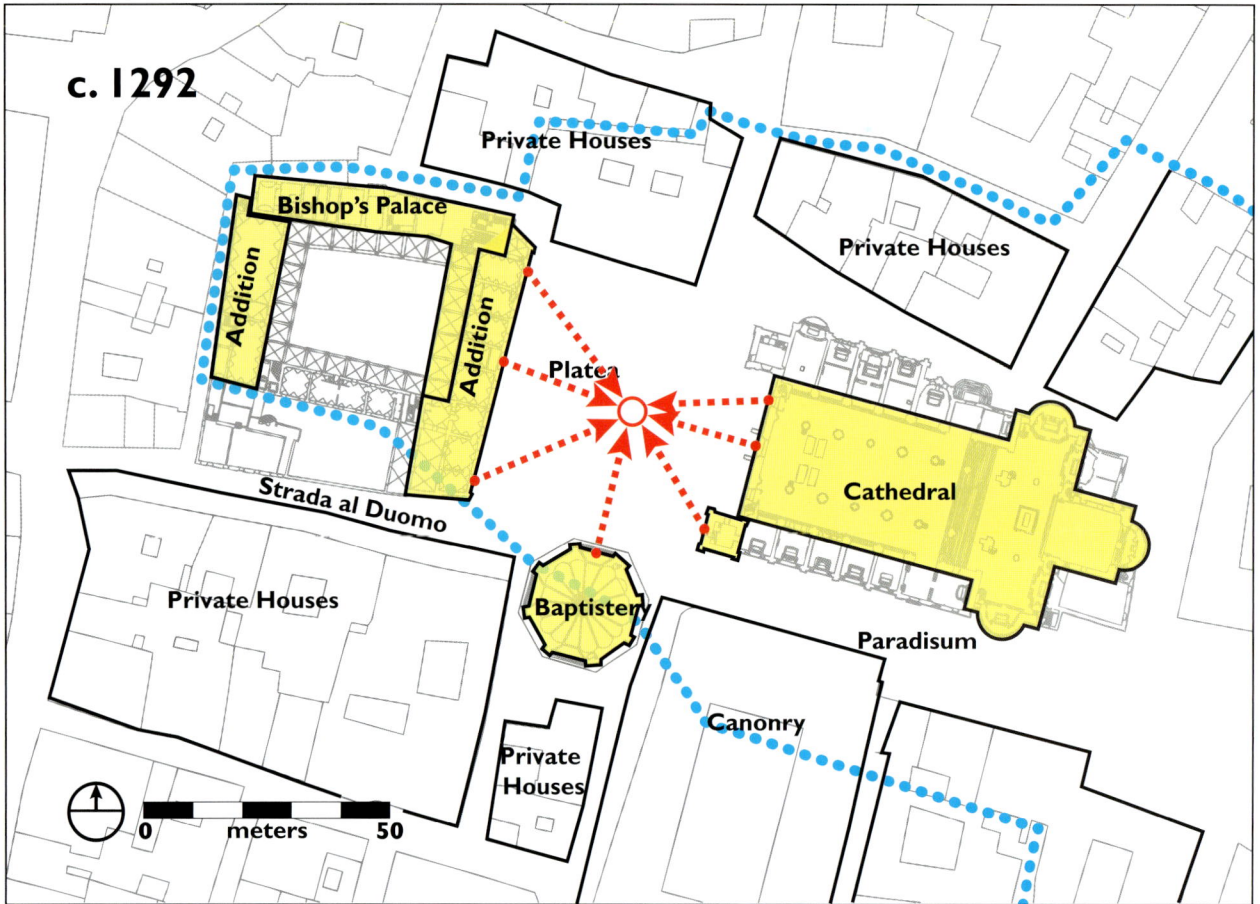

c. 1292

Private Houses

Bishop's Palace

Addition

Addition

Private Houses

Private Houses

Platea

Cathedral

Strada al Duomo

Baptistery

Paradisum

Private Houses

Canonry

Private
Houses

meters   50

betrayal, sharing in the fine collected from the transgressor.[53] Especially given the financial incentive to inform on others, the vast, open, and consequently well-lit new piazzas were fields in which it was difficult to engage in covert action. It would have been difficult to avoid the eyes in, and of, the piazza.

In sum, the new piazzas' characteristic form created a platform for civic rituals, both secular and religious. In producing these environments, Parma's planners also created clearly bounded, large, well-lit open fields in which the behavior of individual citizens was simultaneously extensively regulated and easily monitored. The city's oligarchs and subjects could simultaneously see and be seen in these new spaces. It is important to note that monitoring was not only bidirectional; it was also reflexive. The system facilitated not only the authorities' surveillance of the urban population and vice versa but also the elites' surveillance of each other, as the chroniclers' critique of the spectacles of Castellino Beccaria and Gucius de Malavoltis demonstrate. Persons acting in the piazzas of Parma must have been conscious that their performance was being observed and judged, and

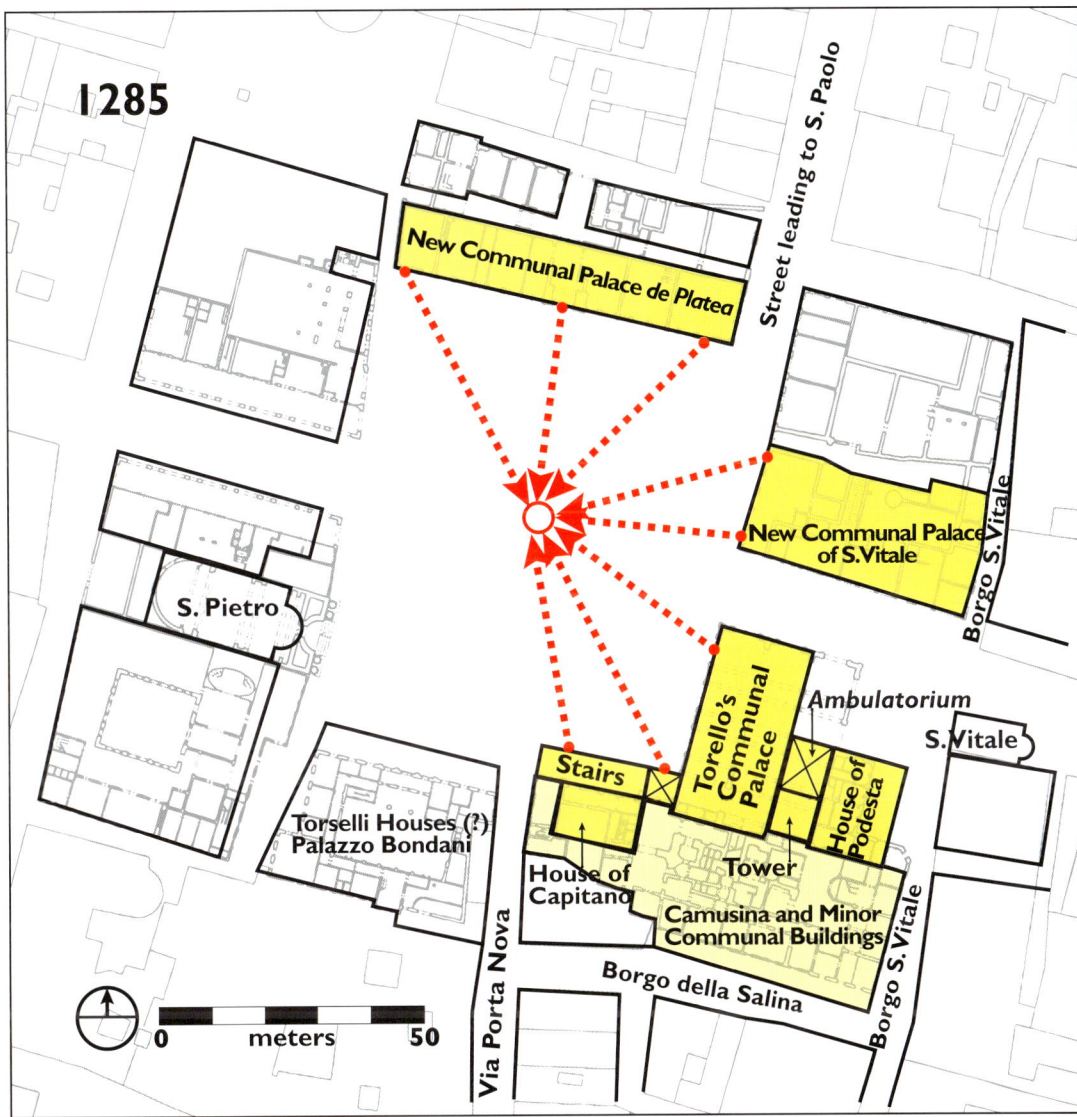

1285

New Communal Palace de Platea

Street leading to S. Paolo

New Communal Palace of S.Vitale

Borgo S.Vitale

S. Pietro

Ambulatorium

S.Vitale

Torello's Communal Palace

House of Podestà

Stairs

Torselli Houses (?) Palazzo Bondani

House of Capitano

Tower

Camusina and Minor Communal Buildings

Borgo S. Vitale

Via Porta Nova

Borgo della Salina

0   meters   50

Fig. 105 Analytical diagram representing the panoptic qualities of the episcopal piazza, Parma, c. 1292.

Fig. 106 Analytical diagram representing the panoptic qualities of the communal piazza, Parma, 1285.

fashioned their behavior accordingly; they became, in Foucault's words, "disciplinary individuals."[54]

But the phenomena of spectacle and surveillance instituted by the oligarchs could be, and were, subverted. The panoramic, panoptic piazza had two major drawbacks in the exercise of control over the city. It gave the city's inhabitants extraordinary access to the representative buildings of the regime, and it provided a large and easily accessible site in which to assemble and from which to express resistance. As Parma's political life became increasingly fractious through the thirteenth and into the fourteenth century, the communal and episcopal piazzas repeatedly became the flash points for revolt against the current regime.[55]

The communal square functioned as one such tinderbox at a turning point in Parma's thirteenth-century history. After vanquishing the Parmesan imperial party at a heated and bloody battle on the banks of the Taro on 16 June 1247, members of the exiled church party marched upon the city, where they massed in the communal square. There, the triumphant crowd appointed its military leader, Gherardo da Correggio, podesta by popular acclaim. Gherardo promptly cemented his battlefield promotion: he expelled the imperial wardens guarding the communal buildings and took control of the palaces and tower.[56] This election by acclamation in the communal square was not unique—Gherardo's kinsman Ghiberto da Correggio was installed as lord of Parma in a similar manner in 1303.[57] Nor was the episcopal piazza free of such mob action. Only five years into Ghiberto da Correggio's rule, rabble sacked the palaces of both communal and episcopal squares. They seized every book and document

they could find and, "crushing and tearing them to shreds, cast them out of the windows" in such quantities that the piazzas were full of mangled sheets. The effect reminded one eyewitness of snowfall.[58]

The medieval piazza's potential for catalysis was not lost on contemporary observers. In the factious early decades of the fourteenth century, Parmesan authorities repeatedly tried to control access to the communal square.[59] In 1317, the commune blocked all entrances to the piazza with heavy chains strung across the streets that opened onto it.[60] Thirty years later, when the Visconti of Milan took definitive control of Parma after decades of political crisis, they hastened to cut off the communal piazza from the surrounding *urbs,* the strangulation of the piazza emphasizing and cementing Visconti subordination of the city. At Luchino Visconti's orders, each and every entrance to Parma's largest square was sealed off by fortifications, and the buildings that formed its perimeter were blinded along their exterior walls. Four closely watched iron-barred gates controlled access into the square, which was denominated Sta in Pace (be, or stay, in peace). The site that had come to represent Parma's political independence was literally imprisoned by the despot, as the city's population lost its freedom.[61]

Repression and Exaltation

Members of Parma's ruling and artisan classes deliberately and systematically produced two public squares of monumental scale and exceptional visual coherence. These vast open spaces, the largest in the city, were bounded by massive and highly visible—indeed, exhibitionistic—buildings. Beyond the strictly functional needs of providing shelter, market space, and so on, the construction of these spaces met broader representational objectives. The form given to the piazzas—the concrete expression of the elite's spatial practice—combined with the elite's "urban imaginary" to produce representational spaces that, as Lefebvre theorizes, "make symbolic use of its objects."[62] The formal composition of each square and the architectural structure and decoration of its perimeter buildings broadcast the oligarchs' noble, Romanizing political program. This does not mean that every viewer of Parma's cityscape would have read each individual fragment of the piazzas in exactly the same way. Rather, each site had what Lefebvre calls a "a *horizon of meanings*: a specific or indefinite multiplicity of meanings, a shifting hierarchy in which now one, now another meaning comes momentarily to the fore, by means of—and for the sake of—a particular action."[63] These monumental ensembles operated nonetheless within a certain semiotic range. They existed only because the society at large—both the elite patrons and their subjects—shared a certain worldview crafted

and imposed by the elite. The Parmesan elite nimbly manipulated noble and ancient Roman products and practices to justify its power and produced two piazzas in which its primacy was proclaimed in space and stone. At the same time, the sites' prestige enhanced the reputation of the whole city. The urban population's access to the elite's showcase public spaces and its participation in the civic rituals that took place therein simultaneously elevated the populace's status and subordinated the participants to the elite's political program.

While the nuances of the piazzas (such as their deliberate quotations of Cremonese urbanism) were intelligible at different levels to different audiences, the squares' scale, openness, and regularity would have immediately disclosed to any able adult spectator the economic and political clout of their patrons. Historical distance has muted the sites' messages, but their survival demonstrates that they have never been silenced altogether. In this project, I have sought to recapture the piazzas' historical specificity and the cultural outlook that produced them, to render them, fleetingly, eloquent spaces once more.

Epilogue
Parma's Spatial Practice Compared

The panoptic quality of Parma's aesthetic differentiates it substantially from the better-known urbanistic aesthetics of Pisa, Siena, and Florence. In these Tuscan cities, piazza spaces act as buffers between individual monuments and the remaining city fabric and as stage sets framing the monument for the viewer. Even when close formal relationships between individual monuments on a site exist, such as in Pisa's Piazza del Duomo, the piazza surrounds its principal monuments (fig. 107); the monuments do not surround the piazza.[1] The viewer is "outside" in the piazza, looking "in" at the monuments. This effect may be a consequence of the Tuscan approach to piazza design. In his analysis of the principles guiding Tuscan urbanism, Trachtenberg has proposed a three-stage model. In the first stage, each newly erected building imposes a buffer zone of clear space around itself that echoes the plan of the building. In the second stage, the clear space attempts to achieve a regular and geometrically idealizing contour. Finally, one or more privileged, perspectival viewpoints of the building from the edge of the clear space are established.[2] The featured buildings influence the size and dimensions of the piazza but do not occupy, much less dominate, most of its perimeter.

Despite this fundamental difference, there are nonetheless four notable correspondences between the urbanistic practices of Parma and those of these three important Tuscan cities. As shown above, builders and planners in both areas created 45-degree angles of view for major buildings or building elements when possible. Second, they also provided visual cues for viewers approaching the piazza from major entrance roads. In the case of Parma's Piazza del Duomo, first a facet of the baptistery and later the new campanile announced the piazza's (and the bishop's) presence to visitors traveling on the strada al Duomo. In Florence, the major roads opening into the Piazza della Signoria frame the tower of the communal palace (fig. 108), and similar mechanisms set off the campanile of Florence and the Palazzo Pubblico of Siena as seen from the entrance roads to the Campo (fig. 109). Third, builders and planners repeatedly refer to the authority of existing buildings in developing the design and ornamentation of new buildings on the site. In Parma's cathedral square, as in Pisa's and Florence's, builders derived the proportions and decorative vocabulary of successive structures from earlier buildings on the site. Finally, both Tuscan and Parmesan patrons used their shaping of the cityscape to manifest their power.

Fig. 107 Episcopal complex, Pisa.

Fig. 108 Piazza della Signoria, Florence.

Fig. 109 Campo, Siena.

The form they gave the major sites associated with their regimes established the spectators' relationship, and submission, to their authority.[3]

Yet despite these similarities, a fundamental difference separates the Parmesan approach to urban design from these Tuscan examples. While Parma's cathedral square certainly aspires to, and partly achieves, a geometrically ideal plan, its principal buildings neither consistently impose buffers around themselves nor systematically pursue narrow perspectival viewpoints. Indeed, Parma's Piazza del Duomo works in the opposite way—the monuments work in concert, not individually, to shape the piazza and embrace the spectator within it. If the Florentine viewer is manipulated by Florentine urbanistic practice into a specific and narrow relationship to the symbolic buildings of that city-state, the Parmesan viewer in the Piazza del Duomo and Piazza Comunale is literally surrounded by the representative buildings of the each political faction. Parma's elites deployed an architectural representation of their power along the perimeter of each of their representative squares. The panorama of the piazza flooded the spectators' visual field with the physical manifestation of its patron's sociopolitical agenda while simultaneously serving as a stage for the religious and civic rituals performed on the site.

It would be unwise, however, to extrapolate either a general Tuscan or Lombard practice from these limited instances. The piazzas of the new towns established by Florence in the first half of the fourteenth century, such as San Giovanni Valdarno and Firenzuola, with their bipolar focus on the church and the house of the commune's executive officer, constitute an entirely different type.[4] Medieval squares whose

designs exhibit panoptic qualities can be found not only in the courtly Lombard-plain cities of Cremona and Modena but also in mercantile, Tuscan Pistoia—alas, none have been studied in detail. I hope that this analysis of Parma's squares will stimulate students and colleagues to launch deeper investigations of these and other sites, so that together we may generate a more comprehensive understanding of the varied urbanistic cultures of Italy's vibrant medieval cities.

Appendix I

On Measurement, Module, and Geometry in Medieval Parma

The prevalent unit of measure usually adopted by scholars of Parma's historic architecture has been a 54.52-centimeter Parmesan *braccio da muro,* a dimension codified in the early nineteenth century. However, when I applied this unit of measure to the city's best-preserved medieval structures and spaces—the Piazza del Duomo's cathedral, baptistery, bishop's palace, and campanile—it did not consistently generate either the elegant whole-number measurements or the geometrically derived irrational dimensions that we have come to expect from late medieval building practices such as modular construction or quadrature.[1] So if the city's medieval builders did not rely on the 54.52-centimeter *braccio,* what did they use instead?[2]

I am not the first to struggle with the problem of Parmesan mensuration in the Middle Ages. Upon studying the question forty-five years ago, Vincenzo Banzola was moved to echo Gaetano De Sanctis's conclusion that historical metrology "is not a science but a nightmare."[3] Although this is by no means a metrological study, my research nonetheless has yielded enough data to intimate a solution to the conundrum of Parma's medieval measures of length. Builders in twelfth- and thirteenth-century Parma seem to have used more than one unit of measure at a given time, and the

unit(s) deployed did not remain static throughout the period. But before reviewing my findings, let us pause to examine the question's parameters.

To establish historical building measurement units, scholars have recourse to three bodies of evidence: period texts referring to mensuration; securely dated, extant historical measurement standards (such as the well-known British imperial foot and yard exemplars in London's Trafalgar Square); and analyses of surviving historical building fabric. All three types of data present challenges in the case of Parma.

First, Parmesan documents of the twelfth to fourteenth centuries refer repeatedly to linear measurement units—the *pertica,* the *pes* (plural *pedes*) and the *brachio* (in Italian, *braccio,* or arm)—but they do not indicate their absolute dimensions or clarify their relationships to one another. The *pertica,* or pole, cited by the ninth century, at different times consisted of either 10 or 12 *pedes,* or feet. The *brachio* turns up for the first time in Parmesan documents in 1228 (*Statuta* 1:143); it supplemented, but did not replace, the *pertica* or *pes,* both of which remained in use throughout the thirteenth century (e.g., *Statuta* 1:83, 146, 445). For illumination, then, scholars have turned to the conversion tables produced in the early nineteenth century as part of the rationalization of the Italian peninsula's highly fragmented systems of weights and measures.[4] These give precise metric dimensions for Parma's local measurement units. But did the units codified in the nineteenth century have the same dimensions as their twelfth- and thirteenth-century namesakes?

There is considerable proof for both the persistence and the mutability of linear measurement units over long epochs. The ancient Roman *pes,* usually defined as 29.57 centimeters, remained in use in Italy, as through other parts of western Europe, into the Middle Ages.[5] However, the length of the original Roman foot itself varied even in antiquity, and later, different versions of the *pes* replaced or coexisted with the Roman standard—a medieval foot could measure as little as 27 centimeters or as much as 37 centimeters.[6] Parma's governments also overhauled standard weights and measures over the centuries, retaining the established terminology but adjusting the dimensions intended—for example, in 1261 (*Statuta* 1:430) and in 1803.[7] Moreover, the metrological culture implied by the nineteenth-century sources differs from that reflected in medieval practice.[8] Though the Ottocento tables present several different versions of certain units—a *braccio da legno o muro* (of wood or wall) equivalent to 0.545167 meters, a *braccio da panno* (of cloth) equivalent to 0.639500 meters, and a *braccio da seta* (of silk) equivalent to 0.587750 meters—the medieval sources refer to a single, unqualified *brachio,* making no distinction between *braccia* used by drapers and those used by builders. To complicate matters further, Valerio Ascani discovered that master builders in thirteenth- and fourteenth-century Italy working away

from their cities of birth sometimes used the measurement units with which they were trained rather than those of their current work site. Nor, he warns, can one assume that the *braccio da muro* would naturally be used for construction. In the Trecento, for example, builders frequently used the Tuscan *braccio da panno* instead.[9]

Second, the date and identity of Parma's surviving premodern length measurement standard are uncertain. The benchmark consists of two metal markers embedded 3.271 meters apart in the west facade of Parma cathedral, between the northern and central portals. In the nineteenth century, the dimension indicated by these markers was considered a *pertica* and was used to benchmark (after dividing it by six) the duchy's *braccio da muro* measurement when the rod that served as the official *braccio* standard could not be located.[10]

Third, dimensional patterns found in historic structures can reveal the units or modules underlying their design, but only if the data are reliable. Two factors compromise analysis of old buildings. Their building fabric presents marked distortions from its original state. It is not unusual for the walls and piers of large masonry structures to deviate from their initial alignments by 10 to 15 centimeters. The problem is especially acute in Parma due to recurrent earthquakes, floods, changes in the water table, and alteration to the ceilings, vaults, and roofs of its historic buildings. In addition, medieval building technology and practices (for example, measuring with mutable organic materials such as rope, rounding off irrational numbers into whole-number lengths for convenience, or adjusting dimensions to accommodate site conditions) sometimes resulted in considerable dimensional variation even among elements that were meant to be identical, or arithmetically or geometrically related. Consequently, we must allow for variation from consistent, ideal dimensions or geometry, but there is little scholarly consensus on what constitute acceptable measurement tolerances—some find variances as large as 5 percent acceptable, but others consider variances even smaller than 1 percent unacceptably large.[11]

To combat these challenges, I employed the strategy proposed by Eric Fernie, who has long studied medieval architecture and its measurements: using the best, most accurate measurements of the extant fabric and comparing them to known historical units of measure, without overlooking irrational numbers generated by geometric, rather than arithmetical, manipulation.[12] I compiled the best modern surveys available. When the measurements given disagreed, I conducted my own focused mensuration campaigns. Since the existing documentation focused on individual buildings at the expense of the piazzas' open space, the subject of my study, I commissioned surveys of Parma's Piazza del Duomo and Piazza Garibaldi. Using this data and keeping in mind the inevitable dimensional distortions presented by centuries-old buildings, I sought to identify potential dimensional patterns and proportional systems, whether arithmetical (the recurrence of multiples of the base unit) or geometrical (such as the 1:$\sqrt{2}$ proportions emerging from a quadrature series, or proportions of 1:$\sqrt{3}$, 1:2, 1:3, etc.). In the cathedral piazza, I found evidence for three distinct systems.

The first derives from a 54.0-centimeter base unit, a plausible variant of the 54.52-centimeter Parmesan *braccio da muro* codified in 1805. It seems to inform the design of the episcopal bell

tower begun in 1284 (fig. 38). Results along a quadrature series originating from a 54.0-centimeter (1 *braccio da muro*) square account for several dimensions of the plan and elevation of the campanile. For example, its corbels are 1 *braccio* apart; each facet between the corner buttresses measures 11⅓ *braccia da muro* (6.12 meters), seven rotations up the series from the 1 × 1 module; its square base measures 16 *braccia* (8.61 meters) per side, eight rotations along; its height to the top of the balustrade is just under 90 *braccia* (48.65 meters), thirteen rotations along, and so forth.

The second prevalent unit measures 58.4 centimeters and appears in buildings built before 1261. A module measuring 7.0 meters or twelve times this "older" *braccio* establishes the dimensions of several elements of the cathedral, baptistery, and bishop's palace. It does not seem to be used in the later campanile. It is interesting to remark that the unit is nearly identical to the Tuscan *braccio da panno,* 58.36 centimeters (12 Tuscan *braccia da panno* = 7.00 meters). It is also very close to (within 1 percent of) the Parmesan *braccio da seta* of 58.77 centimeters (12 *Parmesan braccia da seta* = 7.05 meters) and varies less than 2 percent from the length of a pair of 29.57-centimeter Roman feet, 59.14 centimeters (24 Roman feet = 7.10 meters). Using this heretofore unidentified, 58.4-centimeter "older *braccio*" produces elegant whole-number measurements for key design components of the older buildings in the Piazza del Duomo complex.[13]

For example, the cathedral transept is 46.2 meters wide, including its semicircular apses, which equals 80.0 older *braccia* (or 85.7 Parmesan *braccia da muro*). Not including the apses, the transept measures 39.7 meters in width, which equals 68.0 older *braccia* (or 72.8 Parmesan *braccia da muro*). The cathedral's west facade is 27.9 meters wide, which equals 47.8 older *braccia*, close to the round-number dimension of 48 *braccia* (compared to the more awkward 51.52 Parmesan *braccia da muro* proposed by Blasi and Coïsson) (fig. 12). The cathedral's center door is 3.5 meters wide, or 6.0 older *braccia* (or 6.5 Parmesan *braccia da muro*), as are several of the three-light windows adorning its facade. The three-light windows on the bishop's palace piazza facade and the openings of the palace's ground-story arcade also measure 3.5 meters, or 6.0 older *braccia*, in width, a dimension repeated in the distance between the intrados of the portico's arches and the string course at the *piano nobile* windows' bases (fig. 29). And the distance between the string course and the top of the corbel table above them is 7.0 meters, or 12.0 older *braccia*.

This 12-older-*braccio* module also seems to account for several components of the baptistery's elevation, such as the average width of the arches of the blind facades (12 older *braccia*, or 7.0 meters) (fig. 18). Moving one rotation up the quadrature series, to 17 older *braccia*, or 10.0 meters, also accounts for the tripartite vertical division of the elevation: the heights of the ground story (from the top of the socle to the bottom of the first gallery), the middle section of the baptistery (from the bottom of the first gallery to the top of the third gallery), and its top section (from the top of the third gallery to the top of the corner piers, below the bell cotes). Moving four rotations down from the basic module of 12 older *braccia* generates the average height of the trabeated galleries' colonnettes, 3 older *braccia*, or 1.75 meters.

But further analysis of the baptistery's elevation also reveals another recurrent quadrature series, one that apparently relies on a measurement unit of 51.85 centimeters and manipulates a 6.2-meter module (12 × 51.85 centimeters). It accounts for the spacing of the engaged columns of the ground-story blind facades (three rotations down the series, 2.2 meters), the height of the blind arches of the ground story (one rotation up the series, 8.8 meters), and the height of the topmost, blind arcade (two rotations down the series, 3.1 meters).

However, neither multiplication or division of these whole-number units nor quadrature (1:√2) alone account for all of the dimensional decisions made by the designers of the piazza's perimeter buildings. For example, the relationship of the cathedral nave and its twelfth-century side aisles seems to rely instead on the proportions 1:√3:1 (corresponding to [the outer wall, side aisle, and half the nave-arcade pier]:[nave and two half-piers]:[half the nave-arcade pier, side aisle, and outer wall]). The relationship of the length of the transept to the length of the nave is also 1:√3.

While there are certainly precedents for the use of more than one module or measurement unit within a single medieval structure, it is important to emphasize that the evidence presented here is suggestive but not conclusive.[14] Definitive answers to the problem of Parma's medieval measurement system await systematic, comprehensive, computerized metrological analysis of the masses of data generated by the recent surveys of each of the piazza's perimeter buildings.

Appendix II

The Communal Buildings of Parma: Evidence and Interpretation

This appendix comprises one entry for each of the major communal buildings on the communal square, listed in chronological order, plus a combined entry on the piazza's minor communal structures. Every entry presents a summary of my conclusions regarding each building's identity and chronology, followed by the primary textual and physical evidence about the building and the most important secondary bibliography. Please note that I do not present here every reference made to these buildings in the primary sources, but only the ones that provide crucial data about their foundation, location, and form.

A. The *porticus communis*

Summary

Schulz hypothesizes that the *porticus communis* may be either of two structures near or on the site of the Roman forum, the "portico milites sancti petri" or the "porticus sancti Vitalis," mentioned in 1228 and 1259 statutes, respectively (Schulz, "Communal Buildings," 307, 307 nn. 14 and 15; *Statuta* 1:182 and 398). However, neither of these porticos is identified in any surviving text explicitly as a *communal* portico; they are merely porticos on a site that in the

course of the thirteenth century became associated with the commune. No evidence suggests that the forum site had communal associations in the twelfth century, nor are the porticos of San Vitale and San Pietro the only ones mentioned by the statutes. But what of the portico on the southern side of the communal piazza prominently portrayed in sixteenth-century and later views of the site (figs. 47, 53, and 55)? Thirteenth-century documents about the commune's purchase of the properties occupying that location (see chapter 2) make no reference to a portico, nor is it mentioned in either of the two contemporary Parmesan chronicles.

The surviving thirteenth-century evidence explicitly locates the *porticus communis,* not on or near the forum, but rather on the Piazza del Duomo. Salimbene reports that in 1285 Guidolino da Enzola moved from borgo Santa Cristina, where the rest of his family lived, to "Parma near the cathedral of the Glorious Virgin. . . . And when he was not engaged in church offices he sat with his neighbors under the community portico [*porticus communis*] near the bishop's palace" (*Chronicle of Salimbene,* 616). The most likely site for this communal portico is along the northern boundary of the Piazza del Duomo, since the bishop's palace, baptistery, chapter house (with its own portico), and cathedral occupied the remaining three sides. A statute compiled in the 1255 statute book may refer to this portico as well; it orders that the porticos "that the commune has been accustomed to maintaining" on the episcopal piazza be kept clear (*Statuta* 1:185).

Physical evidence

No visible evidence survives.

Textual evidence

A *porticus communis* is mentioned repeatedly in documents of the late twelfth century, as Schulz documents ("Communal Buildings," 281–82, 307 n. 14). In 1181: Drei, *Le carte . . . dei secoli X–XI*, 2:708, 710. In 1187: ibid., 2:732. In 1192: ibid., 2:754. In 1193: ibid., 2:763. In 1194: ibid., 2:771. In 1196: ibid., 2:783, 787, 578. In 1199: ibid., 2:652. In 1200: ibid., 2:673, 674, 676.

A *porticus communis* was located on the cathedral square, near the bishop's palace, in 1255 and 1285: *Statuta* 1:185; *Chronicle of Salimbene*, 616.

Secondary bibliography

Schulz, "Communal Buildings," 281–82, 307 n. 14.

B. Torello's communal palace

Summary

The first communal palace of Parma was begun in 1221, during Torello da Strada of Pavia's term as podesta of Parma. It was located on the site of the current Palazzo del Municipio, to the southeast of Piazza Garibaldi. Surviving graphic evidence suggests that the palace was a building of the so-called *broletto* type: a large rectangular structure with ground-story arcades, council halls and other rooms in its upper stories, and battlements above. The upper stories of Torello's palace were accessed by means of an external staircase built in 1223. The staircase was more than a mode of ingress. It provided the commune with an external platform for public ceremonies. The palace retained its function as an important seat of communal government even as the commune erected additional buildings to accommodate its needs.

Physical evidence

All that remains of Torello's communal palace above ground is the southwest pier of its ground-story arcade and a fragment of its archivolt (fig. 56). Certain witnesses report but do not officially confirm the existence of massive foundations underneath and to the east of the current principal staircase of the Palazzo del Municipio. These were allegedly uncovered during the installation of the palazzo's new climate-control system in 1999. The Soprintendenza per i Beni Ambientali e Architettonici was not notified of their discovery.

Textual evidence

1. Parma's first communal palace was founded in 1221, under the rule of Podesta Torello da Strada of Pavia: *Chronicon Parmense,* 9; *Chronicle of Salimbene,* 591.
2. The palace was flanked by piazzas to its east

(between it and the church of San Vitale) and to its west, according to a 1263 statute: *Statuta* 1:183.

3. The palace was given a staircase traveling south and west in 1223: *Chronicon Parmense,* 9.
4. By 1268, this staircase had been furnished with a bell: *Chronicon Parmense,* 26.
5. The stairs were of substantial breadth, since they were large enough to support both a melee in 1268 and a public ceremonial (the installation of John, king of Bohemia, as lord of Parma) in 1331: *Chronicon Parmense,* 27, 212–13.
6. The staircase was external, since the commune's *tubatores,* the town criers, issued proclamations from them in 1307: *Statuta* 3:142.

Secondary bibliography

Maurizio Corradi Cervi was the first to suggest that Torello's palace was part of a complex of buildings to the southeast of the piazza, a complex destroyed by the collapse of the communal tower in the seventeenth century ("Evoluzione topografica della Piazza Grande," 40). Schulz confirmed and substantiated Corradi Cervi's intuition, pinpointing the palace's location (Schulz, "Communal Buildings," 282–85). Before Schulz, several scholars, beginning with Angelo Pezzana (*Storia della città di Parma,* 1:9, 3:19 n. 1, 5:26 n. 2), misidentified Torello's palace as the Palazzo Bondani. The Palazzo Bondani, now destroyed, was on the site of the current Banca Commerciale Italiana building, on the southern boundary of Piazza Garibaldi, to the east of via Farini. The Bondani family owned this palazzo in the seventeenth century (Schulz, "Communal Buildings," 307 n. 17 and 309 n. 19).

Although the sources seem straightforward, there nonetheless has been some disagreement about the number and configuration of staircases leading to Torello's palace. Schulz rightly follows Corradi Cervi in concluding that in 1223 a single staircase was built (Schulz, "Communal Buildings," 284–85, 311 n. 32; Corradi Cervi, "Evoluzione topografica della Piazza Grande," 41–43). However, there is no reason to believe the stairs were "unusual" in plan, as Schulz proposes.

C. Communal tower

Summary

The communal tower was located to the east-southeast of Torello's communal palace; the tower was contiguous to the palace and accessible from its upper story. All of the known sixteenth-century views of the city (including figs. 55, 60, and 62) represent the communal tower in this location. Although the drawings and texts support the conclusion that the tower was to the southeast of Torello's palace, its precise relationship to the fabric of the palace cannot be definitively determined, since some views place it behind (to the south of) the palace's southeastern corner, while others place it east of the palace's southeastern corner. Extant copies of Smeraldi's schematic sixteenth-century plan of the city do not provide conclusive evidence one way or the other (fig. 53). On Smeraldi's plan, the communal tower might be either the square inscribed with a circle just to the south of the southeastern bay of Torello's communal palace or the smaller, plain square to the east of that same bay. Sottili's and Bertoia's views suggest the latter position, but the tower's scale exceeds the dimensions implied by the small square on the Smeraldi map (figs. 55 and 62); Sottili also represents a two-story *ballatoio* connecting Torello's communal palace, the tower, and the House of the Podesta (see section D below). Ponzoni's view suggests the former position; he places the tower southeast of Torello's palace and behind the *ballatoio* (fig. 60). In the view painted for the Palazzo Farnese at Caprarola in 1569, Bertoia represents the tower between a smaller gabled structure to its east (the House of the Podesta) and a larger gabled structure to its west (Torello's communal palace). Bertoia was from Parma and knew the city well. It is unlikely that he would deliberately misrepresent one of the major monuments of his hometown, especially when it was the seat of his patron's government.

Schulz's hypothesis that the tower was built atop the extant arched building to the east of the Palazzo del Municipio—and consequently to the east of Torello's palace—is invalidated by the graphic and textual evidence (Schulz, "Communal Buildings," 284).

Physical evidence

The tower collapsed in 1606. No traces of the tower remain visible above ground. However, one witness to the discovery of massive foundations underneath and to the left of the current principal staircase of the Palazzo del Municipio (see section A above), an architect by training, has speculated that they must be the foundations of a tower.

Textual evidence

1. The communal tower received a bell in 1246: *Chronicon Parmense*, 13.

2. In 1287, a wooden belfry was added to the top of the tower, to accommodate a new communal bell: *Chronicon Parmense*, 54.

3. In 1299, the tower was damaged by lightning. It destroyed one merlon and part of the tower's wooden superstructure, as well as a portion of the House of the Podesta: *Chronicon Parmense*, 79.

4. In 1332, the communal tower and the House of the Podesta were again struck by a bolt of lightning and damaged: *Chronicon Parmense*, 219.

5. In 1336, the bell on top of communal tower cracked and was replaced with the bell formerly on the communal palace's staircase. It rung the hours and summoned officials to the palace: *Chronicon Parmense*, 253.

6. Circa 1556, the tower was to the east of the erstwhile communal palace: anonymous report for Bishop Giulio Ascanio Sforza c. 1556, Archivio della Curia Vescovile, Parma, in Schiavi, *Diocesi di Parma*, 2:167–70 n. 1.

7. In the sixteenth century, the communal tower's lower stories were square in plan; its upper stories were octagonal, ornamented with assorted marble pinnacles and colonnettes, and surmounted by a pyramidal spire: Angeli, *Historia della città di Parma*, 15; anonymous report for Bishop Giulio Ascanio Sforza c. 1556, Archivio della Curia Vescovile, Parma, in Schiavi, *Diocesi di Parma*, 2:167–70 n. 1.

Secondary bibliography

For the history of the communal tower, see Drei, "L'antica torre del Comune di Parma." The clock was installed in 1421; the automata that impressed Sforza's emissary were added in 1423.

Other scholars who have discussed it in the context of the communal piazza include Melli, "La piazza maggiore di Parma," 30; Corradi Cervi, "Evoluzione topografica della Piazza Grande," 44; Pellegri, "Parma medievale," 112; and Schulz, "Communal Buildings," 286–87, 312 nn. 45–47. All but Schulz accept the testimony of the visual sources.

D. The House of the Podesta

Summary

The most difficult problem in reconstructing the communal piazza in the thirteenth century is the correct identification of the House (or Lodging) of the Podesta. Much of the evidence concerning it (and the later House of the Capitano del Popolo) is open to multiple interpretations. The earliest documentary reference to the House of the Podesta dates from 1246, although, as Schulz has pointed out, the office of the podesta had existed since 1175 (Schulz, "Communal Buildings," 287). Repeatedly, the documents tell us that the House of the Podesta was connected to the communal palace by means of a *balatorium*. It was probably not located to the north of Torello's palace, on the other side of the via Emilia, because, in order to straddle the road below, any *balatorium* connecting it to the palace would have had to be an enormous structure spanning a gap wider than the entire breadth of Parma's cathedral. Furthermore, accounts testifying to damage undergone by the House of the Podesta when the communal tower was struck by lightning on two separate occasions demonstrate that the podesta's house must have been very close— indeed, contiguous to—the tower. The commu-

nal buildings adjacent to the communal tower were Torello's palace, to its west, and a smaller building represented to the east of Torello's palace and the tower in early views of the city (figs. 54–55 and 65). I propose that this latter building is the House of the Podesta. Its most notable feature, as represented in historic views, is that it was topped by battlements.

An account of the office-taking of Castellino Beccaria of Pavia vividly captures one moment in the life of the communal buildings and attests to their spatial arrangement. Castellino—about to be made vicar, rector, and podesta of Parma on behalf of King Ludwig of Bavaria—left the bishop's palace for the communal piazza, presumably via the former Roman *cardo maximus* (the modern strada Cavour). The ringing bells of the communal tower accompanied his entry into the piazza. Then he solemnly ascended the communal compound by means of the monumental staircase "of the lord captain" (for the House of the Capitano del Popolo and its staircase, see section E, below) and entered Torello's communal palace and the House of the Podesta in sequence.

Other documentary evidence regarding the location of the House of the Podesta is ambiguous. The precise location of the fish market is unclear, the communal canal had many subsidiary spurs, and two different streets led from the communal square to the church of San Giorgio (the former Roman *cardo* and the newer borgo San Vitale, now vicolo di Sant'Ambrogio).

Physical evidence

The House of the Podesta was damaged by the collapse of the communal tower in 1606.

Then the construction of the Palazzo del Municipio in the seventeenth century and its expansion in the early twentieth century obliterated almost all signs of the structure. The only visible surviving trace is a brick wall pierced by colonnetted windows found in a small courtyard behind the Palazzo del Municipio, behind the vaulted passageway between the Municipio and Piazza Garibaldi, no. 1, now repurposed as the city hall's information desk.

Textual evidence

1. The House of the Podesta was located near Torello's communal palace, to which it was connected by means of an *ambulatorium* in 1246: *Chronicon Parmense*, 13.
2. The House of the Podesta was still connected to Torello's communal palace by means of a *balatorium communis* in 1300; banners and emblems hung from it: *Chronicon Parmense*, 80.
3. The *balatorium* between the House of the Podesta and Torello's palace was rebuilt in 1322 by a Cremonese master called Zanonum: *Chronicon Parmense*, 172.
4. In 1253, the House of the Podesta was located in front of a fish market held on the lot formerly belonging to Alberti de Cassio: *Statuta* 1:184.
5. On or before 1255, the House of the Podesta was located near or on a street leading to the church of San Giorgio: *Statuta* 1:134.
6. The House of the Podesta was located above the Canale Communis in 1259 and in 1261: *Statuta* 1:416, 434.
7. The House of the Podesta was located near or on a street leading to the churches of San

Giorgio and San Paolo in 1281 or 1289: *Statuta* 2:287.

8. The House of the Podesta was located sufficiently near the communal tower for a single lightning bolt to have damaged both tower and house in 1299 and again in 1332: *Chronicon Parmense*, 79, 219.
9. On or before 1255, the House of the Podesta had a staircase, a door underneath the staircase, and a back door opening onto an alley, or *viazola*: *Statuta* 1:77–78.
10. In 1307, the House of the Podesta was located behind a staircase leading to Torello's communal palace: *Chronicon Parmense*, 102–3.
11. The podesta's house was located in such a position that in 1332 Ludwig of Bavaria's vicar could enter Torello's communal palace and the House of the Podesta in succession, after ascending a single staircase placed in front of the House of the Capitano (for the House of the Capitano's location, see section E, below): *Chronicon Parmense*, 219.

Secondary bibliography

Many have struggled with the ambiguities and apparent contradictions in the documentary record. For different interpretations of the location of the House of the Podesta, see Schulz, "Communal Buildings," 287–94, and Pellegri, "Parma medievale," 110. Other scholars have argued that the House of the Podesta and the House of the Capitano were the same building; see Pelicelli, *Palazzo Vecchio del Comune e Palazzo del Capitano del Popolo di Parma*, 6–10; Corradi Cervi, "Evoluzione topografica della Piazza Grande," 41–52; Banzola, *Il centro storico di Parma*, 29.

E. The House of the Capitano

Summary

The documentary evidence for the House (or sometimes Palace, Lodging, or Houses) of the Capitano del Popolo is scantier than that for the House of the Podesta, but it is less contradictory. The earliest references to it are from Salimbene, who wrote in the early 1280s, and the statute book dated 1266–1304. The House of the Capitano had a staircase leading to Torello's communal palace. Since the staircase terminated on the street leading to the Porta Nova, it was sited to the west of Torello's palace. Therefore, the House of the Capitano must have corresponded to the surviving medieval structure at Piazza Garibaldi, no. 1, as Schulz has proposed ("Communal Buildings," 298–300). The only complicating factor is the possibility that more than one building was denoted House of the Capitano, including the jail known as the Camusina, as indicated by the plural reference to "domos domini capitanei, seu Camusina," or "houses of the lord captain, or Camusina," in 1294. The Camusina, built in 1263, stood to the south of Torello's communal palace.

Physical evidence

The House of the Capitano stands on the southern perimeter of Piazza Garibaldi, east of via Farini (figs. 66–67). Its thirteenth-century brick facade was restored in 1927 (fig. 68). Although neither the building's original ground-story elevation nor its interior arrangement could be recaptured by modern restorers, the facade nonetheless retains several distinctive features. Its most notable characteristic is the staggered placement of three *trifore* along its center facade. The position of the windows echoes the diagonal path of the now-missing monumental staircase that led from via Farini to Torello's communal palace. Three additional three-light windows, conventionally aligned, illuminate the house's uppermost story. *Rosso di Verona* colonnettes adorn all six windows, though only a few columns, bases, and capitals are original; most are replacements. The 1927 restorers added the swallow-tailed battlements that now surmount the house's piazza facade, although early views consistently show conventional square-topped merlons instead. The historic views of the building differ substantially from each other, and none closely resembles the surviving structure. None depicts the building's characteristic staggered three-light windows.

Textual evidence

1. Salimbene, writing c. 1283–88, reported that the House of the Capitano was located next to Torello's communal palace and characterized it as a "palace" and "very beautiful": *Chronicle of Salimbene,* 529.
2. The House of the Capitano was next to the communal palace in 1317: *Chronicon Parmense,* 150–51.
3. The Houses (plural) of the Capitano, or the Camusina, stood in front of the house for the lion of the commune built in 1294: *Chronicon Parmense,* 67.
4. The Camusina prison was built in 1263, to the south of Torello's communal palace: *Chronicon Parmense,* 22.
5. The House of the Capitano's stables stood near the Camusina prison in 1316: *Chronicon Parmense,* 148.

6. The House of the Capitano had a staircase; a statute dating between 1266 and 1304 commanded that it be guarded: *Statuta* 2:102.

7. In 1322, the stairs "of the lord captain" begin their ascent near the street leading to the Porta Nova, now via Farini: *Chronicon Parmense*, 165.

8. Stairs characterized as "of the communal palace of the lord captain" led not only to that palace but also to the House of the Podesta in 1332: *Chronicon Parmense*, 219.

9. In 1336, stairs leading to Torello's communal palace are described as being "on the side of the captain": *Chronicon Parmense*, 253.

10. Notaries occupied stalls between the stairs "of the lord captain" and Torello's communal palace, on or after 1347: *Statuta* 4:74.

Secondary bibliography

Schulz correctly identifies the House of the Capitano ("Communal Buildings," 298–300). Other scholars have argued, unconvincingly, that the House of the Podesta and the House of the Capitano were the same building, at the location established by Schulz for the House of the Capitano. See Pelicelli, *Palazzo Vecchio del Comune e Palazzo del Capitano del Popolo di Parma*, 6–10; Corradi Cervi, "Evoluzione topografica della Piazza Grande," 41–52; Banzola, *Il centro storico di Parma*, 29. Pellegri conflates the Palazzo del Capitano with the new palace built by the commune in 1281 (discussed below, in section F) and places it on the site of the Palazzo del Municipio ("Parma medievale," 114–15), perhaps because no firmly dated sources refer to the *capitano*'s house or palace before Salimbene's account (*Chronicle of Salimbene*, 523). But as demonstrated by Schulz ("Communal Buildings," 298–300), Pellegri's proposed identification is untenable.

F. The New Communal Palace of San Vitale

Summary

While there is no question that two distinct new communal palaces were built in Parma in the 1280s, the statutory sources are seldom sufficiently specific to distinguish them from each other, or from Torello's old palace. The only documentary source that refers explicitly to the "palatio novo communis de sancto Vitale" is the *Chronicon Parmense*. Despite occasional contradictions, the preponderance of evidence indicates that the New Communal Palace of San Vitale is the Palazzo Fainardi, a long, two-towered structure in front of the church of San Vitale, to the north of the via Emilia (fig. 78). As Schulz has shown, the Palazzo Fainardi is really, behind its unified facade, an agglomeration of preexisting buildings ("Communal Buildings," 297–300). This is consonant with reports that the new palace was built in a single year, since constructing such a large building *ex novo* would likely have taken much longer.

Physical evidence

The New Communal Palace of San Vitale survives, with alterations. It is now known as the Palazzo Fainardi. While its exterior elevation has undergone many changes, we can still discern the row of three-light windows along its *piano nobile* and the two towers flanking its southern facade. The palace's interior arrangement has been radically modified in the intervening centuries.

Textual evidence

1. The New Communal Palace of San Vitale was begun and nearly completed in 1281; the arms of the podesta, *capitano,* and the Society of Crusaders were painted on its exterior: *Chronicon Parmense,* 37, 39.

2. In 1282, the New Communal Palace of San Vitale was complete; seats and benches were installed within it, and the podesta, *capitano, anziani,* and *primicerii* began meeting there: *Chronicon Parmense,* 39.

3. The New Communal Palace of San Vitale was located in front of the church of San Vitale in 1281–82: *Chronicon Parmense,* 37, 39.

4. It sheltered shops in 1281: *Chronicon Parmense,* 37.

5. The New Communal Palace of San Vitale contained the debtor's prison in 1281–82: *Chronicon Parmense,* 37, 43.

6. The New Communal Palace of San Vitale housed a prison in 1289: *Chronicon Parmense,* 57.

7. One of its prisons was contiguous to the Canale Communis, which enabled a group of prisoners to escape by digging through to the canal: *Chronicon Parmense,* 43.

Secondary bibliography

For a different hypothesis regarding the identity of the New Communal Palace of San Vitale (although it does not contradict my broader interpretation of the development of the communal piazza), see Schulz, "Communal Buildings," 297–300. Pellegri erroneously conflates the New Communal Palace of San Vitale with the House of the Capitano and places it on the site of the Palazzo del Municipio ("Parma medievale," 114–15).

G. The New Communal Palace of the Piazza

Summary

As in the case of the New Communal Palace of San Vitale, we must rely on Parma's chroniclers, rather than statutory documents, for details on the location and form of the New Communal Palace of the Piazza, or "palatio novo de platea." As Schulz has stated, the building was a shallow two-story structure that spanned the entire northern border of the newly expanded piazza, justifying its repeated characterization as "magno" (great or large) (fig. 85). At ground level, but not in its upper stories, the building was bisected by an alley, the vicolo di San Marco. The palace seems to have enclosed no large council hall, but rather to have been divided into many small rooms. A series of shops fronted by a wooden portico spread across its piazza facade (Schulz, "Communal Buildings," 301–4).

Physical evidence

The New Communal Palace of the Piazza survives today as the Palazzo del Governatore. Modern, neoclassicizing plaster and decoration hides what remains of the palace's medieval piazza elevation. The general configuration of its ground story is probably very like the original arrangement: several shops flank a central passageway that transverses the building at ground level. There are no visible remains of its interior disposition in the thirteenth century. For discussion of the palace's historic views, see Marina, "Urbanistic Transformation," 241–42.

Textual evidence

1. In 1282, the commune of Parma purchased properties for the site of the New Communal

Palace of the Piazza. Construction began the same year: *Chronicon Parmense,* 44; *Chronicle of Salimbene,* 529.

2. The new communal palace was located on the north side of the piazza: *Chronicon Parmense,* 44, 51, 154.
3. The "great" palace was finished, crenellated, and painted in 1285: *Chronicon Parmense,* 48.
4. The right side of the nearly completed palace collapsed in 1286: *Chronicon Parmense,* 51.
5. The palace's repairs were completed in 1287: *Chronicon Parmense,* 53.
6. The "great" palace was used as a provisional grain storehouse in 1287 and 1317: *Chronicon Parmense,* 53, 151.
7. The palace served as a provisional jail in 1289: *Chronicon Parmense,* 57.
8. The palace housed the recently reduced number of *anziani* beginning in 1317: *Chronicon Parmense,* 154.
9. A bell and a wooden bell cote were installed on a corner of the palace in 1317: *Chronicon Parmense,* 154–55.

Secondary bibliography

Schulz, "Communal Buildings," 301–4; Sitti, *Parma nel nome delle sue strade,* 3; Gambara, Pellegri, and de Grazia, *Palazzi e casate di Parma,* 94–96. Pellegri labels it the Palazzo dei Mercanti, due to the shops that occupied its ground story ("Parma medievale," 115).

H. Other communal buildings

Camusina prison

The Camusina prison was built in 1263 to house the city's worst criminals. It was probably located to the south of the House of the Capitano, near the *capitano*'s stables and the house of the communal lion.

1. The Camusina prison was built in 1263: *Chronicon Parmense,* 22.
2. The Camusina prison was next to the house of the Bocaci in 1272: *Chronicon Parmense,* 29.
3. The Camusina was near the House of the Capitano and the house of the communal lion in 1294: *Chronicon Parmense,* 67.
4. The *capitano* had stables next to the Camusina prison in 1317: *Chronicon Parmense,* 148.

Palace of the Notaries

The Palace of the Notaries was begun in 1287 and finished by 1302; it was located in the parish of San Vitale, near the eastern end of the communal compound: *Chronicon Parmense,* 54, 84.

Belfry

In 1287, a temporary wooden belfry was erected in the communal piazza for the new bell intended for the communal tower: *Chronicon Parmense,* 52.

Lion's house

A house was built for the communal lion behind the House of the Capitano and the Camusina prison in 1294: *Chronicon Parmense,* 67.

Well

A well was built in the communal piazza in 1303: *Chronicon Parmense,* 86; *Statuta* 2:262–63.

Appendix III
Salimbene de Adam's Account of Parma's Late Thirteenth-Century Architectural Projects

The Franciscan friar Salimbene de Adam, a Parmesan native, compiled a chronicle in the late 1280s. While not particularly attentive to works of art in general, he repeatedly comments with pride on the architectural and urbanistic projects of Parma. Toward the end of the chronicle, he provides this summary of the major architectural enterprises of the prior two decades (*Chronicle of Salimbene*, 529):

In earlier years also the Parmese had built many fine buildings in their city. For they had finished the structure of the baptistery including the roof, and they would have completed it long before, save that Ezzelino da Romano, the ruler of Verona, had caused delays, because the baptistery was being built of Veronese, and only Veronese, stone.

Also, they had great lions sculptured, and columns erected in front of the main entrance of the cathedral near the square of the baptistery and the episcopal palace. Moreover, they built three large streets, wide and beautiful: one running from St. Christine Church to the communal palace; the other from Piazza Nuova, where the podesta held public forums, to the Church of St. Thomas the Apostle. And on all these streets they built houses and beautiful palaces here and there.

They also built the very beautiful captain's palace near the old palace, which had been built during the rule of Torello (or Taurello) de Strata of Pavia, the podesta of Parma.

Also under him was begun the Torello castle on the road which leads to Borgo San Donnino. But because the forces of Borgo San Donnino surrendered to Parma, the Parmese stopped the work begun and never did finish the castle.

Also in that same year they enlarged Piazza Nuova, and they bought all the houses around the square for the city. And they had to replace the palace of the Pagani family, which was very beautiful, with another palace and shops for public use, as I saw with my own eyes. Then the city bought the even more beautiful palace of Lord Manfred de Scipione, and in addition the slaughter houses of the butchers, as well as the houses and tower of Lord Ruffino de Vernazzi in the vicinity of the Church of St. Peter.

Notes

Introduction

1. For the rise and fall of the Italian communes, see Philip Jones's exhaustive synthesis, *Italian City-State,* esp. 103–51; for a critical examination of their vast historiography, see Coleman, "Italian Communes." Parts of this introduction were first published in Marina, "Order and Ideal Geometry."

2. It is difficult to estimate Parma's population in the twelfth and thirteenth centuries; its population in 1395 may have numbered around twenty thousand. Parma seems to have been a city of the second tier, significantly smaller than Venice, Milan, or Bologna but on a par with Modena, Piacenza, and Cremona. Ginatempo and Sandri, *L'Italia delle città,* 87.

3. Other important treatments of medieval Italian political history, particularly in relation to the city-states, include Tabacco, *Struggle for Power;* Hyde, *Society and Politics;* Waley, *Italian City-Republics;* and Brezzi, *Comuni cittadini.* Gene Brucker emphasizes the violence and factionalism of the communes in "Civic Traditions."

4. Trachtenberg, *Dominion of the Eye,* 9–16.

5. "Civitas est hominum multitudo societatis vinculo adunata, dicta a civibus, id est ab ipsis incolis urbis pro eo quod plurimorum consciscat et contineat vitas. Nam urbs ipsa moenia sunt, civitas autem non saxa, sed habitatores vocantur." The English translation is by Barney, Lewis, Beach, and Berghoff, in Isidore of Seville, *Etymologies* xv.ii.1; the Latin is from *Isidori Hispalensis Episcopi Etymologiarum.*

6. Barney et al., introduction to Isidore of Seville, *Etymologies,* 3.

7. This problem has been noted by Rees Jones, review of *City and Spectacle in Medieval Europe,* 361. For an example, see Racine, "Naissance de la place civique." This "disciplinary myopia" is not limited to scholars of medieval Europe, as Diane Favro observes, "Meaning and Experience."

8. Racine remarks on the problem, "Naissance de la place," 316: "Il n'y a pas à l'heure actuelle d'ouvrages satisfaisants sur les problèmes urbanistiques concernant les villes italiennes à l'époque communale. La majeure partie des publications actuelles est orientée sur une problématique esthétique, sans que l'urbanisme soit mis en relation avec les structures sociales et politiques." There are a few notable exceptions: McLean, *Prato;* Bruzelius, *Stones of Naples;* and several doctoral dissertations—Russell, "*Vox Civitatis*"; Gruber, "Medieval Todi"; and Grossman, "*Pro Honore Comunis Senensis*"—that have not yet come to press. Greg Hise argues that architectural historians could be more assertive in claiming architecture's role in state formation: "Architecture as State Building."

9. Of course, these are not the only sites in Parma that would benefit from an integrated approach. In particular, many aspects of the city's "vernacular," or nonmonumental, built environment (housing, urban infrastructure, commercial and artisanal spaces, road and water circulation, settlement patterns, etc.) still await rigorous analysis. I regret that they receive little attention here.

10. After Baxandall's felicitous formulation, *Painting and Experience,* 29–40.

11. Enrico Guidoni has asserted the importance of accurate surveys to historians of urban form, *La città dal Medioevo al Rinascimento,* vii–xiii.

12. For a catalogue of historic views and maps of Parma, see Da Mareto, *Parma e Piacenza nei secoli,* and the Web site "Parma: L'immagine della città attraverso i secoli," ed. Giancarlo Gonizzi.

13. *Chronicon Parmense;* the chronicle is also available in an edition by Barbieri, *Chronica Parmensia.* The

standard edition of Salimbene's chronicle is Salimbene de Adam, *Cronica,* ed. Scalia, but *Cronica fratris Salimbene,* ed. Holger-Egger, still has the best critical apparatus. There is a partial English translation: *Chronicle of Salimbene,* ed. and trans. Baird, Baglivi, and Kane; it omits the first section of Salimbene's text, which is heavily indebted to the chronicle of Sicard of Cremona (*PL* 313). English quotations herein are from the Baird translation unless otherwise indicated. The statutes of Parma have been edited by Amadio Ronchini, *Statuta Communis Parmae,* 4 vols. The *Liber iurium* contains records of notarized transactions in which the commune of Parma was a principal; La Ferla Morselli, *Liber iurium.*

14. The fundamental history of Parma (up to 1346) remains that by Ireneo Affò, *Storia della città di Parma,* 4 vols. For a short (and unannotated) history of Parma, see Bernini, *Storia di Parma.* For the medieval period, see also Ronchini's historical introductions to the Parma statutes and V. Banzola's succinct treatment in *Il centro storico di Parma,* 21–32.

15. For example, although Augustine Thompson's focus on "the religious life of ordinary people in high medieval Italy" leads him to emphasize aspects of urban life other than the forces that led to the city's urbanistic transformation, he mines similar sources and frequently touches on shared Parmesan themes in *Cities of God.*

16. Among Bocchi's prodigious bibliography, see especially "Il disegno della città" and "La Piazza Maggiore di Bologna." Crouzet-Pavan, *Sopra le acque salse.*

17. Friedman, *Florentine New Towns.*

18. Trachtenberg, *Dominion of the Eye;* idem, "What Brunelleschi Saw"; and idem, "Scénographie urbaine."

19. McLean, *Prato.*

20. Henri Lefebvre's inquiries into the nature of space have stimulated my inquiry methodologically, although I do not accept certain of his problematic interpretations of space in medieval society; Lefebvre, *Production of Space.*

21. The baptistery of Parma has attracted more scholarly attention than any other medieval Parmesan building, followed by the cathedral and the bishop's palace; see chapter 1 for bibliography. There is no book-length study of any other medieval building on either the Piazza del Duomo or Piazza Garibaldi. Capelli, *Piazza Grande,* is a coffee-table book intended for a general audience.

22. Limited excavations have been conducted in the Piazza del Duomo and Piazza Garibaldi; they have typically been a consequence of discoveries made during maintenance work on the site rather than deliberately planned projects. See Catarsi, "Storia di Parma"; La Ferla Morselli, "Fonti documentarie"; Dall'Aglio, "Il disegno urbano," 106–11.

23. Schumann, *Authority and the Commune;* Greci, *Parma medievale.* To partially redress this deficiency, the new multivolume, multiauthor history of the city sponsored by the press Monte Università di Parma plans to devote two volumes to the medieval centuries.

24. This phenomenon has been noted by Juergen Schulz and others; see Schulz's introduction to the special issue of *Annali di architettura* devoted to the Italian piazza.

25. Paul the Deacon: "Everywhere ruined cities throughout all Illyria and Gaul testify to this, but most of all in unhappy Italy which has felt the cruel rage of nearly all these nations"; "the churches were despoiled, the priests killed, the cities overthrown, the people who had grown up like crops annihilated, and . . . the greater part of Italy was seized and subjugated by the Langobards." *History of the Langobards,* 2, 93.

The debate on the relative degree of urbanization in Italy from the fourth to the fourteenth centuries is discussed in Ward-Perkins and Brogiolo, *The Idea and the Ideal of the Town,* esp. Ward-Perkins, "Re-using the Architectural Legacy"; Wickham, "L'Italia e l'alto Medioevo"; and Wickham and Dean, *City and Countryside.*

26. According to Livy, the Roman colony of Parma was first established in 183 B.C.E. (Livy, *Per.* 39.55). That early settlement was destroyed by Anthony's soldiers in 43 B.C.E. and reestablished under Augustus (Plin., *HN* 3.116). Surprising acrimony surrounds archaeological debates on Roman Parma's urban form. For an analysis of the major questions, a summary of the state of research, and further bibliography, see Catarsi, "Storia di Parma." Two questions are particularly relevant to this study: the contours of the city's forum and the location and constitution of Parma's ancient and late antique fortifications. Parma's archaeologists have yet to agree on the precise contours of the Roman forum, as the archaeological evidence is inconclusive. For the two principal, differing accounts, see Dall'Aglio, "Il disegno urbano," which proposes a rectangular forum with a longer north-south axis sited to the west of the *cardo maximus* and transversing the via Emilia *decumanus,* and Marini Calvani, "Parma nell'antichità," which proposes a

rectangular forum with a longer east-west axis sited to the south of the via Emilia *decumanus* and transversing the *cardo maximus*. Textual evidence from the thirteenth century (see chapter 2 on the commune's acquisition program) supports Marini Calvani's hypothesis. On the contested location of Parma's Roman fortifications, especially in relation to the location of the cathedral complex, see Catarsi, "Storia di Parma," 397–99; Dall'Aglio, "Il disegno urbano"; and La Ferla Morselli, "Fonti documentarie." There is evidence for at least three different sets of early fortifications near the city's episcopal complex: the robust passage of masonry wall uncovered underneath the bishop's palace c. 2000 (definitely enclosing the site of the medieval cathedral), an earlier Roman defense a few yards further north along the path of modern via Melloni and via del Consorzio (just north of the present episcopal complex), and an undated wall passing through the former canonry on the site of the modern Seminario Maggiore (just to the south of the present episcopal complex). Archaeologists have identified the wall beneath the bishop's palace as a section of the city's late third-century northern enceinte. This discovery seems to have settled earlier disagreements regarding the location of the early medieval episcopal complex as a whole, if not the specific siting and dates of its individual buildings.

For the via Emilia in antiquity and the early Middle Ages, see Catarsi, "Storia di Parma," 398, and Conversi, "Le chiese e le necropoli." Reinhold Schumann reports that in the medieval period Parma's *cardo maximus* extended northward from the city all the way to the Po, where a ferry carried travelers across the river; Schumann, *Authority and the Commune,* 27.

27. Catarsi, "Storia di Parma," 397–99; Dall'Aglio, "Il disegno urbano"; and La Ferla Morselli, "Fonti documentarie"; and Conforti, *Le mura di Parma,* 1:37–41.

28. Morigi, "La città dentro la città"; V. Banzola, "Parma barbarica"; and La Ferla, "Parma nei secoli ix e x."

29. V. Banzola, "Parma barbarica," 72–74; Conforti and Erenda, "Il Battistero."

30. Pellegri, "Parma medievale," 98–100; Catarsi, "Parma tra età romana e Medioevo."

31. No contemporary descriptions of the imperial Palazzo dell'Arena survive. Only a few columns, incorporated into an eighteenth-century structure on Borgo Lalatta remain evident today. For the Palazzo dell'Arena, see

Dall'Aglio and Catarsi, "L'anfiteatro di Parma"; Guzzon, "Il Palazzo dell'Arena"; Parmeggiano, "Sulla consistenza e caratteristiche architettoniche del Palazzo dell'Arena."

32. For Parma's 1169 walls, see Conforti, *Le mura di Parma,* 1:42–47, 76–77.

33. Pellegri, "Parma medievale," 85–94, and note 26 above.

34. Morigi, "La città dentro la città"; Pellegri, "Parma medievale"; Barocelli, "San Vitale"; Ghidiglia Quintavalle and Guerra, *La Chiesa di S. Pietro.*

35. Jones, *Italian City-State,* 52. As Jones remarks, Italy had more, and larger, cities than any other region of western Europe. These cities were "filled" with ancient Roman remains; Jones, *Italian City-State,* 85–86.

36. Passages from this section have been published as part of Marina, "Magnificent Architecture," 199–202.

37. Jones, "Economia e società nell'Italia medievale." Jones later expanded upon themes introduced in this article in the masterful and exhaustive *Italian City-State.*

38. Dean, "Rise of the *Signori*"; Guyotjeannin, "Podestats d'Émilie centrale," 349–50, 368–90.

39. Guyotjeannin, "Podestats d'Émilie centrale," 368–90.

40. Schumann, *Authority and the Commune,* passim.

41. See Guyotjeannin, "Podestats d'Émilie centrale," 368–90; Bandieri, "I Rossi di Parma" (pts. 1 and 2); Nasalli Rocca di Cornegliano, "Le origini e la posizione politica dei Rossi"; idem, "La posizione politica dei Sanvitale."

42. Guyotjeannin, "Podestats d'Émilie centrale," 368–90, and *DBI,* s.v. "Correggio, Gherardo da," "Correggio, Guido da," and "Correggio, Giberto da," all by G. Montecchi.

43. See note 41 above, and *DBP,* s.v. "Sanvitale, Giacomo," "Sanvitale, Giovanni," "Sanvitale, Giovanni Quirico," and "Sanvitale, Òbizzo."

44. See notes 41 and 42 above.

45. Cf. Miller, "Religion Makes a Difference." Miller asks for a more nuanced understanding of the differences between the culture of clerical elites and that of lay elites but still acknowledges that they had more in common with each other than with nonelite culture: "There were both secular and clerical dialects within the aristocratic, or 'courtly,' culture of medieval Italy" (1021). Both partook of the elite instrument of magnificent architectural patronage in order to express their claims to authority.

46. Black, *Humanism and Education,* esp. 174–273;

Wieruszowski, "Rhetoric and the Classics," 602; Curtius, *European Literature and the Latin Middle Ages,* 36–75, 154–58; and Paetow, *The Arts Course at Medieval Universities,* 503–95. Ronchini reports that the Parma *Liber Epistolarum Ciceronis* was listed on a c. 1296 receipt whose mutilated parchment surface was later recycled as a book cover; *Statuta* 1:xxxv n. 2.

47. On the importance of public speaking, see Martines, *Power and Imagination,* 115–23; Artifoni, "I podestà professionali"; Latini, *Livres dou Tresor,* 3.1; *Oculus pastoralis* as cited in Artifoni, "I podestà professionali," 699; *Chronicle of Salimbene,* 132; Violante, "Motivi e carattere della *Cronica* di Salimbene."

48. Italian teachers of rhetoric were often active in public life, practicing as lawyers, notaries, and other public functionaries, as Martin Camargo notes, *Ars Dictaminis,* 39–41. Well-known surviving examples of "how-to" manuals include the works of Boncompagno da Signa (e.g., *Rhetorica novissima,* devoted to speeches alone), Guido Faba, Giovanni da Viterbo, and Matteo dei Libri. For bibliography on the *ars arengandi* specifically, see Camargo, *Ars Dictaminis,* 40; von Moos, "Die italienische '*ars arengandi*'"; and Witt, "Medieval '*Ars dictaminis,*'" 14. Emil Polak has catalogued model books for both letters and speeches in the two volumes of *Medieval and Renaissance Letter Treatises and Form Letters:* vol. 1, *A Census of Manuscripts Found in Eastern Europe and the Former U.S.S.R.,* and vol. 2, *A Census of Manuscripts Found in Part of Western Europe, Japan, and the United States of America.*

49. On clerical use of Sallust's *Bellum Jugurthium,* see Black, *Humanism and Education,* 295–96. For the role of rhetoric in clerical speeches, that is, sermons, see Jennings, introduction to *The Ars componendi sermones.*

50. On the role of Cicero, see Cox, "Ciceronian Rhetoric in Late Medieval Italy," 114–19; Milner, "Communication, Consensus, and Conflict," 367; Baron, "Cicero and the Roman Civic Spirit," 82–97; and Skinner, *Visions of Politics,* 2:17–30.

51. For a summary of the issues and extensive bibliography, see Racine, "Noblesse et chevalerie." C. Stephen Jaeger emphasizes the clerical origin of courtly ideas; *Origins of Courtliness.* Aldo Scaglione highlights the role of courtliness in the German imperial court and its impact on Italian notions; *Knights at Court,* 169–87.

52. For example, Rolandino of Canossa as characterized by Salimbene, *Chronicle of Salimbene,* 643: "The greatest leader among these was Lord Rolandino of Canossa, a handsome, noble, courteous, and generous man, who had been podesta many times in Italy." Note, however, that an obsession with courtly practices could be counterproductive, as Salimbene observes in the case of Lord Jacopino da Benezeto: "Lord Jacopino, a handsome knight, was a very rich man in goods and horses and treasure, but he wasted it all on minstrels and feasting and maintaining a lavish court"; *Chronicle of Salimbene,* 618.

53. Keen, *Chivalry,* 108–10.

54. Latini, *Livres dou Tresor,* 396–97; Bolton Holloway, "The Road Through Roncesvalles," 115.

55. For Charles of Anjou as knight and art patron, see Dunbabin, *Charles I of Anjou,* 194–213; Cassidy, *Politics, Civic Ideals, and Sculpture in Italy,* 43–52; and Bruzelius, *Stones of Naples,* 11–74. For an example of Charles's poetic glorification, see *The Romance of the Rose,* 2:235–41, vv. 7013–7119.

56. For a succinct account of the major trends leading to the thirteenth-century situation, with further bibliography, see Tabacco, "Northern and Central Italy in the Eleventh Century," and idem, "Northern and Central Italy in the Twelfth Century." For the emergence of the independent communes, see Jones, *Italian City-State,* 1–103. For the role of faction in medieval Italy's political life, see the work of Jacques Heers, esp. *Parties and Political Life,* and Brucker, "Civic Traditions."

57. Schumann, *Authority and the Commune,* esp. 43–51, 75–166, 202–24. The emperors frequently appointed members of the imperial court or loyal subjects as bishops of Parma; Pochettino, "L'elezione dei vescovi." For Bishop Bernardo, see *DBI,* s.v. "Bernardo degli Uberti, santo."

58. Parma's factionalism is a recurring theme of two medieval chronicles, the anonymous *Chronicon Parmense* and the chronicle of Friar Salimbene de Adam, as well as Affò's *Storia di Parma* (see note 13 above). For Bishop Bernardo II, see *DBI,* s.v. "Bernardo [Vescovo di Parma]."

59. Affò, *Storia di Parma,* 3:188–93.

60. Miller, *Bishop's Palace,* 86–169; Censi, "Il declino del capitolo della cattedrale."

61. Maureen Miller has persuasively associated the construction of new bishops' palaces with bishops' attempts to reassert their weakening authority; Miller, *Bishop's Palace,* 111–13, 115, 145–46. For this practice elsewhere in

Italy, scc also idcm, "From Episcopal to Communal Palaces," and idem, "Vescovi, palazzi e lo sviluppo dei centri civici."

Chapter 1

1. An earlier version of this chapter appeared as Marina, "Order and Ideal Geometry."

2. Unexpectedly, Parma's Piazza del Duomo has largely been ignored by scholars. While there are several specialized studies of the development of the city's communal piazza (now Piazza Garibaldi), there is no systematic study of the form of the Piazza del Duomo. The chronology of the buildings forming the perimeter of the piazza has been discussed by Pellegri, "Parma medievale," and V. Banzola, *Il centro storico di Parma,* 21–32, although neither considers the site's spatio-visual qualities. Paolo Giandebiaggi and Chiara Vernizzi hypothesize that the dimensions of many north Italian episcopal piazzas derive from the diameter of an imaginary circle surrounding the base of their respective baptisteries. They use Parma's baptistery and Piazza del Duomo as a case study; Giande-biaggi and Vernizzi, "Il Battistero di Parma." However, their analysis of Parma's Piazza del Duomo fails to exclude postmedieval structures on the square. Miller has studied Parma's Piazza del Duomo in relation to its bishop's palace; Miller, *Bishop's Palace,* 111–13, 115, 145–46.

3. The postmedieval "improvements" to the bishop's palace facade were removed in (not unproblematic) restoration campaigns undertaken between the First and Second World Wars. The work was spearheaded by Nestore Pelicelli, who was determined to return the palace to its medieval appearance. For contemporary accounts, see De Giorgi, "Il Palazzo Vescovile"; Testi, "Il Palazzo Vescovile"; and Minardi, "Il Vescovado di Parma."

4. See Comune di Parma, *Danni di guerra 1940–1945.*

5. Quite a lot of ink has been spilled over the question of whether Parma's episcopal center was always on this site or was moved there in the mid–eleventh century from a location closer to the city's Roman center. The debate is summarized in Masini, "La cattedrale di Parma." Recent archaeological findings below the bishop's palace and in the piazza have settled the question in favor of the current site, though the precise boundaries of the *curtis* remain uncertain. See note 26 to the introduction, above, and Catarsi, "Storia di Parma," 490–94. For the north Italian

context, see Violante and Fonseca, "Ubicazione e dedicazione delle cattedrali." For discussion of the early Christian basilica, see Catarsi, "Storia di Parma," 490–94, and Fava, "Il complesso episcopale parmense." There is little question that the site had long been associated with imperial power, as Schumann establishes, *Authority and the Commune,* 6, 68, and 139.

6. The recent nine hundredth anniversary of the cathedral's consecration by Pope Paschal II in 1106 stimulated a flurry of new and reissued publications on the basilica. The latest scholarly monograph published on Parma's cathedral is Luchterhandt, *Die Kathedrale von Parma,* with extensive bibliography and the most persuasive account of the building's contested construction history. Luchterhandt proposes a first Romanesque construction c. 1037, during the reign of Bishop Ugo (*reg.* 1027–45), a veteran of Otto II's imperial chancery, and a major reconstruction on mostly the same plan after the damage of the 1117 earthquake, begun under Bishop Bernardo degli Uberti (*reg.* 1106–33) and continued by Bishop Lanfranco (*reg.* 1136–63).

See also Blasi and Coïsson, *Fabbrica del Duomo di Parma;* Quintavalle, *Basilica cattedrale di Parma;* Pellegri, *Basilica cattedrale di Parma;* Ricci, *Basilica cattedrale di Parma;* Quintavalle, *La cattedrale di Parma;* Testi, *La cattedrale di Parma;* and Porter, *Lombard Architecture,* 3:148–67. Affò, too, is attentive to the church's building history; Affò, *Storia della città,* 2:69–72, 130–31, 147–48, 223.

The nave's original flanks and its two minor apses have long since been engulfed by later construction. For the problem of accurately recapturing the original building project in the light of subsequent modifications, see Luchterhandt, *Die Kathedrale von Parma,* and Dezzi Bardeschi, "Il Duomo di Parma."

7. The current facade is the product of a late thirteenth-century remodeling, which added the upper row of galleries and the central portal's monumental porch (1281), and extensive restorations throughout the centuries.

8. Of these structures, nothing visible remains. Many were destroyed when via Cardinal Ferrari was opened up in 1514. Sitti, *Parma nel nome delle sue strade,* 75–76. Parts of the chapel of Sant'Agata were incorporated into the chapels added to the south flank of the cathedral during the fourteenth to the sixteenth centuries. Any remains were lost when the chapter house was replaced by the Seminario

Maggiore in the seventeenth century, which was in turn rebuilt in 1881; Testi, *La cattedrale di Parma,* 33.

9. The definitive construction history of the bishop's palace remains to be written; examination of the palace's heterogeneous masonry suggests a more complicated series of events than has been proposed by scholars to date. See Pelicelli, *Il Vescovado di Parma;* his findings are supplemented, but not entirely superseded, by M. O. Banzola, "Il Palazzo del Vescovado." See also Testi, "Il Palazzo Vescovile." Cf. Zaniboni Mattioli, "Il Palazzo Vescovile."

The original nucleus of the bishop's palace was built during the reign of either Bishop Ugo or his successor, Bishop Cadalo (*reg.* 1045–92). Maria Ortensia Banzola summarizes the arguments for each patron; M. O. Banzola, "Il Palazzo del Vescovado," 26–30. No firm conclusion can be drawn from the documentary evidence. Regardless of who began construction, it is certain that Cadalo had more need of the palace's fortified aspects. He was appointed Pope Honorius II by Emperor Henry IV in 1061, only to be rejected by the reforming cardinals of the church, who elected first Nicholas II and then Alexander II in opposition to Cadalo. After being chased out of Rome, Cadalo took refuge in Parma's turreted bishop's palace. Bernini, *Storia di Parma,* 32–36; Gambara, Pellegri, and de Grazia, *Palazzi e casate di Parma,* 511–14.

Miller observes that Parma's is the first Italian episcopal residence referred to as a palace in the Middle Ages; Miller, *Bishop's Palace,* 89–90. As Miller notes, it was already called "palatio" in 1020; Drei, *Le carte . . . dei secoli X–XI,* vol. 2, no. 26.

10. Pelicelli, *Il Vescovado di Parma,* 17–20; M. O. Banzola, "Il Palazzo del Vescovado," 31–33.

11. The limited archaeological investigations conducted in the Piazza del Duomo have failed to uncover evidence of significant buildings there after the sixth century. The archaeological findings are summarized in Bianchi and Catarsi Dall'Aglio, *Museo Diocesano di Parma,* 26–39; see also Farioli Campanati, "Un'inedita fronte d'altare," and idem, "Note sul problema dell'ubicazione della cattedrale." Cf. Fava, "Il complesso episcopale parmense," who hypothesizes a baptistery on the spot, despite the absence of archaeological or documentary evidence in support of this notion.

12. In his chronicle, Salimbene de Adam states repeatedly that his family and other members of the nobility lived along the Piazza del Duomo; *Chronicle of Salimbene,* 9, 11–12, 30, 46, 523. The Adam family home was next to the baptistery, on the south side of the piazza; ibid., 590. It seems that in Parma, as elsewhere in Italy, the most powerful families would have their family compounds close to the local center of power. Their privileged position may have been due to their status as vassals of the bishop in previous centuries. Some porticos on the north side of the piazza were maintained by the commune, though they may have been erected at private initiative and expense; *Statuta* 1:98–99, 185; *Chronicle of Salimbene,* 616.

13. The question of when the Canale Maggiore was deviated westward from its north-south path to wrap around the *curtis regia* has not been settled, but it already seems to have had that configuration in the twelfth century. Conforti and Erenda, "Il Battistero."

14. Affò, *Storia della città,* 3:10–11; Allodi, *Serie cronologica dei vescovi di Parma,* 1:315–69; and Pelicelli, *Vescovi della chiesa parmense,* 1:172–89. While several documents attest to Òbizzo's energetic expansion of the patrimony of the Parmesan church as well as his own, only one extant record connects him explicitly with a specific building, a suit between him and the abbess of Sant'Alessandro over Òbizzo's erection of a chapel on the grounds of the church of Santo Spirito; Pelicelli, *Vescovi della chiesa parmense,* 1:182.

15. The dispute was triggered by a communal ruling abrogating the bishop's right to hold trials. Censi, "Declino del capitolo," 353.

16. Schumann, *Authority and the Commune,* 75–164. For Otto's diploma, see Societas Aperiendis Fontibus Rerum Germanicarum Medii Aevi, *Diplomatum regum et imperatorum Germaniae,* 1:333–34, doc. 239. On the temporal power of Italian bishops, see Schmidinger and Mor, *Poteri temporali dei vescovi.*

17. Schumann, *Authority and the Commune,* 167–264.

18. For the text of the Constance constitutions in English, see Thatcher and McNeal, *Source Book for Mediaeval History,* 199–202; in Latin, *MGH LL,* fol. ii, 175–80. The regalian rights in question included taxation, toll collection, coinage, collection of fines and criminal penalties, appointment of administrators and civil and criminal judges, control of all public roads, bridges, rivers and their tributaries, riverbanks, harbors, forests, mines, salt mines, fisheries, and royal palaces, among others.

19. Affò, *Storia della città,* 3:12–15, 307–8.

20. Although its foundation date is uncertain, the *laborerium* already existed in Bishop Bernardo I's day, according to Barbarossa's 1162 confirmation of revenues granted to it by the bishop. Ibid., 2:372.

21. Three medieval sources securely date the beginning of the baptistery's construction. The first is an inscription on the lintel of the baptistery's north portal, facing the Piazza del Duomo. It reads: "bis binis demptis / annis de mille / ducentis / incepit dictus / opus hoc scultor / benedictus" (Twice two years before 1200, sculptor Benedictus began this work). The Benedictus named here has been persuasively identified as the same Benedictus Antelami who inscribed the Deposition relief now in the cathedral. Scholars mostly agree on this point, although Quintavalle, *Benedetto Antelami,* 42–45, and Porter, *Lombard Architecture,* 3:146–48, among others, emphasize that "Antelami" was not a family name but a term used in northern Italy during this period to designate anyone who worked with stone on a monumental scale. The prevalence of Benedetto's sculptural style in the work completed by the cathedral workshop supports the conclusion that he directed it. Cf. Testi, *Le baptistère,* 39–40. The second source is Salimbene de Adam's chronicle, written in the 1280s. Salimbene reports that his father laid a stone in the baptistery's foundation ceremony in 1196: "In 1196, the Parmese began construction on the baptistery, and my father placed stones in its foundation as a memorial, as he told me himself. For [nothing interposed itself] between my house and the baptistery." *Chronicle of Salimbene,* 590. The third source is the *Chronicon Parmense;* its terse entry for 1196 records the names of the year's consuls and the foundation of the baptistery; *Chronicon Parmense,* 7.

The baptistery of Parma has attracted more scholarly attention than any other medieval Parmesan building. The more substantive recent literature includes Kerscher, *Benedictus Antelami oder das Baptisterium von Parma;* Quintavalle, *Battistero di Parma: Il cielo e la terra;* idem, *Battistero di Parma;* idem, *Benedetto Antelami;* Duby et al., *Battistero di Parma: La scultura;* Le Goff et al., *Battistero di Parma: La decorazione pittorica;* Woelk, *Benedetto Antelami;* Frugoni, *Benedetto Antelami e il Battistero di Parma;* Schianchi, *Battistero di Parma: Iconografia, iconologia, fonti letterarie;* Calzona, "I maestri campionesi"; Incerti, "Cosmo e architettura"; and Geymonat, "The Parma Baptistery."

Important older treatments of the architecture include Lopez, *Battistero di Parma,* with the most complete published architectural drawings of the building; Testi, *Le baptistère;* and Toesca, *Battistero di Parma.* Also helpful are the discussions of the baptistery by de Francovich, *Benedetto Antelami,* and Porter, *Lombard Architecture,* 3:133–48. The controversies relating to the building's construction history and authorship are summarized by Lomartire in "Introduzione all'architettura."

22. E.g., *Statuta* 3:142.

23. *Rosso di Verona* is quarried exclusively near that city. It was used by the ancient Romans as a building material in Verona and Parma but not elsewhere; Mansuelli, "Il commercio delle pietre veronesi."

24. For an overview of Italian freestanding baptisteries after the year 1000, see Cattaneo, "Il Battistero in Italia dopo il mille"; *Grove Dictionary of Art Online,* s.v. "Baptistery," by Annabel Jane Wharton; Frati, "Lo spazio del battesimo nelle campagne"; Longhi, "Battisteri e scena urbana nell'Italia comunale"; Tosco, "Dal battistero alla cappella battesimale."

25. Lomartire, "Introduzione all'architettura," 209, 233. The classic work on the Florence baptistery remains Horn, "Florentiner Baptisterium," 100–151. For more recent bibliography, see Paolucci, *Battistero di San Giovanni.* For the Cremona baptistery, see Tassini, *Battistero di Cremona.* Note that Cremona's stone cladding and upper galleries were added in the sixteenth century in imitation of Parma. Guidoni has hypothesized that the continual exchange of podestas between Italian communes quickened the exchange of architectural, urbanistic, and political ideas; Guidoni, "Modena e le città europee" (paper delivered at the conference L'urbanistica di Modena medievale, x–xv secolo, Modena, 3 December 1999).

26. For the complex question of Parma's medieval measurement system and the units and modules underlying the cathedral's and baptistery's designs, see appendix 1. Unless indicated otherwise, all the measurements given for the piazza and its perimeter buildings are based on the laser-assisted surveys of the sites conducted by Professor Michela Rossi and Dr. Cecilia Tedeschi of the University of Parma in May 2005. These contemporary instruments are capable of greater consistency and precision than were attainable with medieval technology, particularly at urban scale. Cf. Blasi and Coïsson, "La geometria della fabbrica."

27. The measurements are taken from the level of the socle of the central portal. The ground level of the piazza is now about 80 centimeters higher than in the thirteenth century.

28. I do not argue for any symbolic significance to these numerical or proportional relationships or the ones that follow. Cf. Hiscock, *Wise Master Builder*.

29. The baptistery measurements given here derive from architect Paolo Mancini's unpublished dissertation, "Il Battistero di Parma," which contains the most complete, detailed, and accurate architectural drawings of the baptistery to date. The engravings published by Michele Lopez are nearly as precise, but less complete.

30. Starting from the baptistery's northern portal and going clockwise, the baptistery's facades measure 7.81, 6.20, 6.64, 6.36, 7.27, 7.14, 7.73, and 6.94 meters respectively, within the inside edges of the corner buttresses.

31. For this practice in Florence, see Trachtenberg, *Dominion of the Eye,* 57 and 297 n. 147. The establishment of "dimensional correspondences" between episcopal buildings is not unique to either Florence or Parma, as Trachtenberg shows. The practice was already in use in the planning of the episcopal complex at Pisa. A fourteenth-century Sienese building contract documents the practice of conceiving of a building-facade design as a plane and then bending or folding the structure, in this instance to accommodate the site; see Toker, "Gothic Architecture by Remote Control." I am grateful to David Friedman for bringing this source to my attention.

32. Lomartire, "Introduzione all'archittetura," 233.

33. The baptistery of Cremona originally had three portals, but the southern and western portals were closed in 1592; Tassini, *Battistero di Cremona,* 16.

34. While we cannot be certain of the precise operations the planners deployed, they seem to have arrived at this position by first extending an imaginary 28-meter-long line westward from the cathedral facade along the path of the basilica's central longitudinal axis. Then they extended another, perpendicular line also measuring 28 meters southward from the first line's western endpoint. The second line served as the new baptistery's north-south cross axis. The new building's north portal facade was to be placed at the second line's southern endpoint, perpendicular to the cathedral's west facade.

35. The baptistery's north-south cross axis is 26.95 meters west of the cathedral facade.

36. Traditionally, baptism had to be performed with "living"—that is, running—water, rather than stagnant water, though this may no longer have been considered a requirement by the twelfth century; see Cramer, *Baptism and Change,* 9–10, and Gatti, "Battesimo, mistero dell'acqua," 23–25. Affò notes that the Canale Maggiore provides water for the baptismal font; *Storia della città,* 1:154. The Canale Maggiore may also have functioned as a sort of moat separating the episcopal complex from the rest of the city; ibid., 1:88–92. Conforti and Erenda, "Il Battistero."

37. The same is true of the Florentine baptistery; see Trachtenberg, *Dominion of the Eye,* 42–44.

38. This French practice perhaps began in emulation of the Benedictine abbey church at Cluny. Cluny III's west portal integrated a tympanum scene of Christ in Majesty with a lintel figuring the Last Judgment or Second Coming dated 1109–15; Conant, "The Third Church at Cluny," 335–37.

39. "This baptistery was constructed on the site of the homes of my kinsmen, who, after the demolition of their homes, left the city and became citizens of Bologna, where they took the name of *Cocca*"; *Chronicle of Salimbene,* 12.

40. In the Middle Ages, the former *cardo* led north from the via Emilia to the convent of San Paolo. As a result of Renaissance street widening, today we can also see one-half of the baptistery's west portal from the strada al Duomo. This would not have been possible in the thirteenth century.

41. *DBI,* s.v. "Grazia," by A. Padovani; *DBP,* s.v. "Grazia"; Miller, *Bishop's Palace.*

42. *Chronicle of Salimbene,* 46. On the construction history of the bishop's palace, see note 9 above.

43. The turn away from military architectural language by episcopal patrons in this period has been noted by Miller. For the iconography of the exterior transformations of Grazia's palace, see Miller, *Bishop's Palace,* 107–15. For her analysis of its interior transformations, which are outside the scope of this study, see ibid., 175–89. For the 1476–82 alterations that sealed the portico, see Pelicelli, *Il Vescovado di Parma,* 47–48.

44. Pelicelli, *Il Vescovado di Parma,* 20–28; M. O. Banzola, "Il Palazzo del Vescovado," 33–38.

45. The center of the cathedral facade corresponds to the center of its central portal, that of the baptistery facade to the center of its north portal, and that of the bishop's

palace facade to the center of its fifth (and central) ground-story pier.

46. The Piazza Santissima Annunziata's northern border measures 56.0 meters, while its southern border measures 62.4 meters; its western border measures 79.0 meters, while its eastern border measures 75.8 meters. The necessity to accommodate ideal plans to site conditions was already understood and documented in Vitruvius's day; Vitruvius, *Ten Books on Architecture*, 5.6.7, 6.2.1. See Trachtenberg, *Dominion of the Eye*, 11–14, for the Santissima Annunziata, and 124–40, for analysis of the accommodations made by Florence's Trecento planners at Piazza della Signoria.

47. Quintavalle's revisionist reading of the baptistery's fabric supports his argument that the baptistery was not finished under Benedetto Antelami's supervision; construction continued into the 1270s. Quintavalle, *Battistero di Parma: Il cielo e la terra*, 19–39. Cf. Lomartire, "Introduzione all'archittetura," 213–35.

48. In fact, the bishop was not even in residence for part of it. From 1244 to 1248, when Frederick II occupied Parma, Bishop-elect Alberto Sanvitale (*reg.* 1243–57) was in exile; the bishop's palace became the city's imperial headquarters. In 1249, he was in Lyon with the pope. Alberto was never consecrated bishop but remained bishop-elect throughout his term because he refused to take priestly orders. Affò, *Storia di Parma*, 3:192–93; *DBP*, s.v. "Sanvitale Alberto"; Pellegri, "Parma medievale," 106–18, 124–25.

49. *Statuta* 1:445: "Capitulum quod Potestas teneatur facere fieri et ampliari viam unam a meridie Batisterii per XVIII. pedes et auferri domos, quae ibi sunt, pro ipsa facienda, ita quod opus Batisterii possit videri, et possit in porta quae ibi est entrari, et quod circa Batisterium libere possit iri." This took place while the pro-church faction under the leadership of Bishop Òbizzo Sanvitale (*reg.* 1258–95) was in ascendancy in Parma, in opposition to the faction led by pro-imperial Marchese Òbizzo Pallavicini, who wanted to become lord of the city (Affò, *Storia di Parma*, 3:265–66).

50. See appendix 1 for a discussion of Parma's medieval measurement system.

51. Sensitivity to the visibility of sculpture and architecture, and empirical solutions to the problems it presented, had long been a medieval concern; Trachtenberg, *Dominion of the Eye*, 36–41, 185–205, 223–43.

52. For Òbizzo's leadership of the church faction, see *Chronicle of Salimbene*, 643, 657. On the casting of the bell for the new tower, see *Chronicon Parmense*, 46. The bell was installed on the campanile in 1292; *Chronicon Parmense*, 63. The tower was completed by 1294; *Chronicon Parmense*, 67. The *Chronicon Parmense* reports that an old campanile was demolished, although its exact form and location are unclear. It most likely postdated the 1117 earthquake. Perhaps the old tower stood among the heterogeneous constructions occupying the ground between the cathedral's southern flank and the chapter house. The unfinished tower to the left of the cathedral facade was added in 1602; it now houses the cathedral gift shop.

53. For a short comparative discussion of thirteenth-century Italian bell towers, see Trachtenberg, *Campanile of Florence*, 153. A lightning strike on the night of 22 October 2009 destroyed the modern reproduction of the angel and damaged the central spire's modern lead sheathing, revealing an elegant terracotta tile surface.

54. Most of the campanile's plaster and paint have been lost to weathering and restoration efforts. For a photograph of a fragment of surviving plaster, see Guarisco, *Il Duomo di Parma*, 108.

55. The public road that connects the cathedral square with the monastic complex of San Giovanni Evangelista (now called via Cardinal Ferrari) was opened in 1514, at least in part to display the facade of the newly rebuilt church of San Giovanni; the small piazza in front of it is contemporary. B. Adorni, "Parma rinascimentale," 168–69.

56. A communal statute of 1259 called for the vaulting of this portion of the Canale Maggiore: *Statuta* 1:423.

57. The campanile measures 48.65 meters to the top of its surmounting baluster; it measures 62.66 meters to the top of the spire, but the current spire is merely the latest in a series of postmedieval replacements. Its exact original height is unknown. Quadrature drove other campanile design decisions. For example, each facet between the tower's corner piers measures 6.12 meters, one rotation down from the 8.61-meter dimensions of the base; the distance between the corbels is 0.54 meters, eight rotations down from the 8.61-meter dimension of the base.

58. Trachtenberg, *Dominion of the Eye*, 253–62.

59. Friedman, *Florentine New Towns*, 117–66.

60. For ancient examples in Italy, see Marini Calvani,

"Leoni funerari romani." For the function and signification of Italian church porches, see Verzar Bornstein, *Portals and Politics in the Early Italian City-State.*

61. *Chronicle of Salimbene,* 529; *Chronicon Parmense,* 38. The new portal is also inscribed: "+ In millo dv[e]c[en]to octvag[esim]o p[ri]mo indic[t]io[n]e nona facti fvere leones / p[er] magistrum I[o]an[n]e Bonum d[e] Bixono et t[em]pore fratrum Ghidi / Nicolay B[er]nardini et Be[n] venuti d[e] laborerio." For further discussion of the 1281 cathedral works, see Quintavalle, *Basilica cattedrale di Parma,* 141–52; Luchterhandt, *Kathedrale von Parma,* 489–503, and Testi, *La cattedrale di Parma,* 25, 40–42. Unlike cathedral *opere* elsewhere, Parma's *laborerium* seems to have been administered exclusively by clerics, not laymen, until the fifteenth century; Luchterhandt, *Kathedrale von Parma,* 483–87; cf. Schumann, *Authority and the Commune,* 245–46.

62. *Chronicon Parmense,* 83.

63. In 1307, the final pinnacle was added to the top of the baptistery; *Chronicon Parmense,* 101. In 1321, a lion-shaped capital was installed atop one of the corner buttresses of the baptistery; *Chronicon Parmense,* 164.

64. While the bishop's palace was remodeled several times after the thirteenth century to accommodate changing tastes and functions, its basic footprint was never altered. The most dramatic changes to the palace's Piazza del Duomo facade were the closing of the open arcade on the ground story in the fifteenth century, the raising of the northern portion of the piazza facade to the height of the southern portion in the sixteenth century, and the demolition of the second-story window at the northeastern corner of Bishop Grazia's thirteenth-century facade extension in the eighteenth century; Pelicelli, *Il Vescovado di Parma,* 47–48, 49, 61–62; M. O. Banzola, "Il Palazzo del Vescovado," 39–40, 41, 45.

Until the Allied bombing of 1944, which destroyed the buildings along the piazza's north edge, the shape of Parma's Piazza del Duomo remained unchanged. Access to and from the southeast of the piazza was eased in 1514, when via Cardinal Ferrari was opened. In that same century, the strada al Duomo was widened slightly; Sitti, *Parma nel nome delle sue strade,* 75–76. Today, from the strada al Duomo, we can see more than the single facet of the building the baptistery's designers intended a viewer to see from that vantage point.

Chapter 2

1. Only three medieval facades remain visible on the piazza. The other perimeter buildings either disguise their medieval origins with later facades or have been completely reconstructed in later centuries. All of the facades on the communal piazza were remodeled in Renaissance taste under the direction of Giovan Francesco Testa for the 1566 entry into the city by Mary of Portugal, Prince Alessandro Farnese's wife; Bertini, "L'entrata solenne," 75–76, 78–79. The piazza's Renaissance name was Piazza Grande.

The facades of the buildings lining the communal piazza were remodeled again in 1760, under the direction of Bourbon prime minister Guglielmo Du Tillot; Canali and Savi, "Parma neoclassica," 208–10.

2. See note 26 to the introduction, above.

3. Barocelli, "San Vitale"; Ghidiglia Quintavalle and Guerra, *La Chiesa di S. Pietro.*

4. As in the eleventh-century documents published by Drei, *Le carte . . . dei secoli X–XI,* 2:18, 20, 332. The appellation demonstrates that the writers were aware that the site had been the Roman forum.

5. The first textual references to portico and cemetery do not appear until 1228 and 1264, respectively (*Statuta* 1:182, 458), so it is possible that those features were not present on the site in 1200; if they were not, the site was even less urbanistically distinguished than I state above.

6. The piazza's western edge has suffered the most alteration; its original building line was several feet to the west of today's boundary. It was altered in the eighteenth century, when the church of San Pietro was reoriented toward the piazza, and again in the twentieth century, most recently during the post–World War II reconstruction of the piazza's severely damaged western perimeter. These alterations have encroached upon the piazza's original western boundary. See Canali and Savi, "Parma neoclassica," 208–10, and Comune di Parma, *Danni di guerra 1940–1945.*

7. For example, in 1179 the counselors of the consuls of Parma issued a sentence from the loggia of the bishop's palace; Affò, *Storia della città,* vol. 2, app. 93, p. 389. In 1189 the communal council met in the bishop's palace to make peace with Piacenza; ibid., app. 102, p. 400. This practice was typical of Lombard communes in general; see Miller, "From Episcopal to Communal Palaces," 178–79. However, communal and imperial officials ventured beyond the

episcopal complex to perform their duties: imperial judges and the podesta issued a sentence from the church of Santo Stefano in Parma in 1160 and from Frederick's own palace in Parma, the "Palatio novo domini Federici Imperatori," also known as the Palazzo dell'Arena, in 1164; Affò, *Storia della città*, vol. 2, app. 67, p. 371, and app. 76, p. 377.

For the *porticus communis,* see appendix II, sect. A.

8. The commune sent Matteo da Correggio, Egidio di Giberti, and Bernardo Magno as ambassadors to Frederick II. A similar back-and-forth of imperial diplomas had taken place earlier that decade, while Otto IV was emperor. Throughout the dispute, Bishop Òbizzo insisted on his rights as imperial count. For further details and the pertinent sources, see *DBP,* s.v. "Fieschi Òbizzo," and Drei, "Le decime del vescovo di Parma," 3–9. Affò provides the text of the Frederickian and papal documents in appendixes 37–41; Affò, *Storia della città,* 3:334–39. He summarizes the events of 1219; ibid., 3:100–113.

9. The church gave up most of its temporal jurisdiction and privileges in Parma and its territory (including the right to confirm and invest communal officials) in exchange for an annual settlement of 3,000 imperial pounds, which represented one-half of the annual product of these rights. Pope Honorius III rejected the settlement made by the Parmesan church. Affò concurred, opining that the church got a poor deal; Affò, *Storia della città,* 3:113.

10. Communal palaces were erected in various locations within Italian cities. For a discussion of the phenomenon across the Italian peninsula, see Paul, *Die Mittelalterlichen Kommunalpäläste in Italien,* 42–44; Guidoni, "L'urbanistica dei comuni italiani in età federiciana"; Racine, "Les palais publics"; Soldi Rondinini, "Evoluzione politico-sociale e forme urbanistiche"; Racine, "Naissance de la place civique"; Cherubini, "La Piazza del Duomo nelle città"; Miller, "From Episcopal to Communal Palaces"; and Miller, "Vescovi, palazzi e lo sviluppo dei centri civici."

While a communal palace was new to Parma, palaces in general were not. The bishops of Parma had had a palace since 1020. Indeed, Parma is one of the first cities in Italy to refer to the bishop's house as a *palatium;* Miller, *Bishop's Palace,* 268. The emperor had had a palace in Parma since at least 1164.

11. For the documentary evidence regarding Torello's communal palace, see appendix II, sect. B.

12. Guidoni, *La città,* 74–76.

13. The precise nature and function of Parma's *societas militum* remain shadowy. In other north Italian city-states, it seems to have been associated with the early, consular commune; see Jones, *Italian City-State,* 149, 496–500. The *societas militum* fades from the Parmesan political scene (or at least from its surviving documents) in the mid–thirteenth century.

Their portico is mentioned in the statute book compiled in 1255. In 1228, the commune makes an exception to the statute forbidding encroachments into the piazza on behalf of the Society of Knights; they are allowed to widen their *porticus militum sancti petri* by 2 or 3 *braccia* if they so choose (*Statuta* 1:182–83). No vendors were allowed under the knights' portico either; the statute is undated, but the statute book was compiled in 1255 (*Statuta* 1:345).

14. See appendix II, sect. B.

15. Schulz, "Communal Buildings," 282–85, 309–11 nn. 22–41.

16. Ibid., 283, although the question of sources is more problematic than Schulz lets on. Miller, in particular, argues that the primary typological sources for communal palaces were bishop's palaces rather than imperial palaces, late antique or otherwise; Miller, *Bishop's Palace,* 115–17; she gives further bibliography. The best introduction to communal palace buildings in Italy remains Paul's *Mittelalterlichen Kommunalpäläste in Italien,* including his discussion of the building type's sources, 70–71.

17. Paul, "Commercial Use of Medieval Town Halls in Italy."

18. See appendix II, sect. B. The staircase extended westward (toward San Pietro) along the piazza's southern boundary (which was pierced by a southbound street leading toward Porta Pediculosa and Porta Nova, the southern part of the ancient *cardo*). For discussion of external staircases in medieval Italy, see Miller, *Bishop's Palace,* 153–56; Caterina Belletti and Maria Angela Cavazzini illustrate several examples, "Sub pede turris," 150–51, 174. Parma's staircase was destroyed as part of the modernization of the piazza perimeter undertaken for the wedding celebrations of Maria of Portugal and Alessandro Farnese; see note 1 above.

19. *Statuta* 1:130–31.

20. *Statuta* 1:182–83.

21. Currently, there is no published study on the urban compounds of Parma's nobility. For these compounds in

Europe, especially in Italy, see Heers, *Family Clans,* 141–46, 154–60. Heers provides further bibliography for several Italian cities. For an especially fine analysis of the phenomenon in Florence, see Lansing, *Florentine Magnates,* 84–105. For the situation in a Lombard-plain city, see Heers, *Espaces publics, espaces privés,* 33–45; in Siena, English, "Urban Castles in Medieval Siena."

22. On medieval Italy's well-documented factionalism, see Heers, *Parties and Political Life,* passim; Jones, *Italian City-State,* 149–50, 333–521; and Cracco, "Social Structure and Conflict," 327–28.

23. Parma's political situation was complex. As Salimbene recalls of the period, "there was a fierce, complicated, and dangerous war between the parties of the Church and the empire"; *Chronicle of Salimbene,* 168. Affò's *Storia della città* reports of Parma in the 1240s: civil strife erupts in 1242 (3:184); litigation over the bishop-elect occurs in 1243 (3:185–87); Bernardo Rossi, part of Parma's ruling faction, switches to the papal side in 1244 (3:192); the papal party flees Parma in 1244, the imperial party takes control, and Frederick II takes over the empty bishop's palace (3:192–93); the Parmesan papal party takes Parma from Frederick II's forces and his Parmesan allies in 1246 (3:196–98); Frederick II retakes Parma in 1246 (3:199); Frederick II's forces are expelled from Parma in 1247 (3:200); Frederick besieges Parma in 1247–48 (3:202–10); the Parmesan papal party trounces Frederick's forces in 1248 (3:211–15).

The change of allegiance that precipitated the later events outlined above was triggered by the election of Parmesan canon Sinibaldo Fieschi as Pope Innocent IV in 1244. Before his election, Sinibaldo had been pro-imperial, like most of his family; Affò, *Storia della città,* 3:185–87.

24. From 1244 to 1247, the commune was led by pro-imperial podestas. The tower must have been complete by 1246, the year that a bell was installed upon it: "Et tintinellum com corda aricalchi positum fuit ad turem communis"; *Chronicon Parmense,* 13. For further documentary and other evidence regarding the location and appearance of the communal tower, see appendix II, sect. C.

25. The tower's description appears in an anonymous report written for Bishop Giulio Ascanio Sforza c. 1556, in the Archivio della Curia Vescovile, Parma. The report's description of the communal square, including a detailed analysis of the tower, was published by Antonio Schiavi as a long footnote to his edition of Cristoforo Dalla Torre's "Descriptio omnium civitatis et dioecesis parmensis ecclesiarum, monasteriorum et beneficiorum in eis fundatorum," in *Diocesi di Parma,* 2:167–70 n. 1. See also the tower's depiction in the view of Parma in the background of Giovan Antonio Paganino's fresco *Pier Maria Rossi Hailed as Restorer of Parma's Freedom,* 1557, Salone delle Gesta Rossiane, Castello di San Secondo.

26. Parma's tower may have predated those of Cremona and Modena. The Torrazzo's square tower block was completed in 1267; its spire was added in 1305. Although begun in the twelfth century, the Ghirlandina was not completed until 1319.

27. Parma's tower was frequently damaged by lightning throughout its existence and was continually repaired and renewed. For the history of the communal tower, see Belletti and Cavazzini, "Sub pede turris," 44–55, and Drei, "L'antica torre del Comune di Parma." Bonaventura Angeli reports that the top of the tower was rebuilt in 1414, although he gives no details about the form the reconstruction took; Angeli, *Historia della città di Parma,* 15. Its first clock was installed in 1421; automata were added in 1433. The elaborate superstructure incorporating a series of octagonal spires evident in the sixteenth-century views was added between 1450 and 1472 according to a design by Gherardo Fatuli. The heightened tower was never stable; repairs were performed repeatedly in the succeeding century. The tower collapsed on 27 January 1606, killing twenty-seven people.

28. Lansing, *Florentine Magnates,* 85–88, 97. Heers, *Family Clans,* 185–201; Settia, "Lo sviluppo di un modello."

29. For example, the episcopal bell was rung to call the communal councils to meetings in the episcopal palace, before the commune had its own; Drei, *Le carte . . . del secolo XII,* no. 836.

30. For bells on the communal tower, see appendix II, sect. C.

31. For the commune's use of its bells, see *Statuta* 1:353, 2:192, 198–200, and *Chronicon Parmense,* 13, 45, 155, 253. Cf. Thompson, *Cities of God,* 174–77.

32. E.g.: "Et sonatum fuit concilium," and "sonatum fuit consilium generale communis"; *Chronicon Parmense,* 85, 212. In the normal course of business, the communal council met "at sonum campanae in Palacio communis"; *Statuta* 1:187.

33. *Chronicon Parmense,* 13: "Et hoc anno [1244] facta fuit campana magna communis." For the 1317 installation procession, see *Chronicon Parmense,* 154–55: "et, campana facta, ducta fuit cum magna solemnitate in plateam die martis 20 decembris et conducta super dicto toresino, seu batifolo; et super ipsum batifolum positus fuit unus taurellus lapideus cum cornibus auratis, qui torellus fuit aportatus ab ecclesia maori ad plateam die veneris 23 decembris. Et ad ipsum torellum aportandum fuerunt domini potestas, capitaneus, advocatus mercatorum ancianos judicum, proconsul notariorum, potestates quatuor misteriorum, domini octo et capitaneus Societatis; qui domini ipsum aportaverunt super spalam, existentem super unam assidem copertam de uno paleo aurato, et omnes boni homines totius civitatis, plusquam quatuor mille hominum, ibi fuerunt cum tubis et aliis solemnitatibus et maxima letitia."

34. An official, permanent House of the Podesta may have existed earlier. Schulz is correct to point out that the podesta's office had been instituted by 1175. The podesta must have lived and worked somewhere before the 1240s; Schulz, "Communal Buildings," 287. For the documentary and other evidence concerning the House of the Podesta and its *ambulatorium,* see appendix II, sect. D.

35. The seventeenth-century reconstruction of the communal palace and the interbellum expansion of the Palazzo del Municipio onto the lots formerly occupied by the tower and the House of the Podesta obliterated valuable archaeological evidence.

36. For a discussion of the location of the House of the Podesta, and supporting evidence, see appendix II, sect. D.

37. For examples of imperial legislation restricting the construction of towers and fortifications by private individuals, albeit beyond northern Italy, see Powell, *Liber Augustalis,* 123. For the location of Ugone Sanvitale's house, see La Ferla Morselli, *Liber iurium,* 55, 56.

38. *Statuta* 1:xiv–xvii, 2:iii.

39. For example, like the podesta, the new *capitano del popolo* brought an entourage with him when he took office. He was accompanied by a judge, a *socio,* two notaries, and six knights, and he was to support this staff from his salary of 325 imperial pounds; *Statuta* 2:96–97. The podesta received 600 imperial pounds and supported four judges, two *socii,* and twelve knights; *Statuta* 2:95–96. The Society of Crusaders elected its own *primicerii,* and the guilds and the merchants too chose representatives. All of them participated in the commune's general council, as well as in meetings of their own.

40. *Statuta* 1:469.

41. For discussion of the evidence supporting this identification of the House of the Capitano, see appendix II, sect. E.

42. Extant examples of external staircases attached to government buildings include the staircases of the Palazzo del Popolo, Todi, c. 1228, and the Palazzo del Podesta, Castell'Arquato (about 40 kilometers from Parma), 1293–97. See note 18 above.

43. *Chronicle of Salimbene,* 529 (transcription in appendix III).

44. Note that restorers have replaced most colonnettes with modern facsimiles.

45. Until a recent renovation (c. 2003), the passageway led to a dank and precipitous courtyard in which several medieval *bifore* pierced a heterogeneous mass of brick masonry.

46. *Statuta* 1:472. The street was already in place in 1271, when two notarial documents refer to its new path; La Ferla Morselli, *Liber iurium,* 55 and 56. Cf. Copertini, "La Via Emilia," 34–35.

47. *Statuta* 1:462 (1264) and 2:290 (1293). The house of Ugone Sanvitale was located next to a communal palace, as indicated by a statute requiring its expropriation in 1253, *Statuta* 1:103–4, and another from 1259, *Statuta* 1:398. The street that was extended and improved already existed in 1255; see *Statuta* 1:134. At that time it may only have reached as far as San Giorgio. Intriguingly, this project was revived when Sanvitale power was again in the ascendant, in 1293; see *Statuta* 2:290.

48. *Chronicon Parmense,* 29.

49. For the eastern arm of the via Claudia/Emilia, see *Chronicon Parmense,* 33, and *Chronicle of Salimbene,* 529 (appendix III).

50. *Statuta* 1:458, and again in 1266, *Statuta* 2:286.

51. For documents mentioning the other communal buildings, see appendix II, sect. H.

52. See note 50 above.

53. See notes 46–49 above.

54. La Ferla Morselli, *Liber iurium,* 1–86, docs. 1, 4, 8–11, 14–30, 32–41. Note that some contracts are for the sale of fractions of houses or lots, and some fractional properties

are owned by more than one individual. Salimbene remarked on the phenomenon; see appendix III.

55. Ibid., xxxix–xlii.

56. Ibid., 1–86.

57. One reason why the house of Jacopo da Benezeto (Jacobus de Beneçeto) may have been a prime candidate for communal expropriation was that Jacopo had murdered imperial *massarius* Andrea de Borgarelli below the communal palace in 1247. Jacopo's house suffered substantial damage when a pro-imperial mob descended upon it to avenge the murder; *Chronicon Parmense,* 16.

For the 1253 statute, see *Statuta* 1:103–4. For the 1259 statute about the money changers, see *Statuta* 1:398. For the contract to buy half of the Sanvitale lot in 1260, see La Ferla Morselli, *Liber iurium,* 81–84. For the 1262 statute, see *Statuta* 1:444. The jails are reported complete in 1263; *Chronicon Parmense,* 22. See also appendix II, sect. H, for the communal jails.

The Preytis clan was part of the old aristocracy and politically active within and without Parma; see Guyotjeannin, "Podestats d'Émilie centrale," 388 n. 69.

58. La Ferla Morselli, *Liber iurium,* 1–3, 13–24, 33–35, 41–51, 53–57, 73–74, 84–86 (docs. 1, 8–11, 16, 18–23, 25–27, 32, 36, and 41).

59. These are the only privately owned battlements mentioned in the entire *Liber iurium.* For the Torselli house, see La Ferla Morselli, *Liber iurium,* 42, 44, 56. Although they were "new men," the Torselli clan had an active political career in the Duecento: many members served as officials in other cities. See Guyotjeannin, "Podestats d'Émilie centrale," 389 n. 69. For further discussion of the Palazzo Bondani, see G. Adorni, "Palazzo Bondani," 176, and appendix II, sect. B.

60. The property belonged to the Raxorii. It was purchased by the commune in two separate transactions. La Ferla Morselli, *Liber iurium,* 22–24, 33–35 (docs. 11 and 16).

61. For a discussion of the function of the communal and cathedral piazzas, and the legislation about maintaining order and decorum therein, see chapter 4. For the removal of potentially polluting activities and encumbrances from the streets leading to the communal piazza, see *Statuta* 2:287–88, 289–90, 290.

62. *Statuta* 1:60. Parma had at least two large international market fairs by the 1220s, the nine-day fair of Sant'Ercolano, in September, and the four-day fair of San

Siro, in May. Another statute (undated but amended in 1229) asserts that the May fair must be conducted in the same manner as the September fair; *Statuta* 1:61. Ercolano was a Roman martyr; Amore, "Ercolano, santo, martire di Roma." The cathedral housed his relics at the high altar.

63. *Statuta* 2:287.

64. *Statuta* 2:287; *Chronicon Parmense,* 37; see also note 46 above.

65. For the documentary evidence regarding the New Communal Palace of San Vitale, see appendix II, sect. F.

66. The precise disposition of the facade's windows is problematic. For Schulz's reconstruction of the Palazzo Fainardi, see Schulz, "Communal Buildings," 297–300.

67. See appendix II, sect. F.

68. Our sources are the *Chronicon Parmense* and Salimbene; no communal statute to this effect survives. *Chronicon Parmense,* 41: "Item eo anno [1282] ampliata fuit platea communis a parte de subtus usque ad domum condam domini Prandonis Rubei, et a via nova beccariorum [now via Cavour] usque ad viaçolam de Ruffinis [now vicolo dei Vernacci]; et omnes domus tenentes caput ad plateam pro communi exstimate fuerunt, ut pro communis emerentur." For the passage in Salimbene, see appendix III. It is striking to compare the commune of Florence's decades-long expansion of the Piazza della Signoria to the commune of Parma's swift implementation of its own plan. For the timing of the Piazza della Signoria, see Trachtenberg, *Dominion of the Eye,* 92–105, 138–40.

69. Some, but not all, of these properties had previously been acquired by the commune; see note 54 above.

70. Although I do not know of any medieval text characterizing the communal piazza as a square, one such Renaissance account survives: it is part of a description of the religious institutions of Parma prepared by an anonymous author for Bishop Guido Ascanio Sforza c. 1556, Archivio della Curia Vescovile, Parma, in Schiavi, *Diocesi di Parma,* 2:167–170 n. 1. The writer describes the communal piazza and the principal buildings around it. Schulz reprints part of the Latin text, "Communal Buildings," 323 n. 120. Oddly, Schulz translates the Latin *quadratam* as "rectangular," rather than the more appropriate "square"; ibid., 305. I am not the first art historian to note the squaring of the communal piazza. Guidoni mentions it, although he does not elaborate, in *La città,* 82.

71. The *Chronicon Parmense*, 44, 48, notes the palace's inception, its completion, and its decoration. See appendix II, sect. G.

72. *Chronicon Parmense*, 48. Schulz has reconstructed the medieval palace's original facade type, if not its details, from a sixteenth-century project drawing for its renovation; Schulz, "Communal Buildings," 301–4.

73. *Chronicon Parmense*, 53 (for the palace's use as a provisional warehouse in a famine), 57 (for its use as a provisional jail for *popolari* from Reggio). See also appendix II, sect. G.

74. The *palatium novum de platea* is 66 meters wide along its communal-piazza facade; the bishop's palace's Piazza del Duomo facade is 54 meters wide. While the podesta of Parma continued to be foreign-born, the da Correggio played other leadership roles in the city's political life. For example, Matteo da Correggio had been the commune's ambassador to the pope in 1282, when his mission was to get the pope to lift the excommunication of the commune; *Chronicon Parmense*, 41. Of the period, Salimbene writes: "At this time there was also a great quarrel in Parma between Obizzo of San Vitale and the Lord Guido of Corigia. These two were captains of the two parties in the city at that time. Neither had been chosen by the Parmese, but had themselves assumed the leadership, each one believing himself to be acting reasonably for the good of the city. And the men of that time, according to their allegiance, spoke in praise or blame." *Chronicle of Salimbene*, 657. Salimbene favored Òbizzo over Guido, whom he cursed, wishing that "God delete his [Guido's] name from the Book of Life"; *Chronicle of Salimbene*, 656.

Chapter 3

1. Ottokar, "Criteri d'ordine"; Braunfels, *Mittelalterliche Stadtbaukunst in der Toskana*, 86–130; Bocchi, "Normativa urbanistica"; Stolleis and Wolff, *La bellezza della città*.

2. On the use of statutes as sources, see Keller, "Zur Quellengattung der italienischen Stadtstatuten."

3. *Statuta* 1–4.

4. The relevant statutes date from 1227 and 1228, respectively; *Statuta* 1:130–31, 182–83.

5. *Statuta* 1:185.

6. *Statuta* 1:367, undated.

7. *Statuta* 1:423.

8. *Statuta* 2:285–86.

9. In 1264, sometime after 1266, and again in 1294; *Statuta* 1:458, 2:285–86; *Chronicon Parmense*, 67.

10. *Statuta* 1:367, 2:286–87.

11. This statute was enacted when the Franciscan friar Gherardo Boccabadati of Modena (d. 1257) was podesta of the city; *Statuta* 1:320. The "soil" to which the statute refers seems to be human soil, namely, urine.

12. *Chronicle of Salimbene*, 616. It is noteworthy that Guidolino da Enzola was a member of a prestigious lineage in Parma, second in distinction only to the Rossi, Sanvitale, and da Correggio; see Guyotjeannin, "Podestats d'Émilie centrale," 366.

13. *Statuta* 1:184, 185, 345, 2:203.

14. *Statuta* 1:183–84.

15. Not even the merchants' own infants were allowed in the shops—cribs were expressly forbidden. *Statuta* 1:183–84, 343.

16. *Statuta* 1:29, 60. The Ghiaia, which remains the site of the city's open-air market today, was eventually enclosed by fortifications in 1232. Like the cathedral and communal squares, it was one of very few large open spaces within the city. Unlike the two majestic piazzas, however, it was an unpaved, utilitarian site devoid of monumental architecture. Not only a site for the livestock market and the annual fairs, it sometimes was used as a place to execute criminals and muster troops. Zennoni, "Piazza Ghiaia," 15–20.

17. *Statuta* 1:344 and 345. See appendix I for Parma's medieval units of measure.

18. *Statuta* 2:287. The 1281 statute had precedents; see a series of statutes amended between 1238 and 1241 establishing that butchers were not allowed to hang pork or beef carcasses outside their shops and that benches lining the street must not be higher than one *braccio*. In 1262 these prohibitions were extended to three streets emerging from the piazza. *Statuta* 1:364. See also *Statuta* 1:365, 2:289–90, 290.

19. *Statuta* 1:365–66, 2:289–90, 3:329–30.

20. *Statuta* 1:379.

21. The statute's phrasing is too vague to help us establish the precise location of the problematic canal opening. It is either the Canale Maggiore itself, on the piazza's southeast, or the smaller canal running parallel to the west wall of the bishop's palace; *Statuta* 1:425. Other examples of statutes regarding access to the episcopal square or its buildings include *Statuta* 1:383, 445, 2:290, 3:329–30.

22. *Statuta* 1:319.

23. *Statuta* 2:76.

24. In 1230, *Statuta* 1:215.

25. *Statuta* 1:286–87, for the episcopal square; 1:295–96, for the communal square.

26. *Statuta* 1:390–91.

27. *Statuta* 1:319.

28. The distinctive treatment of behavior in the two piazzas may be linked to the impetus to severely penalize transgressions against property owners when performed on their own property. The property owner was allowed to avenge such insults with a homicidal vendetta; see *Statuta* 1:275. For the penalties in the Piazza del Duomo, see *Statuta* 1:286–87.

29. *Statuta* 1:286–87.

30. *Chronicon Parmense,* 27.

31. *Statuta* 1:370.

32. Before 1228, *Statuta* 1:131–32.

33. *Dugaroli* oversaw certain communal projects as early as 1229; *Statuta* 1:146–51. Their responsibilities expanded quickly; *Statuta* 1:387, 286–87.

34. *Statuta* 1:378.

35. *Statuta* 1:76–77, 364, 100–101. For the role of religious in communal administration, see the Arts and Humanitites Research Council research project "Religion and Public Life in Late Medieval Italy c. 1250–1450," directed by Frances Andrews of the University of Saint Andrews, at http://www.ahrc.ac.uk/FundedResearch/Pages/ResearchDetail.aspx?id=128781, as well as the project's forthcoming publications, Frances Andrews, *Regular Bureaucrats,* and Frances Andrews and Agata Pincelli, eds., *Religion and Public Life.*

36. *Statuta* 2:98–99.

37. See note 61 to chapter 1. *Chronicon Parmense,* 164.

Chapter 4

1. Le Goff, "Tentative des conclusions," and idem, "L'immaginario urbano."

2. Le Goff, "Tentative des conclusions," 444–46; Trachtenberg, *Dominion of the Eye,* 245–73; Friedman, *Florentine New Towns,* 39–49.

3. My arguments below reprise passages from Marina, "Magnificent Architecture," 199–209.

4. Jones, *Italian City-State,* passim.

5. Hyde, "Medieval Descriptions of Cities"; Beneš, "Roman Foundations."

6. Meredith, "The Arch at Capua." For a biography of the emperor, see Abulafia, *Frederick II.*

7. A contemporary reports: "Et quia scivit quod antique magnate respiciebant ascendens, cum volebant condere civitatis, et faciebant ipsimet urvum cum aratro, quo circumdabat civitates"; Rolandini Patavini, "Cronica Marchie Trivixane," 84. For ancient Roman city foundation practices, see Owens, *City in the Greek and Roman World,* 9. Isidore of Seville describes the ritual; *Etymologies* xv.ii.3–4.

8. Isidore of Seville, *Etymologies* xv.viii.13, xix.x, xix.xiii.

9. According to Reynolds and Wilson, classical manuscripts, including those of Vitruvius, "were so thick on the shelves of the libraries that their survival was no longer in question." Reynolds and Wilson, *Scribes and Scholars,* 101.

10. Mansuelli, "Il commercio delle pietre veronesi."

11. Greenhalgh, "*Ipsa ruina docet,*" 123–28.

12. For the use of spolia in medieval Italy, see De Lachenal, *Spolia,* 145–247, with further bibliography, and Kinney, "Roman Architectural Spolia." For the prestige and reuse of ancient marbles throughout the medieval Mediterranean, see Greenhalgh, *Marble Past.*

13. Rockwell, "La decorazione plastica." Both original statues have been moved to the new diocesan museum for safekeeping; they have been replaced by copies on the baptistery's exterior.

14. For the problems presented by the imprecise period style label "Romanesque," see Fernie, "Romanesque Architecture"; O'Keeffe, *Archaeology and the Pan-European Romanesque;* and Trachtenberg, "Gothic/Italian 'Gothic.'"

15. The remains of the Septizodium stood on the Palatine Hill in Rome until 1588.

16. Dall'Aglio, "Il disegno urbano," and Marini Calvani, "Parma nell'antichità."

17. *Chronicon Parmense,* 48, 151.

18. Several editions of these texts exist; in English translation, see Morgan Nichols, *The Marvels of Rome,* and Osborne, *Master Gregorius: The Marvels of Rome.*

19. *DBP,* s.v. "Rossi Ugolino di Giacomo."

20. A volume dedicated to the theme, emerging from a 2009 conference held at the University of Illinois, has begun to redress this lacuna. See Jaeger, *Magnificence and the Sublime.* For the question in general, see Jaeger, introduction to *Magnificence and the Sublime;* idem, "Richard of St. Victor and the Medieval Sublime"; and Williamson, "How Magnificent Was Medieval Art?" For the question in relation

to architectural patronage, see esp. Binski, "Reflections," and Marina, "Magnificent Architecture."

21. Aristotle, *Nicomachean Ethics* 4.1–2; Jenkins, "Cosimo de' Medici's Patronage"; Goldthwaite, *Wealth and the Demand for Art,* 220–21.

22. Aristotle, *Nicomachean Ethics* 4.2; idem, *Politics* 6.7; Albertus Magnus, "Politicorum," 599, as observed by Spilner, "Giovanni di Lapo Ghini," 457–61.

23. For the medieval reception of Aristotelian magnificence, see Spilner, "Giovanni di Lapo Ghini," 457–61, and Onians, *Bearers of Meaning,* 123–25. Aquinas, *Summa theologica* II-II, q. 13, and *In decem libros Ethicorum Aristotelis,* 240–49; Orfino da Lodi, *De regimine et sapientia potestatis,* 21.609–82; Flamma [Fiamma], "Opusculum de rebus gestis ab Azone, Luchino et Johanne Vicecomitibus"; Green, "Galvano Fiamma."

24. Suetonius, *Augustus,* 167; for the whole of Suetonius's passage on Augustus's architectural patronage, see 166–71 (or sections 28.3–30.2).

25. Aristotle, *Nichomachean Ethics* 4.1; Keen, *Chivalry,* 52, 82, 237.

26. Miller, "Religion Makes a Difference," 1124.

27. Salimbene, *Cronica* (Scalia ed.), 38.16–21; Baird does not translate the first section of Salimbene's chronicle, which is heavily indebted to the earlier chronicle of Sicardus of Cremona (*PL* 313).

28. *Chronicle of Salimbene,* 46.

29. Indeed, both Roland and Oliver are names repeatedly found in the Adam lineage. Percivallo Fieschi was Pope Adrian V's nephew. Roland is the protagonist of the *Chanson de Roland,* a late eleventh-century text that remained intensely popular in the twelfth and thirteenth centuries; Oliver is his sidekick. Percival is the Arthurian knight who seeks the Holy Grail, as in Chrétien de Troyes's *Le roman de Perceval* or *Le conte du Graal* (c. 1090). For chivalric names in late medieval north Italy, see Guyotjeannin, "L'onomastique émilienne." For the vogue for French chivalric romances in twelfth- and thirteenth-century Italy, see the work of Daniela Delcorno Branca, with further bibliography; a good introduction to the theme is Delcorno Branca, "Tavola rotonda."

30. Witt, *"In the Footsteps of the Ancients,"* 42–43.

31. It also recalls Saint Martin's generous deed; *Chronicle of Salimbene,* 643.

32. *Chronicle of Salimbene,* 7.

33. *Chronicon Parmense,* 165, 188–89. Though Bishop Simone is renowned for his artistic patronage—he sponsored the decoration of the Spanish Chapel at Santa Maria Novella in Florence and the frescoes in the Campo Santo of Pisa—he is not associated with any major artistic projects in Parma.

34. *Chronicle of Salimbene,* 616. Jacopo died while in office, and Salimbene reports that his tomb monument in Modena cathedral portrayed him "with honor" as a knight on horseback; *Chronicle of Salimbene,* 612.

35. These images of soldiers at war can also be understood allegorically, as part of a Christian tradition that calls for spiritual warfare against evil—for example, Ephesians 6:10–19.

36. Racine, "Noblesse et chevalerie," 139. The lady's name is Winlogee; she is the wife of King Yder of Cornwall, the hero of an anonymous French Arthurian romance, *Le roman d'Yder.* Frugoni, *La Porta della Pescheria.*

37. *Chronicon Parmense,* 33, 39, and 80.

38. *Statuta* 1:342.

39. Reynolds and Wilson, *Scribes and Scholars,* 112.

40. Martines, *Power and Imagination,* 127–29; Quaglioni, "The Legal Definition of Citizenship," 160–63; Skinner, *Visions of Politics,* 2:10–117, esp. 23–27, including the Sallust quote on p. 23; Milner, "Citing the *Ringhiera.*"

41. For example, "pro bono et honore et utilitate consorcii e populi parmenses"; *Statuta* 1:398. Similarly, *Statuta* 1:86, 354, 377, 394, 472.

42. *Chronicle of Salimbene,* 187: "In this miniature appeared all the major and principal buildings of the city completely constructed in silver, like the major church. . . . The baptistery was also there and the bishop's palace and the community palace and as many buildings as were necessary for a good likeness of the city."

43. Foucault, *Discipline and Punish,* esp. 195–228.

44. For examples of civic processions elsewhere, see Thompson, *Cities of God,* 156–60.

45. No medieval service books specifying the path of Parma's religious processions survives—the earliest extant, *Ordinarium Ecclesiae Parmensis* (edited by Barbieri in 1864), dates from 1417—nor do specific instructions for lay processions and ceremonies. Nonetheless, some customary practices can be ascertained by combining references in various contemporary texts, for example, *Chronicon Parmense,* 103, 219.

46. Milner, "Communication, Consensus, and Conflict," 375; Hertter, *Podestàliteratur Italiens*; Franchini, *L'istituto del podestà*, 223–64; Pozzi, introduction to *De regimine et sapientia potestatis.*

47. For example, in Cicero's repeated references to the forum, rostra, and senate-house in *De officiis* 2:4, 3:1, 3:30. For a stimulating analysis of Cicero's manipulation of place and space, see Vasaly, *Representations.*

48. For example, the city's *carroccio* was paraded in the cathedral square in 1281; *Chronicon Parmense*, 38. Jousting, music, and dancing in the cathedral and communal squares followed the installation of King John of Bohemia as lord of Parma in 1331; *Chronicon Parmense*, 212–13. (He lost the city the following year.)

49. *Chronicon Parmense*, 219:

Die 2 junij martedì [1332], dominus Castellanus de Beccaria de Papia, per dictum dominum regem factus vicarius seu rector et potestas civitatis Parme, et ipsa die in hora tercia venit Parmam et ivit ad ecclesiam maiorem ad offerendum more solito, et, facta oblatione, ivit ad dominum Carolum, filium dicti domini regis, existentem in palatio episcopatus, et ibi coram domino Carolo juravit regere ad beneplacitum et ad mandata regie maiestatis; quo facto, venit ad plateam, sonantibus campanis turris communitatis, et ivit ad scalas palatij communis domini capitanei, et absque alia solenitate, et per ipsas scalas ascendit palacium communis et domum dictam potestatis; et incontinenti ipsa die et hora incepit regere et mittere banum regiminis more solito; et predecessor non ascendit sed discessit et ivit ad ospitandum quo voluit in Parma.

50. *Chronicon Parmense*, 102–3:

Item eodem tempore [1307] et predicta die lune xiij novembris, quidam miles de civitate Senarum, qui rediebat a regimine civitatis Brixia, ubi per sex menses stererat pro potestate, cui nomen erat Gucius de Malavoltis, com esset hospitatus in burgo sancte Christine cum certa sua familia, invitatus fuit si volebat esse potestas Parme; et, facto sibi magno salario, dictum et factum simul completum fuit, et sic et tali modo ellectus fuit potestas Parma usque ad kalendas mensis julij proxime venturi; et eodem die venit ab hospitio in quo erat ad palatium communis pedes, asociatus a pluribus bonis hominibus civitatis Parme, et ascendit palatium per scalas palatij ante domum potestatis; et cum fuit in palatio, juravit regimen, sine quod aliter sonarent consilium vel arenghum, et eadem die regimen incipit.

51. Foucault, *Discipline and Punish*, 221–22; Bentham, *Panopticon*, 21–24.

52. *Statuta* 1:4, 8–9.

53. For example, the accuser got to keep half the fine paid by someone convicted of blaspheming on the via Emilia; *Statuta* 1:319.

54. Foucault, *Discipline and Punish*, 225–28.

55. *Movimenti di piazza* are recorded in 1247, 1303, 1308, and 1331; see *Chronicon Parmense*, 13–14, 85, 105–6, and 212–13.

56. *Chronicon Parmense*, 13–14.

57. *Chronicon Parmense*, 85:

Item eodoem die et festo sancti Jacobi, post nonam, existente predicto domino Ghiberto de Corigia, filio condam domini Guidonis de Corigia, sub porticu sancti Vitalis com multitudine magna amicorum suorum et com multis de predictis qui redierant, per multos eorum omnium cridatum fuit "Vivat, vivat, vivat dominus Ghibertus" et sic omnes alij existentes per plateam, curentes ad rumorem, omnes clamabant similiter "Vivat, vivat" et tandem dictus dominus Ghibertus per forciam portatus fuit in palatio veteri communis, clamantibus omnibus eodem modo "Vivat, vivat." Et incontinenti factum et sonatum fuit conscilium, et totum palacium plenum omnino fuit de hominibus; et in ipso conscilio factus et vocatus fuit dictus dominus Ghibertus dominus et defensor et protector civitatis, communis et populi Parme, et conservator pacis predicte; et ibi in eodem conscilio investitus fuit de dicto dominio cum vexilo beate Marie et carocij, quod ibi aportatum fuit.

58. *Chronicon Parmense*, 105–6:

Insuper rustici, qui venerant com dicto Rolandino Scorça et ab aliis partibus, et ribaldi et alie viles persone ascenderunt palatia communis, vetus et nova, et domos potestatis et capitanei et gabelle et judicis exactoris averis communis, qui stabat in palatio novo communis, et omnes libros banorum ad taschas maleficiorum et actorum novorum et veterum et reformacionum communis et populi Parme et condepnationum existentes ibi in ipsis domibus et palatiis, fractis omnibus archimbanchis, universaliter astulerunt et fregerunt et delaceraverunt et de fenestris in platea proiecerunt ad modum nevolarum, ita quod tota platea erat plena de cartis laceratis, et tali modo predicti rustici cançelati sunt de suis banis et sua debita persolverunt; robas vero dictorum potestatis et capitani et familie eorum et dicti judicis et arnese eorum spoliaverunt. Etiam multi alij cucurerunt ad palatiium episcopatus, ubi residebat idem dominus Ghibertus com familia sua, et similiter libros et alias scripturas ibi existentes et arnese et robas dicti domini Ghiberti et familie sue totaliter spoliaverunt et abstulerunt.

59. First, Parma fell to local lord Ghiberto da Correggio in 1303. Then, after brief interludes of communal rule, papal rule, and imperial rule, as well as a few short-lived local lordships, Cangrande della Scala became Parma's *signore* in 1334. In 1341, the della Scala were chased out by the da Correggio, who had helped them to power. The da Correggio sold Parma to Òbizzo d'Este, who retained it until 1346. Luchino Visconti took over the city in 1346. Bernini, *Storia di Parma,* 71–80.

60. *Chronicon Parmense,* 154.

61. *Statuta* 4:ix–x. The sealing-off of communal piazzas in their conquered territory was standard Visconti practice; see Racine, "Les Visconti," and Spigaroli, "Piazza in ostaggio." For the fortified enclosure's postmedieval fate, see Covini, "L'urbanistica e la fortificazione," 52–54.

62. Lefebvre, *Production of Space,* 39.

63. Ibid., 222.

Epilogue

1. For Pisa, see Guidoni, *Arte e urbanistica,* 49–52; Smith, *Baptistery of Pisa,* esp. 214–32; and Trachtenberg, *Dominion of the Eye,* 297 n. 147.

2. Trachtenberg, *Dominion of the Eye,* 17–21.

3. For Pisa, see note 1 above. For Siena, see Cunningham, "For the Honour and Beauty of the City," and Grossman, "*Pro Honore Comunis Senensis,*" 356–62. For Florence, see Trachtenberg, *Dominion of the Eye,* passim, esp. 251–71.

4. Friedman, *Florentine New Towns.*

Appendix I

1. Mancini found the same problem in the case of the baptistery; Mancini, "Il Battistero," 65.

2. My conclusions have evolved since my earlier discussion of this question. Cf. Marina, "Order and Ideal Geometry," 544–45.

3. V. Banzola, "Antiche misure," 139.

4. Ibid., 157–75; *Tavole di ragguaglio;* Haros, *Compendio sulle nuove misure.*

5. For example, it was used to plan many small churches in Tuscany; Mandelli and Rossi, *Percorsi religiosi.*

6. Addis, "Measure and Proportion," 59.

7. In 1803, the Parmesan authorities replaced the alien names of the new metric dimensions with the old measurement nomenclature, so that the new 10-meter measure elsewhere called a *decametro,* or decameter, was called a *pertica* in Parma; the new 10-centimeter measure, the decimeter, was called a *palmo;* and so on. V. Banzola, "Antiche misure," 159.

8. For a new study of the metrological culture of medieval Lombardy, see Lugli, "Hidden in Plain Sight."

9. Ascani, *Trecento disegnato,* 150–56.

10. V. Banzola, "Antiche misure," 159.

11. Fernie, introduction to *Ad Quadratum,* 2.

12. Fernie summarizes the recommended approach in ibid., 1–9. For further bibliography on medieval architectural metrology, see also Fernie, "Historical Metrology," and Wu, *Ad Quadratum.*

13. Mancini believes that the baptistery's design is based on the Roman *pes,* and is comfortable with up to 5 percent dimensional variation; Mancini, "Il Battistero," 66–67.

14. Fernie, introduction to *Ad Quadratum,* 7–8.

Bibliography

Abulafia, David. *Frederick II: A Medieval Emperor.* London: Allen Lane, 1988.

Accademia della Crusca. *Vocabolario degli Accademici della Crusca.* Venice: Giovanni Alberti, 1612.

Adani, Giuseppe. *Piazze e palazzi pubblici in Emilia Romagna.* Milan: Silvana, 1984.

Addis, James. "Measure and Proportion in Romanesque Architecture." In *Ad Quadratum: The Practical Application of Geometry in Medieval Architecture,* edited by Nancy Y. Wu, 57–82. London: Ashgate, 2002.

Adorni, Bruno. "Parma rinascimentale e barocca: Dalla dominazione sforzesca alla venuta dei Borboni." In *Parma: La città storica,* edited by Vincenzo Banzola, 149–202. Parma: Cassa di Risparmio di Parma, 1978.

Adorni, G[iovanni]. "Palazzo Bondani." *L'Annotatore* 2 (1858): 176.

Affò, Ireneo. *Memorie di Alberto e di Obizzo Sanvitali vescovi di Parma nel secolo XIII, raccolte dal P. Ireneo Affò.* Venice: Stamperia Coleti, 1784.

———. *Storia della città di Parma.* 4 vols. Parma: Stamperia Carmignani, 1792–95. Facsimiles published in Bologna, 1956, and Parma, 1956–57.

Albertus Magnus. "Politicorum libri VIII." In *Opera Omnia,* edited by Auguste Borgnet. Paris: Louis Vivès, 1891.

Allodi, Giovanni Maria. *Serie cronologica dei vescovi di Parma con alcuni cenni sui principali avvenimenti civili.* 2 vols. Parma: Fiaccadori, 1854.

Amore, Agostino. "Ercolano, santo, martire di Roma." In *Bibliotheca Sanctorum,* vol. 4, cols. 1308–9. Rome: Istituto Giovanni XXIII della Pontificia Università Lateranense, 1964.

Angeli, Bonaventura. *Historia della città di Parma et descrittione del fiume Parma.* Parma: Erasmo Viotti, 1591.

Aquinas, Thomas. *In decem libros Ethicorum Aristotelis ad Nichomachum expositio.* Turin: Marietti, 1932.

Aristotle. *Nicomachean Ethics.* Edited and translated by W. D. Ross. Oxford: Clarendon Press, 1908.

———. *Politics.* Translated by Benjamin Jowett. Oxford: Clarendon Press, 1885.

Artifoni, Enrico. "I podestà professionali e la fondazione retorica della politica comunale." *Quaderni storici* 63 (1986): 687–719.

———. "Sull'eloquenza politica del Duecento italiano." In *Federico II e le città italiane,* edited by Pierre Toubert and Agostino Paravicini Bagliani, 144–60. Palermo: Sellerio, 1994.

Ascani, Valerio. *Il Trecento disegnato: Le basi progettuali dell'architettura gotica in Italia.* Rome: Viella, 1997.

Bandieri, Giovanni. "I Rossi di Parma dalle origini alla metà del secolo XIII." Pt. 1. *Archivio storico per le province parmensi,* 4th ser., 29 (1977): 247–77.

———. "I Rossi di Parma dalle origini alla metà del secolo XIII." Pt. 2. *Archivio storico per le province parmensi,* 4th ser., 30 (1978): 195–225.

Banzola, Maria Ortensia. "Il Palazzo del Vescovado." *Parma nell'arte* 14 (1982): 25–51.

Banzola, Maria Ortensia, and Walter Ferri. "Il Vescovado: Il rilevamento fotogrammetrico." *Parma nell'arte* 13 (1981): n.p., between pp. 130 and 131.

Banzola, Vincenzo. "Le antiche misure parmigiane e l'introduzione del sistema metrico decimale negli Stati Parmensi." *Archivio storico per le province parmensi,* 4th ser., 18 (1966): 139–78.

———. *Il centro storico di Parma: Sue origini e suo sviluppo.* Quaderni del Centro Studi Urbanistici di Parma, 2. Parma: La Nazionale, 1967.

———, ed. *Parma: La città storica.* Parma: Cassa di Risparmio di Parma, 1978.

———. "Parma barbarica: Dal tardo antico ai Franchi." In *Parma: La città storica,* edited by Vincenzo Banzola, 71–82. Parma: Cassa di Risparmio di Parma, 1978.

———. "Parma e l'urbanistica." *Parma nell'arte* 3 (1971): 105–10.

Barbieri, L. Aloisius, ed. *Chronica Parmensia a Sec. XI. ad Exitum Sec. XIV.* Parma: Fiaccadori, 1858.

———, ed. *Ordinarium Ecclesiae Parmensis e Vetustioribus Excerptum Reformatum A. MCCCCXVII.* Monumenta Historica ad Provincias Parmensem et Placentinam Pertinentia. Parma: Fiaccadori, 1864.

Barocelli, Francesco. "San Vitale: Il profilo della storia." In *La Chiesa di San Vitale: Il monumento ritrovato,* edited by Francesco Barocelli, 15–21. Milan: Mazzotta, 2005.

Baron, Hans. "Cicero and the Roman Civic Spirit in the Middle Ages and the Early Renaissance." *Bulletin of the John Rylands Library* 22 (1937): 72–97.

Baxandall, Michael. *Painting and Experience in Fifteenth Century Italy: A Primer in the Social History of Pictorial Style.* Oxford: Clarendon Press, 1972.

Belletti, Caterina, and Maria Angela Cavazzini. "Sub pede turris: Il Palazzo Comunale e l'evoluzione del nucleo civico a Parma tra XII e XX secolo." Politecnico di Milano, Facoltà di Architettura, Dipartimento di Conservazione e Storia dell'Architettura, 1997.

Benassi, Umberto, ed. *Codice diplomatico parmense.* Vol. 1. Parma: Reale Deputazione di Storia Patria, 1910.

Benassi, Umberto, and Tullo Bazzi. *Storia di Parma.* Parma: Battei, 1908.

Beneš, Carrie Elizabeth. "Roman Foundations: Constructing Civic Identity in Late Medieval Italy." Ph.D. diss., University of California, Los Angeles, 2004.

Bentham, Jeremy. *Panopticon; or, The Inspection-House.* Dublin: Thomas Byrne, 1791.

———. *The Works of Jeremy Bentham, Published Under the Superintendence of His Executor, John Bowring.* Edited by William Tait. Vol. 4. Edinburgh: Simpkin, Marshall & Co., 1843.

Bernini, Ferdinando. "La prima signoria in Parma, Giberto della Gente." *Aurea Parma* 25, no. 4 (1941): 132–43.

———. *Storia di Parma.* 3rd ed. Parma: Luigi Battei, 1979.

Bertelli, Sergio. *Il potere oligarchico nello stato-città medioevale.* Florence: Nuova Italia, 1978.

Bertini, Giuseppe. "L' entrata solenne di Maria di Portogallo a Parma nel 1566." In *D. Maria de Portugal princesa de Parma (1565–1577) e o seu tempo,* 69–84. Porto: Centro Interuniversitário de História da Espiritualidade, 1999.

Bianchi, Alfredo, and Manuela Catarsi Dall'Aglio, eds. *Il Museo Diocesano di Parma.* Parma: Silva, 2004.

Binski, Paul. "Reflections on the 'Wonderful Height and Size' of Gothic Great Churches and the Medieval Sublime." In *Magnificence and the Sublime in Medieval Aesthetics: Art, Architecture, Literature, and Music,* edited by C. Stephen Jaeger, 129–56. New York: Palgrave Macmillan, 2010.

Black, Robert. *Humanism and Education in Medieval and Renaissance Italy: Tradition and Innovation in Latin Schools from the Twelfth to the Fifteenth Centuries.* Cambridge: Cambridge University Press, 2001.

Blasi, Carlo, and Eva Coïsson, eds. *La fabbrica del Duomo di Parma.* Parma: Grafiche STEP Editrice, 2006.

———. "La geometria della fabbrica." In *La fabbrica del Duomo di Parma,* edited by Carlo Blasi and Eva Coïsson, 103–9. Parma: Grafiche STEP Editrice, 2006.

Bocchi, Francesca. "Città e campagne nell'Italia centrosettentrionale (secc. XII–XIV)." *Storia della città* 10 (1986): 101–4.

———. "Il disegno della città negli atti pubblici dal XII al XIV secolo." In *Il millennio ambrosiano: La nuova città dal Comune alla Signoria,* edited by Carlo Bertelli, 208–37. Milan: Electa, 1989.

———. "Normativa urbanistica, spazi pubblici, disposizioni antinquinamento nella legislazione comunale emiliana." In *Attraverso le città italiane nel Medioevo,* edited by Francesca Bocchi, 107–24. Bologna: Grafis, 1987.

———. "La Piazza Maggiore di Bologna." In *La Piazza del Duomo nella città medievale (nord e media Italia, secoli XII–XVI): Atti della giornata di studio, Orvieto, 4 giugno 1994,* edited by Lucio Riccetti, 135–46. Orvieto: Istituto Storico Artistico Orvietano, 1997.

Bolton Holloway, Julia. "The Road Through Roncesvalles: Alfonsine Formation of Brunetto Latini and Dante— Diplomacy and Literature." In *Emperor of Culture: Alfonso X the Learned of Castile and His Thirteenth-Century Renaissance,* edited by Robert I. Burns, 109–23. Philadelphia: University of Pennsylvania Press, 1990.

Bonazzi, Giuliano, ed. *Chronicon Parmense: Ab anno*

MXXXVIII usque ad annum MCCCXXXVIII. Rerum Italicarum Scriptores: Raccolta degli storici italiani dal cinquecento al millecinquecento, edited by Ludovico A. Muratori, Giosuè Carducci, and Vittorio Fiorini, 9.9. Città di Castello: S. Lapi, 1902.

Boucheron, Patrick. "De l'urbanisme communal à l'urbanisme seigneurial: Cités, territoires et édilité publique en Italie du Nord (XIIIe–XVe siècle)." In Pouvoir et édilité: Les grands chantiers dans l'Italie communale et seigneuriale; Études réunies par Elisabeth Crouzet-Pavan, 41–77. Rome: École Française de Rome, 2003.

Branner, Robert. Saint Louis and the Court Style in Gothic Architecture. London: Zwemmer, 1965.

Braunfels, Wolfgang. Mittelalterliche Stadtbaukunst in der Toskana. Berlin: Verlag Gebr. Mann, 1953.

Brezzi, Paolo. I comuni cittadini italiani: Origine e primitiva costituzione (secoli X–XIII). Milan: Istituto per gli Studi di Politica Internazionale Varese, 1940.

———. "Politica, vita economica, istituzioni, strutture urbanistiche nelle città italiane del Medioevo." Quaderni catanesi 1 (1979): 417–34.

Brogiolo, Gian Pietro. "A proposito dell'organizzazione urbana nell'alto Medioevo." Archeologia medievale 14 (1987): 27–46.

———. "Ideas of the Town in Italy During the Transition from Antiquity to the Middle Ages." In The Idea and the Ideal of the Town Between Late Antiquity and the Early Middle Ages, edited by Bryan Ward-Perkins and Gian Pietro Brogiolo, 98–126. Leiden: Brill, 1999.

———. Le città nell'alto Medioevo italiano. Rome: Laterza, 1998.

Brucker, Gene. "Civic Traditions in Premodern Italy." Journal of Interdisciplinary History 29 (1999): 357–78.

Brühl, Carlrichard. "Königs-, Bischofs- und Stadtpfalz in den Städten des 'Regnum Italiae' von 9. bis zum 13. Jahrhundert." In Historische Forschungen für Walter Schlesinger, edited by Helmut Beumann, 400–419. Cologne: Böhlau Verlag, 1974.

———. "'Palatium' e 'Civitas' in Italia dall'epoca tardo-antica fino all'epoca degli Svevi." In I problemi della civiltà comunale: Atti del Congresso storico internazionale per l'VIII centenario della prima Lega lombarda 1967, edited by Cosimo Damiano Fonseca, 157–66. Bergamo: Comune di Bergamo, 1971.

———. "Il 'palazzo' nelle città italiane." In La coscienza cittadina nei comuni italiani del Duecento, Convegno, 11, edited by Centro di Studi della Spiritualità Medievale, 265–69. Todi: Presso l'Accademia Tudertina, 1972.

Bruzelius, Caroline. The Stones of Naples: Church Building in Angevin Italy, 1266–1343. New Haven: Yale University Press, 2004.

Cadei, Antonio. Review of Battistero di Parma, by Arturo Carlo Quintavalle. Arte medievale, 2nd ser., 5, no. 1 (1991): 212–16.

Calzona, Arturo. "I maestri campionesi e la 'Lombardia': L'architettura del Battistero di Parma." In Medioevo: Arte lombarda, edited by Arturo Carlo Quintavalle, 367–87. Milan: Electa, 2004.

Camargo, Martin. Ars Dictaminis, Ars Dictandi. Turnhout: Brepols, 1991.

Cammarosano, Paolo. Italia medievale: Struttura e geografia delle fonti scritte. Rome: Nuova Italia Scientifica, 1991.

Campi, Antonio. Cremona fedelissima città et nobilissima colonia de Romani rappresentata in disegno col suo contado: Et illustrata d'una breve historia delle cose più notabili appartenenti ad essa et dei ritratti naturali de duchi et duchesse di Milano e compendio delle lor vite. Cremona: Hippolito Tromba & Hercoliano Bartoli, 1585.

Canali, Guido, and Vittorio Savi. "Parma neoclassica: Architettura e città dai primi ai secondi Borboni." In Parma: La città storica, edited by Vicenzo Banzola, 203–75. Parma: Cassa di Risparmio di Parma, 1978.

Capacchi, Guglielmo. Castelli parmigiani. Parma: Silva, 1997.

Capelli, Gianni. Piazza Grande: Da Parma romana al Duemila. Parma: Battei, 1989.

Carrari, Vincenzo. Historia de' Rossi parmigiani. Vol. 1. Ravenna: Francesco Tebaldini, 1583.

Cassidy, Brendan. Politics, Civic Ideals, and Sculpture in Italy, c. 1240–1400. London: Harvey Miller, 2007.

Catarsi, Manuela. "Parma tra età romana e Medioevo: Trasformazioni urbanistiche e aspetti di vita quotidiana, il contributo dell'archeologia." In Vivere il Medioevo: Parma al tempo della cattedrale, edited by Giovanna Damiani, 21–34. Cinisello Balsamo: Silvana, 2006.

———. "Storia di Parma: Il contributo dell'archeologia." In

Parma romana, edited by Domenico Vera, 367–499. Parma: Monte Università Parma, 2009.

Catarsi Dall'Aglio, Manuela, and Massimo Fava. *Museo diocesano.* Parma: Fondazione Cassa di Risparmio di Parma, 2003.

Cattaneo, Enrico. "Il battistero in Italia dopo il mille." In *Miscellanea Gilles Gérard Meersseman,* 171–95. Padua: Antenore, 1970.

Cavalieri, Marco. "La basilica civile nel *de Architectura* di Vitruvio: Prassi e codificazione in Italia e a Parma." *Archivio storico per le province parmensi,* 4th ser., 53 (2001): 517–33.

Censi, Umberto Primo. "Il declino del capitolo della cattedrale di Parma nei secoli XI–XIV." *Archivio storico per le province parmensi,* 4th ser., 43 (1991): 335–86.

Cherubini, Giovanni. "La Piazza del Duomo nelle città dell'Italia centro-settentrionale tra il XII e il XV secolo." In *La Piazza del Duomo nella città medievale (nord e media Italia, secoli XII–XVI): Atti della giornata di studio, Orvieto, 4 giugno 1994,* edited by Lucio Riccetti, 11–18. Orvieto: Istituto Storico Artistico Orvietano, 1997.

Coleman, Edward. "The Italian Communes: Recent Work and Current Trends." *Journal of Medieval History* 25, no. 4 (1999): 373–97.

Comune di Parma. *Danni di guerra 1940–1945.* Photo album. Parma, 1949. ASCP.

Conant, Kenneth John. "The Third Church at Cluny." In *Medieval Studies in Memory of A. Kingsley Porter,* edited by Wilhelm R. W. Koehler, 327–58. Cambridge: Harvard University Press, 1939.

Conforti, Paolo. *Le mura di Parma.* Vol. 1, *Dalle origini alla soglie del Ducato (1545).* Parma: Luigi Battei, 1979.

Conforti, Paolo, and Cristina Erenda. "Il Battistero e il tracciato del Canale Maggiore." *Archivio storico per le province parmensi,* 4th ser., 48 (1996): 253–60.

Conversi, Roberta. "Le chiese e le necropoli urbane di età longobarda a Parma." *Archivio storico per le province parmensi,* 4th ser., 44 (1992): 233–48.

Copertini, Giovanni. "La Via Emilia e l'aspetto icnografico-artistico di Piacenza, Parma, Reggio e Modena." *Aurea Parma* 18, no. 1 (1934): 25–39.

Corradi Cervi, Maurizio. "Evoluzione topografica della Piazza Grande di Parma dall'epoca romana alla fine del secolo XIII." *Archivio storico per le province parmensi,* 4th ser., 14 (1962): 31–52.

Covini, Nadia. "L'urbanistica e la fortificazione della città in epoca sforzesca." In *Parma e l'umanesimo italiano: Atti del convegno internazionale di studi umanistici (Parma, 20 ottobre 1984),* 39–54. Padua: Antenore, 1986.

Cox, Virginia. "Ciceronian Rhetoric in Late Medieval Italy: The Latin and Vernacular Traditions." In *The Rhetoric of Cicero in Its Medieval and Early Renaissance Commentary Tradition,* edited by Virginia Cox and John O. Ward, 109–43. Leiden: Brill, 2006.

Cracco, Giorgio, ed. *Comuni e signorie nell'Italia nordorientale e centrale.* Vol. 1, *Veneto, Emilia-Romagna, Toscana.* Turin: UTET, 1987.

———. "Social Structure and Conflict in the Medieval City." In *City-States in Classical Antiquity and Medieval Italy: Athens and Rome, Florence and Venice,* edited by Anthony Molho, Kurt Raaflaub, and Julia Emlen, 309–29. Stuttgart: Franz Steiner, 1991.

Cramer, Peter. *Baptism and Change in the Early Middle Ages, c. 200–c. 1150.* Cambridge Studies in Medieval Life and Thought, 4th ser., 20. Cambridge: Cambridge University Press, 2002.

Crouzet-Pavan, Elisabeth. *Sopra le acque salse: Espaces, pouvoir et société à Venise à la fin du Moyen Âge.* Rome: École Française de Rome, 1992.

Cunningham, Colin. "For the Honour and Beauty of the City: The Design of Town Halls." In *Siena, Florence, and Padua: Art, Society, and Religion, 1280–1400,* edited by Diana Norman, 29–54. New Haven: Yale University Press, 1995.

Curtius, Ernst Robert. *European Literature and the Latin Middle Ages.* New York: Pantheon, 1953.

Dall'Aglio, Pier Luigi. "Il disegno urbano di Parma." In *Una città e la storia: Parma attraverso i secoli,* edited by Francesco Barocelli, 89–123. Parma: Comune di Parma, 2000.

———. *Parma e il suo territorio in età romana.* Quaderno, 5. Sala Baganza (Parma): Editoria Tipolitotecnica, 1990.

Dall'Aglio, Pier Luigi, and Manuela Catarsi. "L'anfiteatro di Parma." *Archivio storico per le province parmensi,* 4th ser., 47 (1995): 227–46.

Dalla Torre, Cristoforo. "Descriptio omnium civitatis et dioecesis Parmensis ecclesiarum, monasteriorum et beneficiorum in eis fundatorum." [1564.] In *La diocesi di Parma,* edited by Antonio Schiavi, 2:104–226. Parma: Fresching, 1940.

Da Mareto, Felice, ed. *Parma e Piacenza nei secoli: Piante e vedute cittadine delle antiche e nuove province parmensi.* Parma: La Nazionale, 1975.

Dean, Trevor. "The Rise of the *Signori*." In *The New Cambridge Medieval History, c. 1198–c. 1300,* edited by David Abulafia, 5:458–78. Cambridge: Cambridge University Press, 1999.

de Francovich, Gèza. *Benedetto Antelami, architetto e scultore e l'arte del suo tempo.* 2 vols. Milan: Electa, 1952.

De Giorgi, L. "Il Palazzo Vescovile." *Gazzetta di Parma* (1920).

De Lachenal, Lucia. *Spolia, uso e reimpiego dell'antico dal III al XIV secolo.* Milan: Longanesi, 1995.

Delcorno Branca, Daniela. "Tavola rotonda." In *Dizionario critico della letteratura italiana,* edited by Vittore Branca, 3:471–76. Turin: UTET, 1973.

Dezzi Bardeschi, Marco. "Il Duomo di Parma: Materiali per un'altra storia." In *Il Duomo di Parma: Materiali per un'altra storia,* edited by Gabriella Guarisco, 6–15. Florence: Alinea, 1992.

Drei, Giovanni. "L'antica torre del Comune di Parma." *Aurea Parma* 7, no. 4 (1923): 203–8.

———. *Le carte degli archivi parmensi dei secoli X–XI.* 2 vols. Parma: Fresching, 1924–28.

———. *Le carte degli archivi parmensi del secolo XII.* Parma: Archivio di Stato, 1950.

———. "Le decime del vescovo di Parma." *Archivio storico per le province parmensi,* n.s., 20 (1920): 1–46.

Duby, Georges, Giovanni Romano, Chiara Frugoni, Peter Rockwell, and Bruno Zanardi. *Il Battistero di Parma: La scultura.* Milan: Franco Maria Ricci, 1992.

Dunbabin, Jean. *Charles I of Anjou: Power, Kingship, and State-Making in Thirteenth-Century Europe.* London: Longman, 1998.

English, Edward D. "Urban Castles in Medieval Siena: The Sources and Images of Power." In *The Medieval Castle: Romance and Reality,* edited by Kathryn Reyerson and Faye Power, 175–98. Dubuque, Iowa: Kendall/Hunt, 1984.

Eusebio, Ludovico. *Compendio di metrologia universale e vocabolario metrologico.* Bologna: Forni, 1967.

Farioli Campanati, Raffaella. "Un'inedita fronte d'altare paleocristiano e una nuova ipotesi sulla cattedrale di Parma." *Feliz Ravenna* 127 30 (1985): 201 15.

———. "Note sul problema dell'ubicazione della cattedrale di Parma." In *La cattedrale in Italia (Actes du XIe Congres d'archéologie chretienne, Lyon, 1986),* edited by Pasquale Testini, Gisella Cantino Wataghin, and Letizia Pani Ermini, 1:249–55. Collection de l'École Française a Rome, 123, Vatican City: École Française, 1989.

Fava, Massimo. "Il complesso episcopale parmense tra tarda antichità e Medioevo: Dalla basilica paleocristiana alla cattedrale romanica." In *Vivere il Medioevo: Parma al tempo della cattedrale,* edited by Giovanna Damiani, 71–88. Cinisello Balsamo: Silvana, 2006.

Favro, Diane. "Meaning and Experience: Urban History from Antiquity to the Early Modern Period." *Journal of the Society of Architectural Historians* 58, no. 3 (1999): 367–68.

Fernie, Eric. "Historical Metrology and Architectural History." In *Romanesque Architecture: Design, Meaning, and Metrology,* 346–62. London: Pindar, 1995.

———. Introduction to *Ad Quadratum: The Practical Application of Geometry in Medieval Architecture,* edited by Nancy Y. Wu, 1–9. London: Ashgate, 2002.

———. "Romanesque Architecture." In *A Companion to Medieval Art: Romanesque and Gothic in Northern Europe,* edited by Conrad Rudolph, 295–313. Oxford: Blackwell, 2006.

Flamma, Gualvanei de la. "Opusculum de rebus gestis ab Azone, Luchino et Johanne Vicecomitibus ab anno MCCCXXVIII usque ad annum MCCCXLII." Edited by Carlo Castiglioni. In *Rerum Italicarum Scriptores,* rev. ed., edited by Giosuè Carducci, Vittorio Fiorini, and Pietro Fedele, vol. 12, pt. 4. Bologna: Zanichelli, 1938.

Foucault, Michel. *Discipline and Punish: The Birth of the Prison.* New York: Vintage, 1979. [Originally published in France as *Surveiller et punir: Naissance de la prison.* Paris: Gallimard, 1975.]

Franchini, Vittorio. *L'istituto del podestà dei comuni medievali.* Bologna: Zanichelli, 1912.

Frati, Marco. "Lo spazio del battesimo nelle campagne medievali." In *L'architettura del battistero: Storia e progetto,* edited by Andrea Longhi, 85–103. Milan: Skira, 2003.

Friedman, David. *Florentine New Towns: Urban Design in the Middle Ages.* Cambridge: MIT Press, 1988.

Frugoni, Chiara, ed. *Benedetto Antelami e il Battistero di Parma.* Turin: Giulio Einaudi, 1995.

———. *La Porta della Pescheria nel Duomo di Modena.* Modena: Franco Cosimo Panini, 1991.

Gambara, Lodovico, Marco Pellegri, and Marco de Grazia. *Palazzi e casate di Parma.* Parma: Nazionale, 1971.

Gatti, Vincenzo. "Battesimo, mistero dell'acqua nella storia della Salvezza: Le Scritture, i Padri, la liturgia." In *L'architettura del battistero,* edited by Andrea Longhi, 17–31. Milan: Skira, 2003.

Geymonat, Ludovico. "The Parma Baptistery and Its Pictorial Program." Ph.D. diss., Princeton University, 2006.

Ghidiglia Quintavalle, Augusta, and Egidio Guerra. *La Chiesa di S. Pietro Apostolo in Parma nella storia e nell'arte.* Parma: Fresching, 1948.

Giandebiaggi, Paolo, and Chiara Vernizzi. "Il Battistero di Parma: Analisi grafica e confronti nella morfologia urbana." *Archivio storico per le province parmensi,* 4th ser., 48 (1996): 283–89.

Ginatempo, Maria, and Lucia Sandri. *L'Italia delle città, il popolamento urbano tra Medioevo e Rinascimento (secoli XIII–XVI).* Florence: Le Lettere, 1998.

Goldthwaite, Richard. *Wealth and the Demand for Art in Italy, 1300–1600.* Baltimore: Johns Hopkins University Press, 1993.

Gonizzi, Giancarlo, ed. "Parma: L'immagine della città attraverso i secoli." Collegio dei Geometri della Provincia di Parma, http://biblioteche2.comune.parma.it/BibParma/Cartografia/PARMAICO.HTM (1997).

Greci, Roberto. *Parma medievale: Economia e società nel Parmense dal Tre al Quattrocento.* Parma: Battei, 1992.

Green, Louis. "Galvano Fiamma, Azzone Visconti, and the Revival of the Classical Theory of Magnificence." *Journal of the Warburg and Courtauld Institutes* 53 (1990): 98–113, pls. 9–10.

Greenhalgh, Michael. "*Ipsa ruina docet:* L'uso dell'antico nel Medioevo." In *Memoria dell'antico,* edited by Salvatore Settis, 1:115–70. Turin: Einaudi, 1984.

———. *Marble Past, Monumental Present: Building with Antiquities in the Medieval Mediterranean.* Leiden: Brill, 2008.

Grossman, Max Elijah. "*Pro Honore Comunis Senensis et Pulchritudine Civitatis:* Civic Architecture and Political Ideology in the Republic of Siena, 1270–1420." Ph.D. diss., Columbia University, 2006.

Gruber, Samuel D. "Medieval Todi: Studies in Architecture and Urbanism." Ph.D. diss., Columbia University, 1998.

Guarisco, Gabriella. *Il Duomo di Parma: Materiali per un' altra storia.* Florence: Alinea, 1992.

Guidoni, Enrico. *Arte e urbanistica in Toscana, 1000–1315.* Rome: Mario Bulzoni, 1970.

———. *La città dal Medioevo al Rinascimento.* Bari: Laterza, 1981.

———. "La storia delle piazze." *Storia della città* 15 (1993): 3–6.

———. *Storia dell'urbanistica: Il Duecento.* Rome: Laterza, 1990.

———. *Storia dell'urbanistica: Il Medioevo, secoli VI–XII.* Rome: Laterza, 1991.

———. "L'urbanistica dei comuni italiani in età federiciana." In *La città dal Medioevo al Rinascimento,* edited by Enrico Guidoni, 70–99. Bari: Laterza, 1981.

Guyotjeannin, Olivier. "L'onomastique émilienne (XIe–milieu XIIIe siècle)." *Mélanges de l'École Française de Rome: Moyen Âge–Temps modernes* 106 (1994): 381–446.

———. "Podestats d'Émilie centrale: Parme, Reggio et Modene (fin XIIe–milieu XIVe siècle)." In *I podestà dell'Italia comunale,* vol. 1, *Reclutamento e circolazione degli ufficiali forestieri (fine XII sec.–metà XIV sec.),* edited by Jean-Claude Maire Vigueur, 349–403. Rome: École Française de Rome, 2000.

Guzzon, Claudio. "Il Palazzo dell'Arena." *Archivio storico per le province parmensi,* 4th ser., 47 (1995): 247–61.

Haros, Ch. *Compendio sulle nuove misure introdotte nell'Impero francese: Con tavole di rapporto tra le nuove misure e le parmigiane.* Parma: Luigi Mussi, 1805.

Heers, Jacques. *Espaces publics, espaces privés dans la ville: Le "Liber terminorum" de Bologne (1294).* Cultures et civilisations médiévales, 3. Paris: Centre National de la Recherche Scientifique, 1984.

———. *Family Clans in the Middle Ages: A Study of Political and Social Structures in Urban Areas.* Amsterdam: North Holland, 1977.

———. *Parties and Political Life in the Medieval West.* Europe in the Middle Ages, edited by Richard Vaughan, 7. Amsterdam: North Holland, 1977.

Hertter, Fritz. *Die Podestàliteratur Italiens im 12. und 13. Jahrhundert.* Leipzig: B. G. Teubner, 1910.

Hiscock, Nigel. *The Wise Master Builder: Platonic Geometry in Plans of Medieval Abbeys and Cathedrals.* London: Ashgate, 2000.

Hise, Greg. "Architecture as State Building: A Challenge to the Field." *Journal of the Society of Architectural Historians* 67, no. 2 (2008): 173–76.

Horn, Walter. "Das Florentiner Baptisterium." *Mitteilungen des Kunsthistorischen Institutes in Florenz* 5, no. 2 (1938): 100–151.

Hyde, J. K. "Medieval Descriptions of Cities." *Bulletin of the John Rylands Library* 48 (1966): 308–40.

———. *Society and Politics in Medieval Italy: The Evolution of the Civil Life, 1000–1350.* London: Macmillan, 1973.

Incerti, Manuela. "Cosmo e architettura." In *Vivere il Medioevo: Parma al tempo della cattedrale,* edited by Giovanna Damiani, 130–33. Cinisello Balsamo: Silvana, 2006.

Isidore of Seville. *The Etymologies of Isidore of Seville.* Translated by Stephen A. Barney, W. J. Lewis, J. A. Beach, and Oliver Berghoff. Cambridge: Cambridge University Press, 2006.

Jaeger, C. Stephen. Introduction to *Magnificence and the Sublime in Medieval Aesthetics: Art, Architecture, Literature, and Music,* edited by C. Stephen Jaeger, 1–16. New York: Palgrave Macmillan, 2010.

———, ed. *Magnificence and the Sublime in Medieval Aesthetics: Art, Architecture, Literature, and Music.* New York: Palgrave Macmillan, 2010.

———. *The Origins of Courtliness: Civilizing Trends and the Formation of Courtly Ideals, 939–1210.* Philadelphia: University of Pennsylvania Press, 1985.

———. "Richard of St. Victor and the Medieval Sublime." In *Magnificence and the Sublime in Medieval Aesthetics: Art, Architecture, Literature, and Music,* edited by C. Stephen Jaeger, 157–78. New York: Palgrave Macmillan, 2010.

Janelli, Giovanni Battista. *Dizionario biografico dei parmigiani illustri.* Italica Gens, 97. Genoa: G. Schenone, 1877. Reprint, Bologna: Forni, 1978.

Jenkins, A. D. Fraser. "Cosimo de' Medici's Patronage of Architecture and the Theory of Magnificence." *Journal of the Warburg and Courtauld Institutes* 33 (1971): 162–70.

Jennings, Margaret. Introduction to *The Ars componendi sermones of Ranulph of Higden,* 1–23. Leiden: Brill, 1991.

Jones, Philip. "Economia e società nell'Italia medievale: La legenda della borghesia." In *Storia d'Italia: Dal feudalismo al capitalismo,* 187–372. Turin: Einaudi, 1978.

———. *The Italian City-State: From Commune to Signoria.* Oxford: Clarendon Press, 1997.

Keen, Maurice. *Chivalry.* New Haven: Yale University Press, 1984.

Keller, Hagen. "Zur Quellengattung der italienischen Stadtstatuten." In *La bellezza della città: Stadtrecht und Stadtgestaltung im Italien des Mittelalters und der Renaissance,* edited by Michael Stolleis and Ruth Wolff, 29–46. Tubingen: Max Niemeyer Verlag, 2004.

Kerscher, Gottfried. *Benedictus Antelami oder das Baptisterium von Parma: Kunst und kommunales Selbstverständnis.* Munich: W. Angerer, 1986.

Kinney, Dale. "Roman Architectural Spolia." *Proceedings of the American Philosophical Society* 145, no. 2 (2001): 138–49.

La Ferla, Graziella. "Parma nei secoli IX e X: 'Civitas' e 'suburbium.'" *Storia della città* 18 (1981): 5–32.

La Ferla Morselli, Graziella. "Fonti documentarie e fonti archeologiche: La cattedrale di Parma ed il suo rapporto con il *murus antiquus civitatis.*" *Archeologia medievale* 28 (2003): 571–82.

———, ed. *Liber iurium communis Parme.* Parma: Deputazione di Storia Patria per le Province Parmensi (La Nazionale Editrice), 1993.

Lansing, Carol. *The Florentine Magnates: Lineage and Faction in a Medieval Commune.* Princeton: Princeton University Press, 1991.

Latini, Brunetto. *Li Livres dou Tresor.* Berkeley: University of California Press, 1948.

———. *La rettorica.* Edited by Francesco Maggini. Preface by Cesare Segre. Florence: Le Monnier, 1968.

Lavedan, Henri, and Jeanne Hugueney. *L'urbanisme au Moyen Âge.* Paris: Arts et Metiers Graphiques, 1974.

Lefebvre, Henri. *The Production of Space.* London: Blackwell, 2000.

Le Goff, Jacques. "L'immaginario urbano nell'Italia medievale (secoli V–XV)." *Storia d'Italia, Annali* 5 (1982): 5–43.

———. "Tentative des conclusions." In *Les élites urbaines au Moyen Âge: XXVII Congrès de la Société des Historiens Médiévistes de l'Enseignement Supérieur Public, Rome, mai 1996,* 443–56. Collection de l'École Française de Rome, 238. Rome: École Française de Rome, 1997.

Le Goff, Jacques, Véronique Rouchon Mouilleron, Enrica Pagella, Massimo Ferretti, and Bruno Zanardi. *Il Battistero di Parma: La decorazione pittorica.* Milan: Franco Maria Ricci, 1993.

Lomartire, Saverio. "Introduzione all'architettura del Battistero di Parma." In *Benedetto Antelami e il Battistero di Parma,* edited by Chiara Frugoni, 145–250. Turin: Giulio Einaudi, 1995.

Longhi, Andrea. "Battisteri e scena urbana nell'Italia comunale." In *L' architettura del battistero: Storia e progetto,* edited by Andrea Longhi, 105–27. Milan: Skira, 2003.

Lopez, Michele. *Il Battistero di Parma.* 2 vols. Parma: Giacomo Ferrari, 1864.

Luchterhandt, Manfred. *Die Kathedrale von Parma: Architektur und Skulptur im Zeitalter von Reichskirche und Kommunebildung.* Römische Studien der Bibliotheca Hertziana, 24. Munich: Hirmer, 2009.

———. "Die Kathedrale von Parma: Untersuchungen zur Bauarchitektur und Kirchengeschichte im 11. und 12. Jahrhundert." Ph.D. diss., University of Würzburg, 1997.

Lugli, Emanuele. "Hidden in Plain Sight: The *Pietre di Paragone* and the Preeminence of Medieval Measurements in Communal Italy." *Gesta* (forthcoming).

Maire Vigueur, Jean-Claude, ed. *I podestà dell'Italia comunale: Reclutamento e circolazione degli ufficiali forestieri (fine XII sec.–metà XIV sec.).* 2 vols. Rome: École Française de Rome, 2000.

Mancini, Paolo. "Il Battistero di Parma: La geometria della forma costruita." Ph.D. diss., Università degli Studi di Firenze, 1998.

Mandelli, Emma, and Michela Rossi. *Percorsi religiosi nel Mugello: Pievi e pivieri.* Florence: Alinea, 1999.

Mansuelli, G. A. "Il commercio delle pietre veronesi nella regione VIII." In *Il territorio veronese in età romana,* 83–92. Verona: Accademia di Agricultura, Scienze e Lettere, 1973.

Marina, Areli. "Magnificent Architecture in Late Medieval Italy." In *Magnificence and the Sublime in Medieval Aesthetics: Art, Architecture, Literature, and Music,* edited by C. Stephen Jaeger, 193–214. New York: Palgrave Macmillan, 2010.

———. "Order and Ideal Geometry in Parma's Piazza del Duomo." *Journal of the Society of Architectural Historians* 65, no. 4 (2006): 520–49.

———. "The Urbanistic Transformation of Parma in the Age of the Commune, 1196–1347." Ph.D. diss., New York University, 2004.

Marini Calvani, Mirella. "Leoni funerari romani in Italia." *Bollettino d'arte* 6 (1980): 7–14.

———. "Parma nell'antichità." In *Parma: La città storica,* edited by Vicenzo Banzola, 18–67. Parma: Cassa di Risparmio di Parma, 1978.

Martindale, Andrew. *Gothic Art from the Twelfth to the Fifteenth Century.* New York: Praeger, 1967.

Martines, Lauro. *Power and Imagination: City-States in Renaissance Italy.* Baltimore: Johns Hopkins University Press, 1979.

Masini, Celide. "La cattedrale di Parma: Un problema aperto." *Corso di cultura sull'arte ravennate e bizantina* 42 (1995): 565–83.

McLean, Alick Macdonnel. *Prato: Architecture, Piety, and Political Identity in a Tuscan City-State.* New Haven: Yale University Press, 2008.

———. "Sacred Space and Public Policy: The Establishment, Decline, and Revival of Prato's Piazza della Pieve." Ph.D. diss., Princeton University, 1993.

Melli, Giuseppe. "La piazza maggiore di Parma nel Medioevo." *Aurea Parma* 1, nos. 3–4 (1912): 25–37.

Meredith, Jill. "The Arch at Capua: The Strategic Use of Spolia and References to the Antique." In *Intellectual Life at the Court of Frederick II Hohenstaufen,* edited by William Tronzo, 109–28. Washington, D.C.: National Gallery of Art, 1994.

Micalizzi, Paolo. *Storia dell'architettura e dell'urbanistica di Gubbio.* Rome: Officina, 1988.

Micheli, Giuseppe. "Le corporazioni parmensi d'arti e mestieri." *Archivio storico per le province parmensi* 5 (1896 [1899]): 3–115. Issued in 1903.

Miller, Maureen C. *The Bishop's Palace: Architecture and Authority in Medieval Italy.* Ithaca: Cornell University Press, 2000.

———. "From Episcopal to Communal Palaces: Places and Power in Northern Italy (1000–1250)." *Journal of the Society of Architectural Historians* 54, no. 2 (1995): 175–85.

———. "Religion Makes a Difference: Clerical and Lay Cultures in the Courts of Northern Italy, 1000–1300." *American Historical Review* 105 (October 2000): 1095–1130.

———. "Vescovi, palazzi e lo sviluppo dei centri civici nella civiltà dell'Italia settentrionale, 1000–1250." In *Albertano da Brescia: Alle origini del razionalismo* economico, del umanesimo civile, della grande Europa, 27–42. Brescia: Grafo, 1996.

Milner, Stephen J. "Citing the *Ringhiera:* The Politics of Place and Public Address in Trecento Florence." *Italian Studies* 55 (2000): 53–82.

———. "Communication, Consensus, and Conflict: Rhetorical Precepts, the *Ars Concionandi,* and Social Ordering in Late Medieval Italy." In *The Rhetoric of Cicero in Its Medieval and Early Renaissance Commentary Tradition,* edited by Virginia Cox and John O. Ward, 365–408. Leiden: Brill, 2006.

Minardi, Alessandro. "Il Vescovado di Parma dopo gli ultimi restauri." *Crisopoli* 3 (1935): 553–60.

Morigi, Alessia. "La città dentro la città: Le trasformazioni di Parma antica." In *Parma romana,* edited by Domenico Vera, 659–93. Parma: Monte Università Parma, 2009.

Muratori, L. A. "Oculus pastoralis sive libellus erudiens futurum rectorem populorum." In *Antiquitates Italicae Medii Aevi,* vol. 4, diss. XLVI [46], pp. 93–132. Milan, 1741.

Nasalli Rocca di Cornegliano, Emilio. "Le origini e la posizione politica dei Rossi." *Archivio storico per le province parmensi,* 4th ser., 21 (1969): 83–104.

———. "La posizione politica dei Sanvitale dell'età dei comuni a quella delle signorie." *Archivio storico per le province parmensi,* 4th ser., 23 (1971): 135–54.

Nichols, Francis Morgan, ed. *The Marvels of Rome (Mirabilia Urbis Romae).* 2nd ed. New York: Italica, 1986.

O'Keeffe, Tadhg. *Archaeology and the Pan-European Romanesque.* Duckworth Debates in Archaeology. London: Duckworth, 2007.

Onians, John. *Bearers of Meaning: The Classical Orders in Antiquity, the Middle Ages, and the Renaissance.* Princeton: Princeton University Press, 1988.

Orfino da Lodi. *De regimine et sapientia potestatis.* Introduction, translation, and notes by Sara Pozzi. Quaderni di studi lodigiani, edited by Sara Pozzi, 7. Lodi: Archivio Storico Lodigiano, 1998.

Osborne, John, ed. *Master Gregorius: The Marvels of Rome (Mirabilia Urbis Romae).* Toronto: Pontifical Institute of Medieval Studies, 1987.

Ottokar, Nicola. "Criteri d'ordine, di regolarità e d'organizzazione nell'urbanistica ed in genere nella vita

fiorentina dei secoli XIII–XIV." In *Studi comunali e fiorentini,* 143–49. Florence: Nuova Italia, 1948.

Owens, E. J. *The City in the Greek and Roman World.* London: Routledge, 1991.

Paetow, Louis J. *The Arts Course at Medieval Universities with Special Reference to Grammar and Rhetoric.* Champaign: University of Illinois Press, 1910.

Paolucci, Antonio. *Il Battistero di San Giovanni a Firenze: The Baptistery of San Giovanni, Florence.* Edited by Salvatore Settis. 2 vols. Modena: Franco Cosimo Panini, 1994.

Parmeggiano, G. "Sulla consistenza e caratteristiche architettoniche del Palazzo dell'Arena in Parma." *Aurea Parma* 53, no. 1 (1964): 66–73.

Paul the Deacon. *History of the Langobards by Paul the Deacon.* Edited and translated by William Dudley Foulke. Philadelphia: University of Pennsylvania, 1907.

Paul, Jürgen. "Commercial Use of Medieval Town Halls in Italy." *Journal of the Society of Architectural Historians* 28, no. 3 (1969): 222.

———. *Die mittelalterlichen Kommunalpäläste in Italien.* Diss., Albert-Ludwigs-Universität. Cologne, 1963.

Pelicelli, Nestore. *Palazzo Vecchio del Comune e Palazzo del Capitano del Popolo di Parma.* Parma: Fresching, 1927.

———. *Il Vescovado di Parma.* Parma: Fresching, 1922.

———. *I vescovi della chiesa parmense.* 2 vols. Parma: Officina Grafica Fresching, 1936.

Pellegri, Marco, ed. *Basilica cattedrale di Parma: Novecento anni di arte, storia, fede.* Vol. 2. Parma: Grafiche STEP Editrice, 2005.

———. "Parma medievale: Dai Carolingi agli Sforza." In *Parma: La città storica,* edited by Vincenzo Banzola, 84–148. Parma: Cassa di Risparmio di Parma, 1978.

Pezzana, Angelo. *Storia della città di Parma.* 5 vols. Parma: Ducale Tipografia, 1837–59. Facsimile published in Bologna, 1956.

La piazza nel Medioevo e Rinascimento nell'Italia settentrionale (Annali di architettura 4–5 [1992–93]). Edited by Centro Internazionale di Studi di Architettura Andrea Palladio. A volume containing papers presented at the IX Seminario internazionale di storia dell'architettura, Vicenza, 3–8 September 1990.

Pirenne, Henri. *Medieval Cities: Their Origins and the Revival of Trade.* Princeton: Princeton University Press,

1925. [Originally published as *Les villes du Moyen Âge.* Paris, 1925.]

Pochettino, Giuseppe. "L'elezione dei vescovi di Parma nell'età feudale." *Archivio storico per le province parmensi,* 2nd ser., 22 bis (1922): 419–40.

Polak, Emil J. *Medieval and Renaissance Letter Treatises and Form Letters.* Vol. 1, *A Census of Manuscripts Found in Eastern Europe and the Former U.S.S.R.* Davis Medieval Texts and Studies, 8. Leiden: Brill, 1993.

———. *Medieval and Renaissance Letter Treatises and Form Letters.* Vol. 2, *A Census of Manuscripts Found in Part of Western Europe, Japan, and the United States of America.* Davis Medieval Texts and Studies, 9. Leiden: Brill, 1994.

Porter, Arthur Kingsley. *Lombard Architecture.* 3 vols. New Haven: Yale University Press, 1917.

Powell, James M., ed. *The Liber Augustalis; or, Constitutions of Melfi, Promulgated by the Emperor Frederick II for the Kingdom of Sicily.* Syracuse: Syracuse University Press, 1971.

Pozzi, Sara. Introduction to *De regimine et sapientia potestatis,* edited by Sara Pozzi, 13–55. Lodi: Archivio Storico Lodigiano, 1998.

Quaglioni, Diego. "The Legal Definition of Citizenship in the Late Middle Ages." In *City-States in Classical Antiquity and Medieval Italy: Athens and Rome, Florence and Venice,* edited by Anthony Molho, Kurt Raaflaub, and Julia Emlen, 154–67. Stuttgart: Franz Steiner, 1991.

Quintavalle, Arturo Carlo, ed. *Basilica cattedrale di Parma: Novecento anni di arte, storia, fede.* Vol. 1. Parma: Grafiche STEP Editrice, 2005.

———. *Il Battistero di Parma.* Parma: Artegrafica Silva, 1990.

———. *Il Battistero di Parma: Il cielo e la terra.* Parma: Università degli Studi di Parma, 1989.

———. *Benedetto Antelami.* Milan: Electa, 1990.

———. *La cattedrale di Parma e il romanico europeo.* Parma: Università di Parma, Istituto di storia dell'arte, 1974.

———, ed. *Medioevo: I modelli; Atti del convegno internazionale di studi di Parma, 27 settembre–1 ottobre 1999.* Milan: Electa, 2002.

Racine, Pierre. "Naissance de la place civique en Italie." In *Fortifications, portes de villes, places publiques dans le monde méditerranéen,* edited by Jacques Heers, 301–21.

Cultures et civilisations médiévales, 4. Paris: Presses de l'Université de Paris–Sorbonne, n.d. [1985].

———. "Noblesse et chevalerie dans les sociétés communales italiennes." In *Les élites urbaines au Moyen Âge: XXVII Congrès de la Société des Historiens Médiévistes de l'Enseignement Supérieur Public, Rome, mai 1996,* 137–52. Collection de l'École Française de Rome, 238. Rome: École Française de Rome, 1997.

———. "Les palais publics dans les communes italiennes (XII–XIIIe siècles)." In *Le paysage urbain au Moyen-Âge: Actes du XIe Congrès des historiens médiévistes de l'enseignement supérieur,* 135–53. Lyon: Presses Universitaires de Lyon, 1981.

———. "Les Visconti et les communautés urbaines." In *Les relations entre princes et villes aux XIVe–XVIe siècles: Aspects politiques, économiques et sociaux,* 187–99. Paris: Centre europeén d'études bourguignonnes, 1993.

Rees Jones, Sarah. Review of *City and Spectacle in Medieval Europe,* edited by Barbara A. Hanawalt and Kathryn L. Reyerson. *Medium Aevum,* no. 2 (Fall 1997): 361.

Reyerson, Kathryn L., and Barbara A. Hanawalt, eds. *City and Spectacle in Medieval Europe.* Minneapolis: University of Minnesota Press, 1994.

Reynolds, L. D., and N. G. Wilson. *Scribes and Scholars: A Guide to the Transmission of Greek and Latin Literature.* 3rd ed. Oxford: Clarendon Press, 1991.

Riccetti, Lucio, ed. *La Piazza del Duomo nella città medievale (nord e media Italia, secoli XII–XVI): Atti della giornata di studio, Orvieto, 4 giugno 1994.* Orvieto: Istituto Storico Artistico Orvietano, 1997.

Ricci, Franco Maria, ed. *Basilica cattedrale di Parma: Novecento anni di arte, storia, fede.* Vol. 3. Parma: Grafiche STEP Editrice, 2005.

Rockinger, Ludwig. *Briefsteller und Formelbücher des eilften bis vierzehnten Jahrhunderts.* Quellen und Erörterungen zur bayerischen und deutschen Geschichte, 9. Munich: Georg Franz, 1863.

Rockwell, Peter. "The Creative Reuse of Antiquity." In *History of Restoration of Ancient Stone Sculptures,* edited by Janet Burnett Grossman, 75–86. Los Angeles: Getty Publications, 2001.

———. "La decorazione plastica." In *Il Battistero di Parma: La scultura,* edited by Georges Duby, 219–48. Milan: Franco Maria Ricci, 1992.

Rolandini Patavini. "Cronica Marchie Trivixane *or* Cronica

in factis et circa facta Marchie Trivixane (AA. 1200 cc.–1262)." Edited by Antonio Bonardi. In *Rerum Italicarum Scriptores,* 2nd ed., edited by L. A. Muratori, Giosuè Carducci, and Vittorio Fiorini, vol. 8, pt. 1 (in 4 numbers). Città di Castello: S. Lapi, 1905–8.

The Romance of the Rose. Translated by W. Lorris and J. Clopinel. 2 vols. London: F. S. Ellis, 1901.

Ronchini, Amadio, ed. *Statuta Communis Parmae ab anno 1266 ad annum c. 1304.* Monumenta historica ad provincias parmensem et placentinam pertinentia. Vol. 2. Parma: Fiaccadori, 1857.

———. *Statuta Communis Parmae ab anno 1316 ad 1325.* Monumenta historica ad provincias parmensem et placentinam pertinentia. Vol. 3. Parma: Fiaccadori, 1859.

———. *Statuta Communis Parmae anni 1347: Accedunt leges vicecomitum Parmae imperantium usque ad annum 1374.* Monumenta historica ad provincias parmensem et placentinam pertinentia. Vol. 4. Parma: Fiaccadori, 1860.

———. *Statuta Communis Parmae digesta anno 1255.* Monumenta historica ad provincias parmensem et placentinam pertinentia. Vol. 1. Parma: Fiaccadori, 1855–56.

Russell, Robert Douglass. "*Vox Civitatis:* Aspects of Thirteenth-Century Communal Architecture in Lombardy." Ph.D. diss., Princeton University, 1988.

Salimbene de Adam. *Chronica.* Monumenta historica ad provincias parmensem et placentinam pertinentia. Parma: Fiaccadori, 1857.

———. *The Chronicle of Salimbene de Adam.* Edited and translated by Joseph L. Baird, Giuseppe Baglivi, and John Robert Kane. Binghamton, N.Y.: Medieval & Renaissance Texts & Studies, 1986.

———. *Cronaca.* Translated by Bernardo Rossi. Bologna: Radio Tau, 1987.

———. *Cronica.* Corpus Christianorum, Continuatio Mediaevalis, 125–125A. 2 vols. Edited by Giuseppe Scalia. Turnhout: Brepols, 1998–99.

———. *Cronica.* Scrittori d'Italia, 187–88. 2 vols. Edited by Ferdinando Bernini. Bari: Laterza, 1942.

———. *Cronica.* Scrittori d'Italia, 232–33. 2 vols. Edited by Giuseppe Scalia. Bari: Laterza, 1966.

———. *Cronica fratris Salimbene de Adam Ordinis minorum.* Edited by Oswald Holder-Egger. Monumenta

Germaniae historica inde ab anno Christi quingentesimo usque ad annum millesimum et quingentesimum, Scriptorum, 32. Hannover: Imp. bibliopolii Hahniani, 1905–13.

Salvemini, Gaetano, ed. *Iohannis Viterbiensis: Liber de regimine civitatum.* Bibliotheca Juridica Medii Aevi, 3:217–80. Bologna: Monti, 1901.

———. "Il 'Liber de regimine civitatum' di Giovanni da Viterbo." *Giornale storico della letteratura italiana* 41 (1903): 284–303.

Sardi, Gian Pietro. *La città di Parma, delineata, e divisa in isole colla descrizione degli attuali possessori di tutte le case, chiese, monasteri &c. dei cannali, cavi, canadelle, condotti, coli e fontane, che vi scorrono sotterra, ricavata dal piano originale della medesima eseguita, e compilata in quest'anno MDCCLXVII.* [Alternate title: *Atlante Sardi.*] Facsimile of the 1767 map. Parma: PPS Editrice, 1993.

Scaglione, Aldo. *Knights at Court: Courtliness, Chivalry, and Courtesy from Ottonian Germany to the Italian Renaissance.* Berkeley: University of California Press, 1991.

Schianchi, Giorgio, ed. *Il Battistero di Parma: Iconografia, iconologia, fonti letterarie.* Milan: Vita e Pensiero, 1999.

Schiavi, Antonio. *La diocesi di Parma.* 2 vols. Parma: Fresching, 1940.

Schmidinger, Heinrich, and Carlo Guido Mor, eds. *I poteri temporali dei vescovi in Italia e Germania nel Medioevo.* Bologna: Mulino, 1979.

Schulz, Juergen. "The Communal Buildings of Parma." *Mitteilungen des Kunsthistorischen Institutes in Florenz* 26 (1982): 279–324.

———. Introduction to *La piazza nel Medioevo e Rinascimento nell'Italia settentrionale* (*Annali di architettura* 4–5 [1992–93]), 113.

Schumann, Reinhold. *Authority and the Commune, Parma, 833–1133.* Parma: Deputazione di Storia Patria per le Province Parmensi, 1973.

Settia, Aldo A. "Lo sviluppo di un modello: Origine e funzioni delle torri private urbane nell'Italia centrosettentrionale." In *Paesaggi urbani dell'Italia padana nei secoli VIII–XIV,* 155–72. Studi e testi di storia medioevale, 15. Bologna: Cappelli, 1988.

Settis, Salvatore, ed. *Memoria dell'antico nell'arte italiana.* Vol. 1, *L'uso dei classici.* Turin: Einaudi, 1984.

Sitti, Giuseppe. *Parma nel nome delle sue strade*. Parma: Fresching, 1929.

Skinner, Quentin. *Visions of Politics*. Vol. 2, *Renaissance Virtues*. Cambridge: Cambridge University Press, 2002.

Smith, Christine. *The Baptistery of Pisa*. Outstanding Dissertations in the Fine Arts. New York: Garland, 1978.

Societas Aperiendis Fontibus Rerum Germanicarum Medii Aevi, ed. *Diplomatum regum et imperatorum Germaniae*. 18 vols. Monumenta Germaniae historica inde ab anno Christi quingentesimo usque ad annum millesimum et quingentesimum. Hannover: Hansche Buchhandlung, 1879–.

Soldi Rondinini, Gigliola. "Evoluzione politico-sociale e forme urbanistiche nella Padania dei secoli XII–XIII: I palazzi pubblici." In *La Pace di Costanza 1183: Un difficile equilibrio di poteri fra società italiana ed impero*, 85–89. Bologna: Cappelli, 1984.

Spigaroli, Marcello. "La piazza in ostaggio: Urbanistica e politica militare nello stato visconteo." *Storia della città* 54–56 (1990): 33–40. [Also published in *Bollettino storico piacentino* 87 (1992): 145–68.]

Spilner, Paula. "Giovanni di Lapo Ghini and a Magnificent New Addition to the Palazzo Vecchio, Florence." *Journal of the Society of Architectural Historians* 52, no. 4 (1993): 453–65.

Stolleis, Michael, and Ruth Wolff, eds. *La bellezza della città: Stadtrecht und Stadtgestaltung im Italien des Mittelalters und der Renaissance*. Reihe der Villa Vigoni, 16. Tubingen: Max Niemeyer Verlag, 2004.

Suetonius. *Augustus*. In *Works*, translated by J. C. Rolfe, 1:123–287. Loeb Classical Library. London: W. Heinemann, 1913.

Tabacco, Giovanni. "Northern and Central Italy in the Eleventh Century." In *The New Cambridge Medieval History*, vol. 4, pt. 2, *c. 1024–c. 1198*, edited by David Luscombe and Jonathan Riley-Smith, 72–93. Cambridge: Cambridge University Press, 2004.

———. "Northern and Central Italy in the Twelfth Century." In *The New Cambridge Medieval History*, vol. 4, pt. 2, *c. 1024–c. 1198*, edited by David Luscombe and Jonathan Riley-Smith, 422–41. Cambridge: Cambridge University Press, 2004.

———. *The Struggle for Power in Medieval Italy: Structures of Political Rule*. Cambridge: Cambridge University Press, 1989.

———. "Vescovi e comuni in Italia." In *I poteri temporali dei vescovi in Italia e Germania nel Medioevo*, edited by Carlo Guido Mor and Heinrich Schmidinger, 253–82. Bologna: Mulino, 1979.

Tassini, Sonia. *Il Battistero di Cremona*. Cremona: Turris, 1988.

Tavole di ragguaglio fra le nuove e le antiche misure e fra i nuovi e gli antichi pesi della Repubblica Italiana pubblicate per ordine del Governo in esecuzione dell'articolo XIII della legge 27 ottobre 1803. Milano: Veladini, 1803.

Testi, Laudedeo. *Le baptistère de Parme: Son histoire, son architecture, ses sculptures, ses peintures*. Florence: Sansoni, 1916.

———. *La cattedrale di Parma*. Bergamo: Istituto Italiano d'Arti Grafiche, 1934.

———. "Il Palazzo Vescovile di Parma e i suoi restauri." *Aurea Parma* 4, no. 6 (1920): 325–35.

Thatcher, Oliver J., and Edgar H. McNeal, eds. *A Source Book for Mediaeval History*. New York: Charles Scribner's Sons, 1905.

Thompson, Augustine. *Cities of God: The Religion of the Italian Communes, 1125–1325*. University Park: Pennsylvania State University Press, 2005.

Toesca, Pietro. *Il Battistero di Parma: Architetture e sculture di Benedetto Antelami e seguaci, affreschi dei secoli XIII e XIV*. Milan: Silvana, 1960.

Toker, Franklin. "Gothic Architecture by Remote Control: An Illustrated Building Contract of 1340." *Art Bulletin* 67, no. 1 (1985): 67–95.

Tosco, Carlo. "Dal battistero alla cappella battesimale: Trasformazioni liturgiche e sociali tra Medioevo e Rinascimento." In *L'architettura del battistero: Storia e progetto*, edited by Andrea Longhi, 63–83. Milan: Skira, 2003.

Trachtenberg, Marvin. *The Campanile of Florence Cathedral: "Giotto's Tower."* New York: New York University Press, 1971.

———. *Dominion of the Eye: Urbanism, Art, and Power in Early Modern Florence*. Cambridge: Cambridge University Press, 1997.

———. "Gothic/Italian 'Gothic': Toward a Redefinition." *Journal of the Society of Architectural Historians* 50, no. 1 (1991): 22–37.

———. "Scénographie urbaine et identité civique: Réflexion

sur la Florence du Trecento." *Revue de l'art* 102 (1993): 11–32.

———. "What Brunelleschi Saw: Monument and Site at the Palazzo Vecchio in Florence." *Journal of the Society of Architectural Historians* 47, no. 1 (1988): 14–44.

Turnbull, David. "The Ad Hoc Collective Work of Building Gothic Cathedrals with Templates, String, and Geometry." *Science, Technology, and Human Values* 18, no. 3 (1993): 315–40.

Vasaly, Ann. *Representations: Images of the World in Ciceronian Oratory.* Berkeley: University of California Press, 1993.

Vasina, Augusto. "L'area emiliana e romagnola." In *Comuni e signorie nell'Italia nordorientale e centrale,* vol. 1, *Veneto, Toscana, Emilia-Romagna,* 361–559. Storia d'Italia, edited by Giuseppe Galasso, 7. Turin: UTET, 1987.

Verzar Bornstein, Christine. *Portals and Politics in the Early Italian City-State: The Sculpture of Nicholaus in Context.* Parma: Università degli Studi di Parma, Istituto di storia dell'arte, Centro di studi medievali, 1988.

Vignoli, A. "La basilica cattedrale di Parma studiata nelle sue origini e principali vicende." In *Il mosaico paleocristiano del Duomo di Parma e le nozze d'oro dell'Arcivescovo Monsignor Evasio Colli,* 17–33. Fidenza: Tipografia la Commerciale, 1955.

Violante, Cinzio. "Motivi e carattere della *Cronica* di Salimbene." In *La "cortesia" chiericale e borghese nel Duecento,* 13–80. Saggi di Lettere Italiane, 49. Florence: Leo S. Olschki, 1995. [Originally published in *Annali della Scuola Normale Superiore di Pisa, classe di lettere,* 2nd ser., 22 (1953): fasc. I–II, pp. 3–49.]

Violante, Cinzio, and Damiano Fonseca. "Ubicazione e dedicazione delle cattedrali dalle origini al periodo romanico nelle città dell'Italia centro-settentrionale." In *Il Romanico pistoiese nei suoi rapporti con l'arte romanica dell'Occidente: Atti del 10 Convegno . . . Pistoia-Montecatini terme, 27 settembre–3 ottobre 1964,* 303–46. Prato, 1966.

Vitruvius Pollio. *Vitruvius: Ten Books on Architecture.* Translated by Ingrid D. Rowland. New York: Cambridge University Press, 1999.

von Moos, Peter. "Die italienische *'ars arengandi'* des 13. Jahrhunderts als Schule der Kommunikation." In

Rhetorik, Kommunikation und Medialität, 127–52. Berlin: LIT Verlag, 2006.

Waley, Daniel. *The Italian City-Republics.* New York: McGraw-Hill, 1969.

Ward-Perkins, Bryan. "Re-using the Architectural Legacy of the Past, *entre idéologie et pragmatisme.*" In *The Idea and the Ideal of the Town Between Late Antiquity and the Early Middle Ages,* edited by Bryan Ward-Perkins and Gian Pietro Brogiolo, 225–44. Leiden: Brill, 1999.

Ward-Perkins, Bryan, and Gian Pietro Brogiolo, eds. *The Idea and the Ideal of the Town Between Late Antiquity and the Early Middle Ages.* The Transformation of the Roman World, 4. Leiden: Brill, 1999.

Wenzel, Siegfried. "The Arts of Preaching." In *The Cambridge History of Literary Criticism,* vol. 2, *The Middle Ages,* edited by Alastair Minnis and Ian Johnson, 84–96. Cambridge: Cambridge University Press, 2005.

White, John. *Art and Architecture in Italy, 1250–1400.* 3rd ed. New Haven: Yale University Press, 1993.

Wickham, Chris. "L'Italia e l'alto Medioevo." *Archeologia medievale* 15 (1988): 105–24, 649.

Wickham, Chris, and Trevor Dean, eds. *City and Countryside in Late Medieval and Renaissance Italy.* London: Hambledon Press, 1996.

Wieruszowski, Hélène. "Art and the Commune in the Time of Dante." In *Politics and Culture in Medieval Spain and Italy,* edited by Hélène Wieruszowski, 465–502. Rome: Edizioni di Storia e Letteratura, 1971.

———. "Rhetoric and the Classics in Italian Education." In *Politics and Culture in Medieval Spain and Italy,* edited by Hélène Wieruszowski, 589–627. Rome: Edizioni di Storia e Letteratura, 1971.

Williamson, Beth. "How Magnificent Was Medieval Art?" In *Magnificence and the Sublime in Medieval Aesthetics: Art, Architecture, Literature, and Music,* edited by C. Stephen Jaeger, 243–62. New York: Palgrave Macmillan, 2010.

Witt, Ronald G. "The Arts of Letter-Writing." In *The Cambridge History of Literary Criticism,* vol. 2, *The Middle Ages,* edited by Alastair Minnis and Ian Johnson, 68–83. Cambridge: Cambridge University Press, 2005.

———. *"In the Footsteps of the Ancients": The Origins of Humanism from Lovato to Bruni.* Leiden: Brill, 2000.

———. "Medieval *Ars dictaminis* and the Beginnings of Humanism: A New Construction of the Problem." *Renaissance Quarterly* 35, no. 1 (1982): 1–35.

Woelk, Moritz. *Benedetto Antelami: Die Werke in Parma und Fidenza.* Münster: Rhema, 1995.

Wu, Nancy Y., ed. *Ad Quadratum: The Practical Application of Geometry in Medieval Architecture.* London: Ashgate, 2002.

Zaniboni Mattioli, Anna. "Il Palazzo Vescovile di Parma nelle fonti del secolo XIII." *Archivio storico per le province parmensi,* 4th ser., 51 (1999): 480–506.

Zennoni, Cinzia. "Piazza Ghiaia dalle origini alla progettazione delle Beccherie." In *Piazza Ghiaia: I volti e la storia,* edited by Guido Conti, Federica Sassi, and Roberto Spocci, 15–24. Parma: Monte Università di Parma, 2005.

Zuccagni-Orlandini, Attilio, ed. *Corografia fisica, storica e statistica dell'Italia e delle sue isole, corredata di un atlante, di mappe geografiche.* 12 vols. Florence: All'insegna di Clio, 1833–45.

Index

Fernie, Eric, 142, 173 n. 12

Fiamma, Galvano, 124

Fieschi, Òbizzo. *See* Òbizzo (bishop of Parma)

Fieschi, Ottobono. *See* Adrian V (pope)

Fieschi, Percivallo, 171 n. 29

Fieschi, Sinibaldo. *See* Innocent IV (pope)

Fieschi family, 16, 72, 125

Florence

    baptistery in, 29, 31, 34, 36, 37, 161 n. 25, 162 n. 31

    Parmesan executive officers in, 15

    Piazza della Santissima Annunziata in, 49, 163 n. 46

    Piazza della Signoria in, 55, 137, *138,* 168 n. 68

Forlì, San Mercuriale, bell tower, 51

fortifications, 20, 41, 49, 78, 134, 160 n. 9, 167 n. 37, 169 n. 16, 173
    n. 61

    Roman, 9, *10,* 11, 156–57 n. 26

forum (Parma), 61, *63,* 65–67, *66,* 123, 156 n. 26

Foucault, Michel, 128, 130, 134

Frederick I Barbarossa (Holy Roman Emperor)

    Bernardo II and, 28

    palace of (*See* Palazzo dell'Arena)

    Peace of Constance signed by, 19

Frederick II (Holy Roman Emperor)

    Parma occupied by, 72, 128, 163 n. 48, 166 n. 23

    Parmesan communal government and, 65

    Roman traditions used by, 115–16

    Rossi (Bernardo di Rolando) in inner circle of, 16, 20

Friedman, David, 57, 115

galleries, trabeated, 58, 119, *122,* 143

gambling, 110

Genoa, Parmesan executive officers in, 15

Ghiaia (Parma), 90, *91,* 109, 169 n. 16. *See also glarea*

"Ghibelline," 20

Ghibelline merlons, 80

Ghirlandina (Modena), 74, 125, *126,* 166 n. 26

Giandebiaggi, Paolo, 159 n. 2

glarea (riverbed), 13, 109

Grazia (bishop of Parma), 41–42, 44, 124, 164 n. 64

Greci, Roberto, 9

Gregory IX (pope), 41

guasti, 110

Gucius de Malavoltis (podesta of Parma), 130

"Guelph," 20

Guelph merlons, 80

Guidoni, Enrico, 161 n. 25

Guido of Corigia. *See* Guido da Correggio

Guyotjeannin, Olivier, 15, 171 n. 29

Heers, Jacques, 166 n. 21

Henry IV (Holy Roman Emperor), 20, 160 n. 9

Henry VI (Holy Roman Emperor), 28

Hise, Greg, 155 n. 8

Hohenstaufen dynasty, 20

Holloway, Julia Bolton, 18

Holy Sepulchre rotunda (Jerusalem), 31

Honorius II (antipope), 19, 160 n. 9

Honorius III (pope), 65, 165 n. 9

Horace, 16, 128

Horn, Walter, 161 n. 25

House of the Capitano (Parma), 150–51

    alterations to, 80, *82,* 150

    architectural features of, 80, 82

    drawing of, *82*

    intermediary structure connecting communal palace to,
        80–83, *83,* 167 n. 45

    location of, 80, *81,* 150

    medieval facades of, 80, *82,* 150

    Roman influences on, 117, *120*

    secondary bibliography on, 151

    staircase of, 80, 148, *149,* 150, 151, 167 n. 42

    textual evidence of, 150–51

House of the Podesta (Parma), 148–49

    architectural features of, 78

    drawing of, *79*

    location of, *73,* 78, *81,* 148, *149*

    remains of, 148–49

    secondary bibliography on, 149

    textual evidence of, 149, 167 n. 34

informants, 131–32

infrastructure, legislation on, 71, 102, 106–12, 128, 169 nn. 11, 18,
    21, 170 n. 28

Innocent IV (pope), 16, 20, 72, 166 n. 23

inzignerios, 111

Isidore of Seville, 5, 116

Italian City-State, The (Jones), 115, 155 n. 1, 157 n. 31

Italy

    education of urban elite in, 16–18, 128

    map of, *2*

    misconceptions about medieval urbanism in, 1

    public building projects in, 124

Jaeger, C. Stephen, 158 n. 51

Jenkins, A. D. Fraser, 123

Jerusalem, Holy Sepulchre rotunda in, 31

John (king of Bohemia), 172 n. 48

Jones, Philip, 14, 115, 155 n. 1, 157 n. 35

Justinian, 128

Justinianic code, 16

Via Maestri, 83. *See also* Via di Porta Nova, *cardo maximo*
violence, fines for, 110–11
Virgil, 16, 128
Visconti family, 134, 173 n. 61
Visconti, Luchino. *See* Luchino Visconti (lord of Milan)
Visdomini family, 41
Vitruvius Pollio, 116, 163 n. 46, 170 n. 9

water, for baptistery, 34–36, 39, 162 n. 36
weapons, fines for possession of, 111

weddings, 125
Welf dynasty, 20
well, 153
Wieruszowski, Hélène, 16
Wilson, N. G., 170 n. 9
Witt, Ronald, 124
Wolff, Ruth, 107
wood bridge (Parma), *12, 13*
World War II, bombing of Parma during, 25, 44, 64, 164 n. 64

Gefesselter Blick

25 kurze Monografien und Beiträge über neue Werbegestaltung

Mit Unterstützung des „Ringes der Werbegestalter des Schweizer Werkbundes" u. a.

herausgegeben und mit einer Einleitung versehen von

Heinz und Bodo Rasch

NEUES BAUEN IN DER W

Lars Müller Publishers   Reprint Collection

"Gefesselter Blick" was originally published by
Wissenschaftlicher Verlag Dr. Zaugg & Co., Stuttgart,
1930.

Reprint 1996 by
Lars Müller Publishers
5401 Baden/Switzerland

ISBN 3-907044-02-9

Reproductions: Reprotechnik Kloten AG
Printing and binding: EBS Editoriale Bortolazzi-Stei,
Verona

Printed in Italy

Die einzelnen Beiträge sind jeweils auf Anordnung ihrer Verfasser
in herkömmlicher Schreibweise oder in Kleinschreibung abgesetzt
worden. Auf Einheitlichkeit in dieser Beziehung wurde grundsätzlich
verzichtet.

Die Frage, ob Groß- und klein- - oder ob Nur-kleinschreibung, ist in
der Einleitung erörtert worden.

Für die Typografie wurde (im Prinzip) Maschinensatz verwendet
(lauter gleichlange Zeilen). Die Zeilenlänge beträgt 65—70 Buch-
staben, und zwar in allen 3 verwendeten Schriftgraden. Dies ist
bei der zur Anwendung gelangten Type die äußerste für das Auge
noch bequem lesbare Länge.

Das in diesem Buche abgebildete Material wurde vom Graphischen
Klub Stuttgart im Februar 1930 ausgestellt. Die Ausstellung wird
auch in anderen Städten gezeigt.

Besonderen Dank für ihre Bemühungen um das Zustandekommen
des Buches sagen die Herausgeber Herrn Kurt Schwitters-Hannover
und Herrn Hans Schmidt-Basel.

Copyright by Wissenschaftlicher Verlag Dr. Zaugg & Co., Stuttgart
Druck von Schöllkopf, Pfund & Cie , Inh. Pfund & Bauer, Stuttgart
Klischees von Haufler & Wiest, Chemigraph. Kunstanstalt, Stuttgart
Cellalineinband D.R.P. a. (Celluloid von WORBLA G. m. b. H., Mann-
heim-Waldhof) - Typografie und Einband Brüder Rasch, Stuttgart